2019-2-015

『十三五』江苏省高等学校重点教材

江苏省高校品牌建设工程资助项目（PPZY2015A012）

江苏省教育科学『十三五』规划课题（J-b/2016/20）

基于学科核心素养的英语教学课例研究

主编 李 箭 周海明

副主编 姜建宇 周 华 韩炳华 林梦茜

U0651990

华东师范大学出版社

·上海·

图书在版编目(CIP)数据

基于学科核心素养的英语教学课例研究/李箭,周海明主编. —上海:华东师范大学出版社,2019
(基于学科核心素养的教学课例研究)
ISBN 978 - 7 - 5675 - 9811 - 9

Ⅰ.①基…　Ⅱ.①李…②周…　Ⅲ.①英语课—教学研究—中学　Ⅳ.①G633.412

中国版本图书馆 CIP 数据核字(2019)第 242037 号

基于学科核心素养的英语教学课例研究
JIYU XUEKE HEXIN SUYANG DE YINGYU JIAOXUE KELI YANJIU

主　　编　李　箭　周海明
策划编辑　李文革
责任编辑　曹祖红
特约审读　周倩丽
责任校对　王婷婷
装帧设计　卢晓红

出版发行　华东师范大学出版社
社　　址　上海市中山北路 3663 号　邮编 200062
网　　址　www.ecnupress.com.cn
电　　话　021 - 60821666　行政传真 021 - 62572105
客服电话　021 - 62865537　门市(邮购)电话 021 - 62869887
地　　址　上海市中山北路 3663 号华东师范大学校内先锋路口
网　　店　http://hdsdcbs.tmall.com

印 刷 者　上海景条印刷有限公司
开　　本　787 毫米×1092 毫米　1/16
印　　张　14.5
字　　数　234 千字
版　　次　2019 年 12 月第 1 版
印　　次　2024 年 8 月第 11 次
书　　号　ISBN 978 - 7 - 5675 - 9811 - 9
定　　价　38.00 元

出 版 人　王　焰

前言

我国英语课程改革至今为止取得了很大的成效。第一,课程性质由单一的工具性向工具性与人文性统一转变。第二,教学理念由以教师为中心向以学生为主体转变。第三,教学目标由掌握语言系统知识向培养综合语言运用能力转变。第四,教学内容由知识点的讲授向语言知识、语言技能、学习策略、情感态度、思维文化品质的综合培养转变。第五,教学方式由单一的讲解向多样化的组织学习方式转变。

《普通高中英语课程标准(2017年版)》以英语学科核心素养为导向,强调学生以主题意义探究为目的,以语篇为载体,在语言实践活动中融合知识、技能的学习与发展,通过感知、预测、获取、分析、概括、比较、评价、创新等思维活动,构建结构化知识;在分析问题、解决问题的过程中发展思维品质,形成文化理解;培养学生的家国情怀、国际视野的文化品格;塑造学生正确的人生观和价值观;促进英语学科核心素养的形成和发展。英语学科的核心素养主要由语言能力、思维品质、文化意识和学习能力四方面构成,而对学生英语学科核心素养的培养应在英语课堂上通过英语学习活动得到落实,因此优秀课例对此有极大借鉴价值。

"课例"是指一个真实的教学案例。"课例研究"是教学研究的一种,起源于20世纪50年代的日本的授业研究,它以学生学习与发展中的问题为研究对象,以教师为主导,基于教师的反思性实践,通过集体合作明确研究主题、设计教学方案、开发课堂观察工具、确定分工与任务、开展课后研讨活动以及撰写研究报告等环节,促进教师专业化发展、促进学生学习和发展,最终达到改进教学、实现教学与研究一体化的目的过程。

本书采取实践取向的视角,以课堂教学案例为载体,为教师如何在英语课堂上培养学生的语言能力、思维品质、文化意识和学习能力提供了重要借鉴。同时,书中所选优秀课例具有典型性和可操作性,便于读者从中参透新课程改革下英语课堂应有的样子,并择其善者而从之,应用于自己的教学实践中。

全书主要包括两大部分。第一部分为理论知识,共包括三章内容,系统地介绍了英语学科核心素养的理论基础、如何在英语课堂上落实对学生核心素养的培养以及英语教师如何将作为教育研究方法之一的课例研究与自身专业化发展相结合。第二部分为实践知识,包括 12 位英语名师的主题式课例,每个课例都包括教学预设、精彩实录以及课例评析三大板块。教学预设部分分析了每堂课的教学内容、教学目标及教学思路、方法与资源。课例评析部分体现了多元评价主体思路,由"学生反响""同行声音""自我反思""专家点评"组成,充分反映了学生、同行及执教者对此课的评析与反思。

鉴于本书既涵盖对理论知识的论证与阐述,又示例了基于英语学科核心素养培养的课堂教学案例及其评析,是一线教师基于核心素养理念下开展的教学探索,因此本书的目标读者既可以是广大中小学英语一线教师,也可以是高等院校英语师范专业本科学生或研究生及高校英语课程与教学论教师等。

本书由盐城师范学院外国语学院和华东师范大学出版社共同组织策划,由盐城师范学院李箭主持,周海明协调统筹。理论篇由李箭、周海明和林梦茜撰写。实践篇中,小学、初中和高中三个学段的英语课例研究分别由一线名师和专家姜建宇(江苏省小学英语特级教师,现任教于江苏省泰州市实验小学)、周华(江苏省中学英语正高级教师、江苏省英语特级教师,现任教于江苏省如皋外国语学校)、韩炳华(江苏省中学英语正高级教师、江苏省中学英语特级教师、江苏省人民教育家培养工程培养对象,现任教于江苏省扬州邗江中学)组稿与编制。全书由李箭统一审定。在本书的编写过程中,我们参考了大量文献资料,吸收了许多专家学者的研究成果,也得到了一线名师专家的支持,为本书的撰写提供了优秀的课例和课例点评,在此一并表示诚挚的谢意。

由于编者水平有限,加上《普通高中英语课程标准(2017 年版)》实施不久,与之配套的新教材还没有全面投入使用,同时新的小学和初中英语课程标准还未出台,书中肯定有诸多不足之处,敬请广大读者批评指正。

编者

2019 年 4 月 30 日

目录

理论篇

实践篇

理论篇

第1章　英语学科核心素养概述

通过本章学习,你将:

1. 了解世界范围内核心素养的定义;
2. 理解英语学科核心素养的构成和涵义;
3. 掌握英语学科核心素养之间的内在关系。

2014 年 4 月,教育部发布了《关于全面深化课程改革落实立德树人根本任务的意见》,①提出了"核心素养"概念,要求将研制与构建学生核心素养体系作为推进我国课程改革深化发展的关键环节,并启动了高中各学科课程标准的修订。2017 年,以"核心素养"为内涵的《普通高中英语课程标准(2017 年版)》(以下简称"《课标(2017版)》")正式颁布。发展学生核心素养,落实立德树人的根本任务是深化课程改革的必然要求。准确理解和解读英语学科核心素养是推进当下基础教育英语课程改革的重要前提,也是促进英语教师专业发展的内在要求。本章简要介绍世界范围内一些国家和国际组织提出的核心素养的定义及其框架内容,简单分析英语学科核心素养的概念以及各要素的内在关系。

---

① 中华人民共和国教育部. 教育部关于全面深化课程改革落实立德树人根本任务的意见[EB/OL]. (2014 - 04 - 24)[2019 - 01 - 27]. http://www.moe.edu.cn/publicfiles/business/htmlfiles/moe/s7054/201404/167226.html.pdf.

1.1 核心素养的定义和框架

1997 年经济合作与发展组织(OECD)首次提出核心素养概念,将核心素养界定为 "A competence is more than just knowledge and skills. It involves the ability to meet complex demands,by drawing on and mobilizing psychosocial resources (including skills and attitudes) in a particular context."之后,还提出了 21 世纪学生发展的十大核心技能。2008 年欧盟委员会(European Commission)对核心素养的阐释是:"A competence is not limited to cognitive elements (involving the use of theory, concepts or tacit knowledge); it also encompasses functional aspects (involving technical skills) as well as interpersonal attributes (e. g. social or organizational skills) and ethical values."①

美国在 2002 年制定了 21 世纪素养框架,在 2007 年进行修订,提出"学习与创新技能""信息媒体与技术技能""生活与职业技能"三大技能领域的若干素养要求。欧盟在 2005 年发布的《核心素养:欧洲参考框架》(Key Competences: A European Reference Framework)中提出"使用母语交流的能力""使用外语交流的能力""数学素养与科技素养""数字化素养""学会学习""社会和公民素养""主动与创新意识"和"文化意识与表达"八项核心素养,作为其成员国推进终身学习以及教育与培训改革的参照框架。澳大利亚在 2008 年发布的《墨尔本宣言》中提出公民必须具有"读写能力""计算能力""信息与通用技术""批判性和创新思维""道德行为""个人和社会能力"和"跨文化理解能力"七项基本素养。新加坡政府于 2010 年提出的核心素养框架包括"核心价值""社交与情绪管理技能"和"新 21 世纪技能"三部分,其中"核心价值"又包括"自我意识""自我管理""社会意识""人际关系管理"和"负责任的决策"五项;"社交与情绪管理技能"包括"交流、合作与信息技能""公民素养、全球意识和跨文化交流技能"和"批判性、创新性思维"三项;"新 21 世纪技能"包括四个理想的教育成果,即培养

---

① 梅德明,王蔷.改什么? 如何教? 怎样考? 高中英语新课标解析[M].北京:外语教学与研究出版社,2018:9.

"充满自信的人""能主动学习的人""积极奉献的人"和"心系祖国的公民"。日本在其2013 年公布的研究报告《培养适应社会变化的素质与能力的教育课程编制的基本原理》中提出了面向国际、立足本国的核心素养框架,该框架是由"基础力""思考力"和"实践力"构成的"21 世纪型能力"。中国台湾教育主管部门在其 2014 年发布的《十二年国民基本教育课程纲要总纲》中指出核心素养包括"自主行动""沟通互动"和"社会参与"三个方面,以及"身心素质与自我精进""系统思考与解决问题""规划执行与创新应变""符号运用与沟通表达""科技信息与媒体素养""艺术涵养与美感素养""道德实践与公民意识""人际关系与团队合作"和"多元文化与国际理解"九大项目。

如上核心素养框架都是针对新时代的国家公民提出的,但是这些素养又不仅仅局限于培养新时代的合格公民,而是旨在培养"完人",即不仅是为了促使"个人社会化",而是在此基础上为实现个体的"社会个性化"努力。这种旨在培养"完人"的趋势正和我国"以人为本、以学生发展为本"的教育目的相契合,对我国学生核心素养框架的构建具有启发性意义。

2016 年 9 月 13 日,《中国学生发展核心素养》在北京正式发布,该文件是我国教育部委托北京师范大学联合国内高校近百位专家成立课题组,历时 3 年完成的研究成果。文件指出,核心素养以培养"全面发展的人"为核心,分为文化基础、自主发展、社会参与三个方面,综合表现为人文底蕴、科学精神、学会学习、健康生活、责任担当、实践创新六大素养,具体细化为国家认同等 18 个基本要点。该核心素养框架根植于社会主义核心价值观的基本要求,强调中华民族传统文化的传承与发展,具有民族性;同时,充分体现我国对塑造"完人"的诉求,体现"以人为本"的科学性;此外,呼应了时代发展的趋势,旨在使培养出的人适应信息化时代和学习型社会的来临,又表现出时代性。该框架在党的教育方针和教育教学实践之间搭建了一座桥梁,促使各科教师在教育教学活动中以培养学生的核心素养为切入点,充分贯彻党和国家对培养人才的期望与诉求。

理论探讨

请尝试从育人角度,谈谈《中国学生发展核心素养》中的六大核心素养和英语学科的关系。

1.2 英语学科核心素养的概念解读

学科核心素养是学科育人价值的集中体现,是学生通过学科学习而逐步形成的正确价值观、适应终身发展和社会发展需要的必备品格和关键能力,突出强调个人修养、社会关爱、家国情怀,更加注重自主发展、合作参与、创新实践。《课标(2017 版)》把英语学科核心素养归纳为语言能力、文化意识、思维品质和学习能力四个方面,取代过去的综合语言运用能力目标,强调英语学科的育人价值。

1.2.1 语言能力

语言能力是指在社会情境中,以听、说、读、看、写等方式理解和表达意义、意图,传递情感态度和价值观的能力,以及在学习和使用语言的过程中形成的语言意识和语感。[①] 语言能力可以进一步细化为以下五种:第一,对英语这门语言及其学习的认识能力;第二,掌握英语语言知识的能力;第三,对各种题材和体裁的口语及书面语篇的理解能力;第四,用英语进行表达的能力;第五,用英语建构与维系良好人际关系的能力。[②]《课标(2017 版)》对"语言能力"的定义首先强调了"社会情境"(不是孤立的课堂或学校情境)这一前提,是因为语言只能通过社会情境传递信息,而离开了情境的语言只是一套没有意义的符号。为此,《课标(2017 版)》相应地提出了"人与自我""人与社会"和"人与自然"三大主题语境,规定成为该"社会情境"的范围。其次,该定义还强调了语言能力的具体表现是听、说、读、看、写五种显性行为,其中听、读、看是信息的输入途径,可以归纳为理解能力;而说、写是信息的输出途径,可归纳为表达能力。[③] 值得注意的是,"看(viewing)"是《课标(2017 版)》中新出现的语言技能,其主要是指对与英语有关的图像、视频、音频、实物、场景等的"看",而且这种"看"不是一扫而过地看,而是在看后提取有用信息从而促进所学英语知识内化的能力,它充分体现了当代学习者

① 中华人民共和国教育部. 普通高中英语课程标准(2017 年版)[S]. 北京:人民教育出版社,2017:7.
② 程晓堂,赵思奇.英语学科核心素养的实质内涵[J].课程·教材·教法,2016,36(5):79—86.
③ 夏谷鸣.深度解读英语学科核心素养(一):提高语言能力需厘清哪六个要素的关系[J/OL].(2017-08-01)[2019-01-28]. https://www.sohu.com/a/161446736_528969.

获取信息的时代特点。而"看"的加入主要是由于当前的英语教学中多媒体和多模态教学资源的逐渐丰富对以纯文本为基础的传统英语教学产生的极大影响。《课标（2017 版）》的语言能力素养要求为英语教学提供一个明确的方向，即英语教学应通过创设情境调动学生多种感官，通过课堂活动培养学生听、说、读、写、看多方面的综合运用语言的能力，从而使学生在走出课堂后也能自如地运用语言，即学生从"情境"（教学情境）中来，到"情境"（社会情境）中去。

1.2.2　文化意识

文化意识指学生对中外文化的理解和对优秀文化的认同，是学生在全球化背景下表现出的跨文化认知、态度和行为取向。"在全球化背景下"首先强调了英语学科的特点之一——人文性。其次，该定义体现了文化意识的两方面内涵：一方面是学生能够对自己的内在世界进行改造与完善，从而使自己成为具有文化素养的人；另一方面是学生能够将内化修炼所形成的文化素养外显，从而在今后的社会生活以及跨文化活动中表现出一定的文化能力和文化素养。值得注意的是，作为英语学科核心素养的文化意识不仅仅局限于跨文化交际能力和文化意识，还包括评价、解释、比较、归纳，以及鉴别语篇反映的文化现象，从而丰富自身文化体验，形成自身文化立场，拥有良好人文素养。可以看出，文化意识已经从单纯的"感知""理解"的范畴进入到"认同""认知""态度"和"行为"的范畴。换一句话说，文化意识素养主要指中外优秀文化，既包括人文知识，也包括科学知识。文化意识是学生在全球化背景下对中外文化的理解和对优秀文化的认同，也是学生在全球化背景下所表现出的跨文化认识、态度和行为取向。[①] 语言和文化紧密相联，语言是文化的载体，在英语语言输入的同时渗透文化意识的培养能帮助学生体察文化差异、加强国际文化理解、形成国际文化视野，从而促使学生了解、接受与鉴赏西方文化以及其他民族的情感态度与价值观，真正达到运用英语实现跨文化交际的目的。

---

① 梅德明，王蔷. 改什么？如何教？怎样考？高中英语新课标解析[M]. 北京：外语教学与研究出版社，2018：22.

1.2.3　思维品质

思维是整个认知的核心,我国教育自古以来就重视对学生思维能力的培养,例如《论语·为政》中用来辩证学习与思考关系的"学而不思则罔,思而不学则殆",以及《中庸》中用来概括整个学习过程的"博学之,审问之,慎思之,明辨之,笃行之"。①《课标(2017版)》对思维品质的定义是"一个人的思维个性特征反映其在思维的逻辑性、批判性、创造性等方面所表现的能力和水平"。其中,思维的逻辑性表现在思维自身的运行规律或是学习者能够正确合理地思考的能力;思维的批判性主要表现为一种质疑和求证的态度,即对于某一观点既不盲目接受,也不武断拒绝,而是采用辩证的态度看待;思维的创造性则表现为不固守旧观点,而是敢于想象、善于改变,从而推陈出新。②作为英语学科核心素养的思维品质指的是与英语及英语学习有关联的思维品质,包括在理解语篇的表层信息之余对语篇的逻辑框架、主题意义、作者观点、情感、意图等有更深层的挖掘,还包括从认知的角度理解英语中概念词的内涵和外延意义、通过英语学习掌握新的概念以及了解英语使用者的思维方式等。《课标(2017版)》对思维品质这一概念的界定将英语学习从简单的符号识记推向更高的领域,而对学生高阶思维能力的培养也不再只是理科独有的魅力,语言教学也可以承担这一责任,进而引发学习者的深度学习。学生只有具备了逻辑和批判思维能力,才能真正在语言运用和解决问题的过程中实现创新。

1.2.4　学习能力

学习能力是英语学科核心素养的发展条件,是指学生积极运用和主动调试英语学习策略、努力拓宽英语学习渠道和提升英语学习效率的意识和能力。③《课标(2017版)》对学习能力的这一定义实则包含两部分的内容。第一是学生掌握与运用某种学习策略的能力。学习策略包括认知策略、元认知策略和资源管理策略。其中,认知策

---

① 刘道义.谈英语学科素养—思维品质[J].课程·教材·教法,2018,38(8):80—85.
② 夏谷鸣.深度解读英语学科核心素养(三):如何因材施教训练思维品质[J/OL].(2017-08-08)[2019-01-27].https://www.sohu.com/a/163124716_528969.
③ 中华人民共和国教育部.普通高中英语课程标准(2017年版)[S].北京:人民教育出版社,2017:7.

略是指学习者对信息加工的方法与技术,英语学习中的认知策略有:利用表格整理文章脉络、通过整合文章结构理解文章大意、通过词源识记词义、创设情境掌握词汇固定搭配等;元认知策略是指学生对自己学习过程的有效监控,从而使学生警觉自己在注意和理解方面可能存在的问题,以便找出并加以修改,主要包括自我监控策略、自我计划策略、自我调节策略、自我评价策略和自我指导策略五个具体策略;而资源管理策略是辅助学生管理可用环境和资源的能力,包括时间管理策略、努力管理策略和学业求助策略三个具体策略。学业求助策略在英语学习中尤为重要,小组成员之间的交流可以使得学生利用"信息差"实现对语篇更全面透彻的理解。另外,听说课中的练习活动如 role play 等也是生生之间互助互进的表现。第二是学生的学习态度(通过"积极""主动""努力"这三个副词体现)。这一定义拓展与超越了"学习能力"原来的意义,从广义上阐述"学习能力",体现了学习能力的时代性,即学习能力不仅局限于某种特定的学习方法或学习策略,还包括学习者在英语学习过程中对学习策略的调控和管理,以及学习者对英语学习的正确认识(例如对英语学习保持持续且较高的兴趣、养成英语学习习惯,以及对英语学习有积极的态度和较强的学习动机等)。《课标(2017 版)》对学习能力这一素养的界定使"学习能力"本身超越了单一的"学习策略",涉及更广泛的学习的情感态度与价值观,使学习者不是被动地使用学习策略,而是能够产生独创性的学习策略,并且有足够的学习动机和学习毅力并持之以恒地加以运用,从而成为一个"会学"且"爱学"的人。

英语学科核心素养的确立是一个以语言为核心的学科教学向以人的发展为核心的学科教育的转变。这一理念的转变是要培养学生成为具有家国情怀、国际视野和跨文化沟通能力的社会主义事业的合格建设者和接班人,真正落实立德树人的根本任务。①

理论探讨

英语学科核心素养表现为语言能力、文化意识、思维品质和学习能力四个方面,请从英语学科教学和英语教育两个角度,分别谈谈英语学科四个核心素养对学生的教育

---

① 梅德明,王蔷.改什么? 如何教? 怎样考? 高中英语新课标解析[M].北京:外语教学与研究出版社,2018:35.

教学价值。

1.3 英语学科核心素养要素关系解析

英语学科核心素养被定义为：在接受相应学段英语课程教育的过程中，学生逐步形成和提升的适应个人终身发展和社会发展需要的必备品格和关键能力，综合表现为四大素养，由语言能力、文化意识、思维品质和学习能力组成。四大素养又可进一步分成两部分：一是必备品格，包括文化意识和思维品质；二是关键能力，包括语言能力和学习能力。

英语学科具有工具性和人文性双重属性。英语学科的工具性要求学生通过学习英语课程获得丰富的语言知识、掌握必备的语言技能、形成一定的交流能力，以及促进自身思维能力的提升等。英语学科的人文性要求学生通过英语课程的学习发展创新能力、形成跨文化意识及良好的品格等。因此，英语课程不仅要考虑学生应学到哪些语言知识、语言技能，将来能用语言做哪些事，还要考虑学生应通过英语课程学到其他哪些方面的知识，形成哪些其他的作为"完人"的关键技能和必备品格。①

语言能力作为英语学科核心素养的基础具有其独特价值，是学生发展文化意识、思维品质和学习能力的依托，也是培养学生核心素养发展的首要保证。英语教育就是在英语语言的学习和运用中发展学生的文化意识、思维品质和学习能力的。同时，英语语言能力的提高有助于学生走出本族语使用者的固有思维方式，更好地促进学生拓展文化视野，去接触、丰富思维方式，体会和发现不同的思维方式，还有助于学生接触更多的文化知识，理解其中的文化内涵，及文化背后的社会背景，从而进一步提高思维能力与水平，扩展文化视野。所以，从一定程度上来说，英语学科教学是让学生在英语语言的学习和运用中发展他们的文化意识、思维品质和学习能力。文化意识则体现了英语学科核心素养的价值取向。学生通过对文化知识的学习、对文化知识内涵的理解、对文化异同之间的比较，加深对文化内涵的挖掘、比较、批判、评价、鉴别，汲取文化精华，形成新的跨文化认识、积极的人生态度和良好的人文素养。文化意识的形成有

---

① 程晓堂.英语学科核心素养及其测评[J].中国考试，2017(5)：7—14.

助于学生树立国际的视野、增强国家的认同感和家国情怀、培养社会责任感。而思维品质则体现学生的心智发展特征和水平。思维品质的形成有助于学生发现问题、分析问题、解决问题能力的提升;有助于学生从跨文化角度观察、体现和认识世界;有助于学生通过语言、思维和文化相结合的英语活动实践对事物做出正确的价值判断,并促进深度学习。学习能力是核心素养发展的必要条件和前提。形成自我管理的良好学习习惯是学生终身发展的重要前提,也是学生学会拓展学习渠道、运用多样化学习资源、提升学习效能的重要保障。①

　　综上所述,英语学科核心素养四要素之间是互相影响、互相促进的关系。语言能力是基础要素,文化意识是价值取向,思维品质是心智保障,学习能力是发展条件。四要素是一个相互联系、密不可分的有机整体。

　　理论探讨

　　英语学科核心素养四要素是一个有机整体,请从认知学角度和教育学角度谈谈它们之间的关系。

---

① 梅德明,王蔷.改什么? 如何教? 怎样考? 高中英语新课标解析[M].北京:外语教学与研究出版社,2018:24.

第 2 章　英语核心素养与英语教学

通过本章学习,你将:

1. 感悟英语教学在培育英语核心素养中的重要作用;
2. 掌握基于核心素养的英语教学研究内容和方法;
3. 了解基于活动观的英语课堂教学设计与实施理念。

在新一轮课程改革中,学科核心素养越来越多地受到学界和业界的关注。本书的第 1 章简要讨论了英语学科核心素养(即语言能力、文化意识、思维品质及学习能力)的概念及意义,但我们希望核心素养不仅仅只是一个抽象概念,还是可教、可学的,即可在课堂教学及学生学习过程中落实。本章将围绕英语核心素养"为什么教?""如何教?"的问题进行简要探讨,具体包括英语教学培育核心素养的价值、英语教学培育英语核心素养的研究范式及基于英语活动观的课堂教学设计与实施的创新理念。

2.1　英语教学培育英语核心素养的价值

2.1.1　英语教学有助于培养学生的综合语言运用能力

综合语言运用能力是学生必备的、能够适应个人终身发展和社会发展需要的关键能力之一。① 随着经济全球化时代的到来,运用语言进行跨文化交流已成为当代公民的一项必备素养,尤其是英语的使用,因为它已成为在世界范围内广泛使用的通用语言。综合语言运用能力的培养具有时代性,它既是《课标(2017 版)》的导向,也是当前英语学科教学最重要的目标之一。

2007 年起开始实施的高中英语新课程改革在教学目标上从"掌握语言系统"向"培养综合语言运用能力"发生转变。这一转变首先是由于"应试教育"向"素质教育"转变导致的,因为"应试教育"模式下的英语教学注重要求学生机械地掌握能够应付升学考试的英语词汇、语音、语法,却忽视了语言的应用性与实践性,也忽视了培养学生运用英语交际的能力,使语言学习趋向"碎片化",②偏向语言知识"片面化"。此外,英语课程的性质由单一的工具性向工具性与人文性双重属性的转变也是导致上述转变的原因之一。

在 20 世纪 80 年代,美国一些教授母语的专家学者提出了"全语言法"(the Whole Language Approach),他们认为语言不应被肢解,语言教学不应将活生生的、动态性的语言分解为单一的词汇、语音、语法等模块来教授,语言学习也不应被机械地分割成听、说、读、写四个部分来学习,长此以往,学生将一直处于"只见树木不见森林"的状态中。③ 语言应被视为一个整体的沟通系统,语言学习应让学习者通过直接经验来学习具有真实交际目的的语言知识与技能。"全语言法"的萌芽使语言教学在培养学生综合语言运用能力方面迈出了一大步。

英语教学在培养学生综合语言运用能力中发挥着很大的作用,当前不少学者提出了多种培养学生综合语言运用能力的英语教学方法。例如,增大英语课堂教学容量,即让教师在有限的英语课堂教学时间内最大化语言的输入与输出,使学生在有限的课堂学习时间内最大化地感知与运用语言。④ 再如,在英语课堂中实行任务型教学(task-based language teaching),教师可以运用真实的语言材料,创设真实问题和任务,

---

① 朱文芳. 英语教学在培育学生发展核心素养中的作用[J]. 科教导刊(中旬刊),2017(8):108—109.
② 王蔷. 从综合语言运用能力到英语学科核心素养——高中英语课程改革的新挑战[J]. 英语教师,2015(16):6—7.
③ Rodgers, S. *Approaches and Methods in Language Teaching* [M]. New York: Cambridge University Press, 2017:108—114.
④ 袁红霞. 增大英语课堂教学容量,提高学生的综合语言运用能力[J]. 贵州教育,2016(8):44—45.

通过师生、生生间的互动、交流、合作、探究等活动,增加学生的体验参与,在解决问题或完成任务的过程中,学生始终处于一种积极思考、积极参与的学习心理状态。这不仅培养了学生的综合语言运用能力,也在教学的过程中,培养了学生的情感态度、学习能力等素养。①

2.1.2 英语教学有助于有效提升学生的人文素养

《义务教育英语课程标准(2011 年版)》(以下简称《课标(2011 版)》)指出,英语课程的总目标是通过英语学习使学生形成初步的综合语言运用能力,促进心智发展,提高综合人文素养。②《课标(2017 版)》更加强调英语课程的人文属性。一个人的人文素养取决于他从事某种或多种文化所获得的价值观,是文化知识在人的头脑中的沉淀,③是一个人能够正确看待文化差异、鉴赏与评价其他文化所蕴含的价值观的能力,它对人的思想、情感、心智和"三观"均有着极大的推动作用。《中国学生发展核心素养》就将"人文底蕴"列为"全面发展的人"的六大必备素养之一。

语言是文化的载体,英语则是西方英语世界的民族文化的载体,它蕴含与凝聚着西方民族长期积累的社会生产生活经验、历史文化、风土人情、价值观念、思想渊源等。因此,教师在英语教学中若是能够发掘语言背后潜藏的文化内涵,带领学生进行深入的情感体验,就能带动学生人文素养的提高,并能在传承文化、促进世界文明交流融合与文化更新方面发挥举足轻重的作用。正如本书前文所提到的,英语是工具性和人文性相统一的学科,提高学生综合人文素养恰恰体现了英语学科的本质属性,也使英语教学回归教育的育人本质。

英语教学在培养学生的综合人文素养中体现出极大的价值,当前也有不少学者提出了各种各样的利用英语教学培养学生综合人文素养的方法。例如,利用文本资源培养学生的人文素养,深入统一文本资源的科学性与思想性。这要求教师要善于合理拓展原有的文本内容,发掘语言材料蕴含的人文内涵、情感素材,以贴近学生生活和联系

---

① 许映梅.运用"任务型"教学途径培养学生综合语言运用能力[J].科教导刊(上旬刊),2013(5):113—114.

② 中华人民共和国教育部.义务教育英语课程标准[S].北京:人民教育出版社,2011:5.

③ 杨卫东,陈葵,戴卫平.英语教学中学生人文素养的培养[J].教学与管理,2009(6):118—119.

学生直接经验的方式呈现,并结合时下社会热点、焦点问题,引发学生的探讨与思考。① 再如,重视发展与丰富英语第二课堂,通过活动带动学生人文素养的提高。② 因为一节英语课时间有限,要想在完成教学任务的基础上提高学生的人文素养还需开设英语第二课堂,如课外阅读活动、文化知识竞赛、辩论赛等。此外,对教学活动进行情感加工,鼓励学生"从做中学",并结合教材话题与活动主体,倡导学生个体进行文化感悟等也有助于使学生发挥主观能动性,从而提高综合人文素养与水平。③

2.1.3　英语教学能够提高学生的思维水平,培养学生的批判性思维能力

随着"思辨能力"这一概念在 1996 年的提出,④以及 1998 年"思辨缺席症"的提出,⑤我国的外语教学研究中思辨能力与外语教学的关系问题日益受到重视。不少学者认为,国内英语教学过于注重对学生听、说、读、写等语言技能技巧的训练,过于强调英语作为一种语言的工具性,却忽略了学生深入思考问题的能力,特别是用批判的眼光看待问题与独立思考问题的能力。

近年来,不少学者从认知、心理等角度对我国英语教学中批判性思维能力的主要内容和基本概念进行深入探讨,构建了多种批判性能力模型。例如,林崇德(2006 年)的"三棱结构模型"、文秋芳等(2009 年)的"层级模型"、阮全友(2012 年)的"思辨能力培养理论框架"以及黄远振等(2014 年)的"三维立体模型"等。

此外,也有学者提出在英语教学中培养学生思维能力的方法,从而发挥英语教学在提升学生思维水平中的价值。例如,以"沉浸式"教学实验(immersion program)为启发,采用内容依托式教学(content-based language teaching),将英语语言学习与学科专业知识学习相结合,并设计一系列思维活动(如解释、分析、评价等),使学生养成勤思考、爱思考、敢质疑的学习习惯。⑥ 再如,在英语写作教学中提高学生的读者意识(reader consciousness),即在写作过程中作者心中存有一位"隐在读者"(implied

---

① 肖琼. 谈高中英语教学中学生人文素养的培养[J]. 英语教师,2015,15(6): 142—144.
② 谢蜀苏. 浅谈高中英语教学中学生人文素养的培养[J]. 课程教育研究,2018(35): 121.
③ 吴长宏,衡清芬. 高中英语教学中学生人文素养的提高[J]. 教学与管理,2010(30): 127—129.
④ 钱坤强. 外语习得与思辨能力[J]. 山东外语教学,1996(3): 72—75.
⑤ 黄源深. 思辨缺席[J]. 外语与外语教学,1998(7): 1,19.
⑥ 杨德祥,赵永平. 内容依托式教学对英语专业学生思辨能力的影响[J]. 外语教学,2011,32(5): 61—64.

reader),通过预测读者的需要来建构文章框架,引导"真正读者"能深入理解作者观点、产生共鸣。而作者在预测读者期待的同时,也是对读者的思想、心智、价值观、态度、情感等多方面的分析,从而在此过程中培养与提升学生的思辨能力。① 此外,在英语阅读教学中,教师可以利用预测、分析、推断、评价等思辨方法,帮助学生深刻理解阅读材料;在阅读问题设置上,通过高阶思维问题(text-independent questions)以及上位问题的设置激活学生思维;同时,思维导图与概念图等的使用,也可帮助学生在头脑中构建知识体系。

2.1.4 英语教学能够培养学生的自主学习能力

随着教育社会化和学习型社会的到来,当代教育不断向终身性方向发展,教育超越了学校的局限扩展到人类生活的整个阶段和全部空间,终身学习能力也成为未来社会公民的一个必备能力。简言之,自主学习能力体现了这样一句话:"教是为了不教。"

本书在第 1 章第 1 节列举了一些对核心素养内容的界定,由于研究视角不同,这些核心素养框架在内容上存在一定差异。但是"学会学习"这项素养几乎得到了所有地区和组织的共同认可。

随着自主学习理念被引入英语教学领域,英语课堂教学的组织模式发生了巨大的转变:从传统英语课堂的"教师中心"模式转变为教师的权威性逐步淡化的英语课堂。学习的主动权重新回到学生手中,教师也从课堂的统治者、决策者转变为学生自主学习的引导者。在英语教学过程中,教师应充分发挥英语课程在培养学生的自主学习能力和学习策略中的重要作用,让学生的自主学习这一核心素养得到很好的提升。

理论探讨

英语教学在培养学生综合语言运用能力、提升学生人文素养、提高学生思维水平及培养学生自主学习能力方面具有不可替代的作用。请结合自身教学经历或学习经历,举例说明英语教学在培养学生核心素养过程中的价值。

---

① 李莉文. 英语写作中的读者意识与思辨能力培养——基于教学行动研究的探讨[J]. 中国外语,2011,8(3):66—73.

2.2 英语教学培育英语核心素养的研究范式

学生发展的核心素养是指学生应具备的、能够适应个人终身发展和社会发展需要的关键能力和必备品格。针对当前英语教学的现状，教师不仅要向学生传授语言知识，还要培养学生的核心素养，从而使其具备完善而健全的人格。

2.2.1 研究内容

就研究内容而言，基于核心素养的英语教学研究至少应包括以下几个方面：

第一，从课程内容六要素（主题语境、语篇类型、语言知识、文化知识、语言技能和学习策略）出发，系统研究分析教学目标的达成情况；

第二，从单元整体设计入手进行研究，注重单元内部板块间的融合性、递进性、整体性；

第三，注重教学"过程"研究，即教学的"生成性"和"弹性"，而不是"预成性"和"刚性"；

第四，强调教学评价研究，使教学评价摆脱终结性评价，向终结性评价与形成性评价、发展性评价相结合的综合评价模式迈进；

第五，开展主题式课例研究，即"以课为例"——选择一节课的教学内容作为载体，围绕一个研究主题或教学问题开展教学改进活动，促成核心素养在课堂教学中落实。

2.2.2 研究方式

根据《课标（2017 版）》，英语教学培育核心素养的思路和途径可以从以下四个方面入手：

1. 关注主题意义，设计单元整体教学目标

英语课程内容的三大主题语境为：人与自我、人与社会和人与自然，它们不仅是英语学科核心素养培养与发展的主要依据，还是教学目标制定及学习活动开展的关键

因素。① 同时,单元是承载和体现主题意义的基本单位,基于单元整体进行教学设计是为了在教学时形成向心合力,避免教学内容的碎片化及整体目标的缺乏。主题单元教学设计是以一个单元为整体,引导学生从整体入手,统筹安排,把握单元整体主题,紧扣单元整体训练项目,把相关知识串成一条教学线索,使单元教学整体运转。

制定单元整体目标有三个前提条件。首先,应从认真分析单元教学内容出发,整合能够体现主题意义的语言知识、文化知识、语言技能及学习策略;其次,以学生实际认知水平为基础,加之教师教学主要内容、学生学习任务难度及学生学习需求,统筹进行教学设计;最后,教学活动不仅应以主题意义为出发点,还应以主题意义为归宿点,并在活动过程中不断拓展主题意义。②

另外,制定单元整体目标还要注意以下三点。首先,应以学生核心素养的发展为根本宗旨与依据,以主题引领的英语学习活动为基础,从整体上考虑进行设计。其次,应特别注意调整好单元整体教学目标和分课时教学目标的关系,做好大小目标的衔接后再考量语篇整体设计。再次,教师在根据单元整体目标教学一个单元时,至少要经历三个维度对单元整体目标的研究和理解,并据此设计和展开教学活动,才能算得上单元整体教学。这三个维度分别是:编者意图、学生状态(即学情)以及教师的个性化理解和创造。其中,前两个维度是第三个维度的基础,三个维度的融合才促成了真正意义上的单元整体教学。最后,学习目标的整体性不仅意味着学习内容、学习活动的整体性,还必然意味着学习目标、学习内容及学习活动的系统性,系统性强调的是内在的联系,是逻辑的体现,是真正意义上的创新、创造。

2. 深入研读语篇,把握教学核心内容

语篇是英语教学的基础资源。语篇使语言学习摆脱杂乱无章、漫无目的的碎片化的语言材料,使语言学习有主题、有情境、有内容,而研读语篇则是对语篇的主题、内容、结构、文体、语言、作者立场与态度等进行深入地解读。研读语篇有利于教师多层面、多角度、多方向地探寻语篇所传递的主题意义,以及所呈现的行文风格、语言特色

---

① 中华人民共和国教育部. 普通高中英语课程标准(2017 年版)[S]. 北京:人民教育出版社,2017:47—48.
② 梅德明,王蔷. 改什么? 如何教? 怎样考? 高中英语新课标解析[M]. 北京:外语教学与研究出版社,2018:69—70.

和表达的观点、立场,从而以此为依据合理设计教学活动,最终帮助学生深刻理解语篇。[①]

目前西方关于语篇研读主要有三种理论:三中心论、语篇分析理论及图式理论。三中心论要求从文本、作者、读者三中心解读文本;语篇分析理论要求从衔接性、连贯性、意图性、可接受性、信息性、情境性及互文性七项标准解读文本;而图式理论则要求从内容、语言、文体三大图式对文本进行解读。

国内学者张秋会、王蔷(2016)认为,教师研读语篇的水平决定着其教学设计的效果,也影响着学生的"学习体验的程度、认知发展的维度、情感参与的深度和学习成效的高度",她们将教师对语篇的研读角度分为以下五个:主题意义、主要内容、作者意图、语言修辞和文体结构。[②] 其中主题意义和主要内容属于 what 问题,作者意图属于 why 问题,而语言修辞和文体结构属于 how 问题。

3. 实践英语学习活动观,促进核心素养养成

活动是英语学习的基本形式,是学习者学习语言知识、形成多元思维、发展文化品质、培养学习能力的主要途径,也就是说,学生学习语言不可能仅仅依靠单方面去"理解"语言材料,还应在丰富多彩的学习活动中体验、运用语言,表达意义,将语言的 input 转化为 intake,最终促进其核心素养的形成与发展。[③] 除此之外,课外英语学习活动还是课堂教学的拓展和延伸,它对于巩固课堂教学,以及将语言知识转化为语言技能、培养与激发学生学习语言的兴趣、升华师生关系有着不可替代的作用。学习活动被分为内部活动(思维活动)和外部活动(言语行为和动作行为),也有人将学习活动细分为思维活动、建构活动、探究活动、创新活动与社会活动,而《课标(2017 版)》则将学习活动分成三类,即学习理解类活动、应用实践类活动和迁移创新类活动。

设计英语学习活动时应注意以下五点:

第一,活动情境的创设应符合真实性、简洁性、有效性,并与学生的直接经验和实际生活紧密结合;

① 中华人民共和国教育部. 普通高中英语课程标准(2017 年版)[S]. 北京: 人民教育出版社,2017:49—50.
② 张秋会,王蔷. 浅析文本解读的五个角度[J]. 中小学外语教学(中学篇),2016(11):11—16.
③ 梅德明,王蔷. 改什么? 如何教? 怎样考? 高中英语新课标解析[M]. 北京: 外语教学与研究出版社,2018:76.

第二,教师应善于利用各种工具和手段帮助学生在活动中整合、梳理信息;

第三,教师课堂提问应富有层次、条理清晰,同时引发学生的反思与讨论,最终促进学生思维从低阶向高阶层层递进;

第四,活动情境的创设还应充分考虑地点、场合、对象、人物关系、交际目的等;

第五,英语学习活动在设计时也应有不同层次。①

4. 立足学生学习能力的提升,为培养学生学习素养创造条件

"学习活动是人的全部生命投入的过程。"②学会学习,即学习能力是英语学科核心素养之一。新的课程标准指出,高中阶段不仅要教语言,更为重要的是以语言为基础、以语言学习为途径,培养学生的学习能力。教师应在教学过程中为学生学习能力的培养与提高创造条件,帮助学生在学习过程中学会计划、监督、调控、评价自身的学习进程,并且促使学生自主学习能力、合作学习能力及探究式学习能力的提升。

教师在培养学生学习能力时应特别注意以下三点。首先,在培养学生自主学习能力时应做好以下两方面工作:一是教师应学会放手,即教师在给学生布置任务时应做幕后引导者,而不应全部包办、不给学生留自主的余地;二是教师应相信学生、敢于放手,即不论是学习成绩优秀的学生还是学习成绩落后的学生,教师都应满足其自主学习的愿望。其次,在培养学生合作学习能力时,教师首先应尝试基于建构主义学习观看待学习,即学习是在社会文化背景下,通过人与人、人与物之间的互动,主动建构意义的过程,而不是直接接受现成结论的过程。③ 同时,由于建构主义者认为学习具有主动建构性、社会互动性和情境性,据此,在教学中教师应使学生首先以自身经验为基础,在情境化的社会实践活动中充分利用"学习共同体"的理论,促使学生间相互促进、共同提高,完成各自头脑中知识的建构。最后,在培养学生探究式学习能力时,教师应旨在促进学生的深度学习,反对机械记忆知识点和非批判性地盲目接受知识。教师可以从以下几方面入手:第一,确立高阶思维能力发展的教学目标、整合意义关联的学习内容,引导学生学习理解;第二,创设真实情境、引入新问题情境,引导学生实践体验

① 中华人民共和国教育部. 普通高中英语课程标准(2017年版)[S]. 北京:人民教育出版社,2017:53.
② 李润洲,石中英. 人·学习·学习能力——构建学习型社会的哲学思考[J]. 教育学报,2006(1):62—67.
③ 丰玉芳. 建构主义学习设计六要素在英语教学中的应用[J]. 外语与外语教学,2006(6):33—36.

并迁移创新;第三,设置持续关注的评价模式,引导学生深度反思。①

理论探讨

本节讨论了英语教师在培育学生英语核心素养时应关注的内容和研究思路,请谈谈教师在这一过程中扮演的角色及作用。

2.3　基于英语活动观的课堂教学设计与实施理念的创新

2.3.1　英语学习活动观概念解读

《课标(2017 版)》指出:"普通高中英语课程倡导指向学科核心素养的英语学习活动观和自主学习、合作学习、探究学习等学习方式。教师应设计具有综合性、关联性和实践性特点的英语学习活动,使学生通过学习理解、应用实践、迁移创新等一系列融语言、文化思维为一体的活动获取、阐释和评判语篇意义,表达个人观点、意图和情感态度,分析中外文化异同,发展多元思维和批判性思维,提高英语学习能力和运用能力。"②

从以上表述可以归纳出英语学习活动观的三个最基本特征:第一,英语学习活动观指向学科核心素养发展,即英语学习活动将成为联系英语教学内容和教学目标的纽带,也就是说,英语学习活动旨在深刻反映课程内容的基础上培养语言能力、培育文化意识、提升思维品质、增强学习能力;第二,英语学习活动观重视课程内容的整合性学习以及六要素的共同作用,即以主题语境为背景,依托体裁丰富、形式多样的语篇,使学生在具有综合性、关联性和实践性特点的英语学习活动中,通过发现、分析、解决问题,获得语言知识与文化知识,提升语言技能,养成学习策略,最终实现核心素养的整体发展;第三,英语学习活动观体现外语学习的认知性特点和实践性特点,且关注英语学习活动的各种类型。③

总之,学习活动观的根本要义是以发展学科核心素养为最终目标,并通过学习活

---

① 安富海. 促进深度学习的课堂教学策略研究[J]. 课程·教材·教法,2014,34(11):57—62.

② 中华人民共和国教育部. 普通高中英语课程标准(2017 版)[S]. 北京:人民教育出版社,2017:52.

③ 高洪德. 英语学习活动观的理念与实践探讨[J/OL]. (2018-03-26)[2019-02-27]. http://www.flts.cn/node/1074.

动观的指导进行英语课程设计与实施,从而培养与提升学生的学用能力。它从根本上体现了英语学科工具性与人文性相统一的双重属性,也体现了英语学习的"活动"本质和学生主体性,为创建有中国特色的英语教学提供了崭新的理论基础与实践路径。

2.3.2 基于英语学习活动观的教学设计与实施

1. 基于活动理论的立体化英语教学活动设计

活动是实施英语学习的基本形式和主要途径。Engestrom 于 1987 年提出了一个研究人类不同活动形式的跨学科概念框架,即"活动理论三角模型"(见图 2.1),该框架将主体、客体、中介工具、规则、学习共同体、劳动分工、成果等之间的诸多交互活动编织成一个系统网络。在该模型中,单单是主体和客体相互作用不足以产生最终的学习成果,还需要在中介工具(mediating artifact)、规则(rule)、学习共同体(learning community)、劳动分工(division of labor)四者的共同力量下产生意义建构才能产生学习成果。因此可以看出,英语课堂并不只是教师与学生间简单的互动活动,英语教师应通过借助直观教具、激发学生间同伴互助,以及布置学习任务等方式设计立体化的教学活动,从而帮助学生对所学内容进行意义建构,提升英语学习的成效。

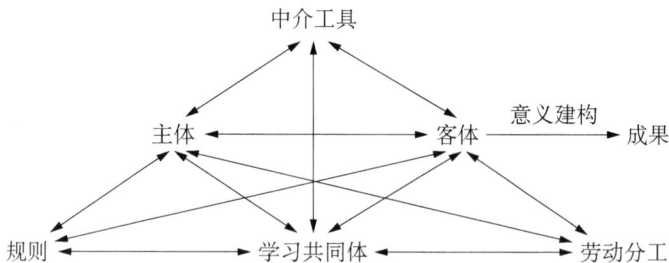

图 2.1　活动理论三角模型①

基于英语学习活动观的英语活动设计可被概括为"六要素六层次"设计范式。②

---

① 张军,程晓龙."活动理论"视阈下中国英语学习者的同伴反馈策略实证研究[J]. 外语教学,2018,39(6):57—63.

② 梅德明,王蔷. 改什么? 如何教? 怎样考? 高中英语新课标解析[M]. 北京:外语教学与研究出版社,2018:93—94.

"六要素"即英语课程内容六要素,包括主题语境、语篇类型、语言知识、文化知识、语言技能和学习策略。"六层次"则是在"六要素"的基础上梳理的:

第一个层次为,根据既定主题创设语境,语境的创设要满足真实性、简洁性、有效性,要能激活学生头脑中已有的直接经验。在情境创设后应根据情境提出问题,问题可以由教师提出,也可以由学生在教师的引导下提出。

第二个层次为,在情境创设、已知激活、问题提出的基础上,梳理细节信息,引导学生获取新知,弥补先前知识框架的空缺。

第三个层次为,在梳理细节信息、获取新知的基础上,进而开始概括、整合、重组信息,使学生在获取零散信息的基础上形成新的知识结构框架,从而对主题意义有一个新的认识。

第四个层次为,在新的知识结构框架构建起来的基础上,开展语言实践类活动,旨在对先前获得的语言新知进行产出,并且在语言产出与进行活动的交融中达到语言新知由外部向内部的转化。

第五个层次为,在语言新知内化的基础上,分析语言结构并使语言形式与主题意义发生联系,使学生在情境中体验与感受语言的运用。

第六个层次为,在以上五个层次的基础上开展迁移创新活动,即教师应引导和激励学生将所内化的语言知识与技能、文化知识、学习策略等迁移到新的、实际的生活情境中去,解决真实生活情境中的实际问题。

由此可以看出,这六个层次的层层递进实际是实现了学习理解类活动、应用实践类活动、迁移创新类活动三类活动的层层递进、逐步升华,并最终服务于学生英语核心素养的形成。

2. 正确认识传统的英语学习活动方式

当下,英语学习方法中,建构性学习、交际法和任务型学习等方法兴起,而传统的例如语法、翻译、背诵、句型操练等方法的弊端日益凸显。但是,这些看似过时的学习方法并没有因此销声匿迹,甚至在使用新的英语学习方法时或多或少会以传统的学习方法为基础。这是因为,英语与汉语的语言符号系统相去甚远,而中国又不具备使用英语的环境,因此要在有限时间内掌握并运用英语,就不能排斥语言形式的学习,不能忽视基于不同认知机制的操练。例如,语言学家 John Carroll 就曾把"语法敏感度"

(grammatical sensitivity)和"死记硬背的能力"(rote learning ability)列入外语学习能力(aptitude)。① 可见,英语学习不可能只遵循某种或几种学习途径,语法知识的学习以及适当的操练、记诵有助于所学的语言知识与技能内化。另外,对语篇中的长难句进行剖析与翻译,有助于精准理解语篇内涵,避免理解上的模糊和似是而非,从而有助于进一步对语篇进行更深层次的探索。

3. 学习活动观体现于单元教学整体设计

单元是一个相对完整的学习单位,也是一个相对完整的学习过程。单元整体教学是实践核心素养的一种重要的实施路径和方式。在单元学习过程中,学生通过教师的具体主题的引领,以形式多样的语篇为依托,选择和运用适当的学习策略,学习语篇中所呈现出的语言知识和文化知识,进行深度思考、挖掘和分析语篇的内涵,用英语交流、探讨语篇的主题意义,逐步发展语言能力、文化意识、思维品质和学习能力,最终达到学科育人、知行合一的目的。

进行单元整体教学时,教师应从以下四个方面予以关注。首先,关注单元教学目标设计,特点如下:一是目标均以描述行为方式的词句呈现,从而同时强调了学习过程和学习结果;二是目标应明确,既可操作也可评价,防止使用标签式用语;三是目标应整合课程内容六要素,同时内嵌核心素养四方面;四是目标中的活动设计应层层递进,从学习理解类活动到实践应用类活动再到迁移创新活动。其次,关注教学板块之间的融合性与整合性,这体现在各板块之间不是相互独立,而是"你中有我,我中有你"、相互渗透、层次递进。再次,关注教学活动的循环性和持续性,其循环性体现在教学内容螺旋式组织以及教学活动的不断复现和逐步提升上,持续性则体现在学生在一个单元的学习后所掌握的学习策略对后续学习的支持。最后,关注教学评价的灵活性和多样性,如牛津初中英语的 Self-assessment 板块不能流于形式地仅仅让学生在评价栏中勾选或填写一个评价性的单词或短语,而应通过后续教学活动真正落实评价目标的达成情况,同时教师也可以自行制定出更有趣味性、针对性和实效性的评价方式。②

---

① 戴炜栋,何兆熊. 新编简明英语语言学教程[M].上海:上海外语教育出版社,2013:164.
② 杨玲.基于英语学科核心素养的单元整体教学设计[J].中国教师,2018(12):60—64.

4. 学习活动观激发学生深度学习

指向核心素养的学习一定是深度学习,深度学习是学科核心素养发展的基本途径,是引导学生掌握学科本质的学习。"深度学习"的四个特征是高认知、高投入、真实任务以及反思。[①] 教师要想在外语课堂上激发学生进行深度学习,就要抓住"三大根本":抓住学生的根本(触发心灵)、抓住教材的根本(学科本质)以及抓住学习的根本(参与实践)。抓住这"三大根本"的课堂才能产生学习者的深度学习,这是以学为本的课堂,是从身体到心灵、从表层到本质都获得深度学习的课堂。在深度学习中,学生是具有主观能动性的学习者;教师不再是课堂的"统治者",而是学生学习活动的引导者、促进者、维持者;学生的学习目标是学用结合、学以致用;学生的学习内容是蕴含实际意义的任务,是真实情境的问题解决;教学过程中是高投入、高认知、高表现的学习,也是输入输出最大化的学习;学习评价是形成性、发展性的评价;教学方案是教师开给学生的学习"处方",让学生知道自己的问题是什么、怎么解决、怎么做才能解决等。[②]

理论探讨

结合英语学习活动观的英语活动设计的"六要素六层次"范式,谈谈英语课程内容六要素如何在六个层次中得到落实。

---

① 崔允漷. 指向学科核心素养的教学——即让学科教育"回家"[J/OL]. (2019 - 02 - 20)[2019 - 03 - 07]. http://www. jsgyzx. net/jiaoyushiye/2019-02-20/2195. html.
② 安桂清. 课例研究[M]. 上海:华东师范大学出版社,2018:24—27.

第3章　课例研究与英语教师课例研究素养

通过本章学习,你将:

1. 了解英语教学课例研究的概念与特点;

2. 掌握英语教学课例研究设计流程和方法;

3. 领会英语教师课例研究素养。

3.1　英语教学课例研究的内涵

3.1.1　课例研究的概念

"课例"是指一个真实的教学案例。"课例研究"是教学研究的一种,起源于20世纪50年代日本的授业研究,它以学生学习与发展中的问题为研究对象,以教师为主导,基于教师的反思性实践,通过集体合作明确研究主题、设计教学方案、开发课堂观察工具、确定分工与任务、开展课后研讨活动以及撰写研究报告等环节,促进教师专业化发展、促进学生学习和发展,最终达到改进教学、实现教学与研究一体化的目的。

对教师而言,通过课例研究,教师可以发展自身有关教学、学科、学生的知识,提升改进教学过程的使命感、责任感,也为自身专业化发展挖掘资源上的支持;①对学生而言,课例研究可以窥见学生的学习面貌,为学生的学习构建积累实践知识;对教学而言,课例研究通过研究一个个真实的教学案例,使教学研究回归到最真实的教学生活。②

3.1.2　英语教学课例研究的特点

1. 实践性

首先,课例研究少不了上课这一环节,而上课实际就是教师实践的过程。值得注意的是,课例研究上的是研究课而不是传统教研活动中的示范课,后者的目的是择其善者而从之,而前者的目的更在于发现其不善者而改之。

其次,课例研究是从真实课堂中潜存的实践性问题出发,促使广大中小学教师发现问题后在自己所在的教师群体中确定研究问题,并在教师们思维的火花经历不断碰撞后发现解决问题的方法,共享实践经验与理性提炼的成果。③

再次,课例研究为教师实践性知识的获得与生长提供了良好的平台,包括课前准备知识、课堂教学技能、课后反思能力等,成为教师专业发展的实践路径。

最后,课例研究的最终目的是"实践的理论化",即将由课例研究得到的实践性理论再进一步用来指导教学实践。因此,可以说,课例研究虽来源于教学实践但又高于教学实践。

2. 反思性

教师是课例研究的主导者,课例研究实际上是教师行动研究的一种,是教师的"反思性实践"。教师的反思既是核心也是重点。

首先,反思是"边行动边反思",反思是教师对自己的思考,除了具有反身性(即使思考从课程回到自身),还要引起自身教学行为的变化与改进,而不是纯思辨。

其次,反思是"合作中的反思",即反思的过程不仅是独立思考,更强调教师之间的合作交流,因为课例研究是由一个教师群体共同完成的。从这个角度看,课例研究中的"教师"既是一个"孤独的行者"又是"学习共同体"中的一员。

---

① 安桂清. 课例研究:信念、行动与保障[J]. 全球教育展望,2007(3):42—46,85.

② 安桂清. 课例研究[M]. 上海:华东师范大学出版社,2018:24—27.

③ 胡庆芳. 课例研究,我们一起来:中小学教师指南(第二版)[M]. 北京:教育科学出版社,2016:22.

再次，反思是"理论指导下的反思"，反思既强调从实践经历中学习的重要性，又不否定学习理论为教师的反思提供新的视角的事实。

最后，反思是"高于教学的反思"，即反思不能仅局限于教学技术领域，这样的反思可能会丧失批判性，而应是对教师全部生活方式的全方位、多角度的审视。

3. 情境性

课例研究的情境性是指"课例研究是一个融合教学实践、知识、心智模式、人际关系、支持合作性研究的结构与工具等要素的复杂的教师学习体系"[①]。而以上五个教学因素在不同的教学情境下具有可变性和不可复制性，因而课例研究的最终目的不是归纳总结出一套万能的、可供所有教师操作的模式，而是依据对一个个具体教学情境的分析和研究探讨教师教学行动中共同面临的问题和可供解决的方式。

4. 以学习为中心的研究模式

以学习为中心的研究模式是指在课例研究的过程中，应以"学生的学"为出发和归宿，要在课例研究的各个步骤（见本章第 2 节）中渗透和突显"以学习为中心""以学生为本"的精髓。

第一，明确课例研究主题时应体现"教学合一"的思想，即在将某个教学实践难题确定为研究主题前应先向自己发问：这些难题是否与学生的学习息息相关？

第二，设计教学方案时应从学情分析出发，做到"因学设教"，这要求教师不仅要在设计教学方案前通过观察法、访谈法、测试法等考察学情，还要在设计教学方案时增加能体现学生主体的活动。

第三，实施课堂观察时应做到"以学观教"，即不仅要开发用于记录学生学习情况的观察工具（例如学生课堂参与度观察表、小组话语权分布表、学生在学习共同体中的角色分配表等），还应在实施课堂观察时把学生学习行为作为观察的焦点，通过学生学习实况对教师教学情况进行考察和评价。

第四，开展课后研讨活动时做到"以学论教"，即分析研讨时应首先站在"学生的学"的立场，从学生学习的实际情况出发并展开讨论。

第五，在撰写课例研究报告时应做到"依学改教"，从"学"中出现的问题出发指导

---

① 安桂清.课例研究[M].上海：华东师范大学出版社,2018：21.

教学改进的方向和重点。①

理论探讨

课例研究本质是一种教师的行动研究,本节探讨了课例研究的概念及英语教学课例研究的特点。请结合自身教学或学习经历谈谈课例研究对教师专业发展的作用。

3.2　英语教学课例研究的设计

3.2.1　明确课例研究主题

明确课例研究主题是课例研究的出发点,同时它指导着课例研究各个环节的进行。

课例研究的主题应满足以下几个特征:第一,主题应从现实出发,即课例研究的主题必须基于英语教学实践中的具体教学问题,从教师日常教学行为入手;第二,主题应由反思促成,即教师应具备良好的反思能力和问题意识,善于在日常教学活动中发现问题、以小见大,并反思这个问题是否典型、是否普遍、是否值得研究等;第三,主题应"小题大做"、切实可行,即研究的主题应当可操作、小而具体;第四,主题所涉及的研究问题的答案应具有开放性,那些已经有唯一的、已知的答案的问题使研究失去了意义,显然不适合作为研究主题。

实际操作过程中,课例研究主题的来源可以从很多维度进行划分,例如:教学的重点、教学的难点和教学的兴奋点;与学科知识及课程知识有关的主题、与学习者有关的主题、与教师有关的主题以及与教学法有关的主题等。

3.2.2　合作设计教学方案

设计教学方案即对一堂课的教学的预设,这个过程应由教师群体合作完成。教学方案的设计至少应当包含如下三个要素:教学内容分析、教学目标分析,以及思路、方法与资源。

第一,教学内容分析中应包括课标要求、教材分析、重难点及学情分析等部分。

---

① 安桂清.课例研究[M].上海:华东师范大学出版社,2018:150—154.

第二,教学目标分析中应包括知识目标、能力目标、情感价值观目标这三维目标。

第三,思路、方法与资源中应包括整体思路、模式方法、推荐资源等板块。

3.2.3 开发课堂观察工具

课堂观察工具的开发可以从四个维度出发,即学生学习、教师教学、课程性质,以及课堂文化。这四个维度又可以分成以下相应视角(见图3.1),课堂观察工具则可以根据不同的视角进行设计。

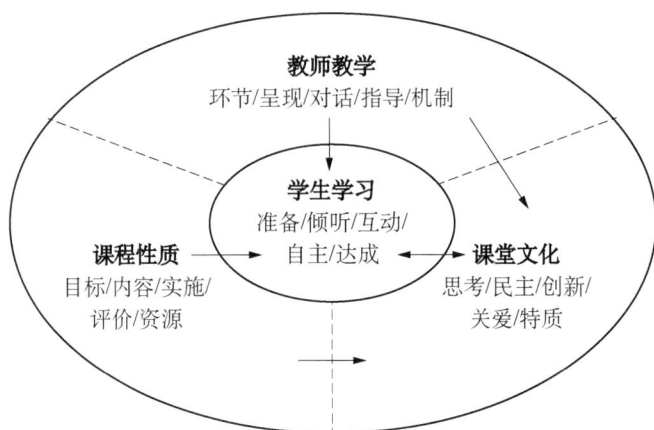

图 3.1 课堂观察框架示意图①

3.2.4 确定分工观察任务②

课堂观察视角的分类是多种多样的,除了可以按照前文的四个维度进行观察任务的分配,还可以从以下五个视角进行:主体互动、知识呈现、教学环节、课堂知识和目标达成。这五个视角分别体现了一堂课的"人""方法""结构""关系"以及"目标"因素。

第一,主体互动是指教学活动主体之间通过言语或行动进行信息共享、传达、接收,没有主体互动的课堂便成为了教师一个人的独舞。主体互动包括师生间的互动与

---

① 沈毅,林荣凑,吴江林,崔允漷. 课堂观察框架与工具[J]. 当代教育科学,2007(24):17—21,64.
② 胡庆芳. 课例研究,我们一起来:中小学教师指南(第二版)[M]. 北京:教育科学出版社,2016:40—45.

生生间的互动。主体互动的衡量标准包括互动的"质量"和互动的"机会"。前者意为互动不在于量的多少而在于其是否能激起学生的学习兴趣、适当活跃课堂氛围、引起学生积极深入且批判性地思考、形成合理反馈以及促成主体间"1＋1＞2"的合作学习等；后者意为课堂氛围是否民主平等、学习共同体内的每一位成员是否都有互动的机会，以及其是否在整个互动过程中都扮演着自己必不可少的角色等。

第二，知识呈现成功与否是教学目标是否成功达成的一项重要标准，而判断知识呈现好坏应观察知识呈现的"时机"与"形式"。前者意为新知呈现前是否有足够的导入，例如相关情境的创设、旧知识的铺垫，以及学生学习兴趣的激发等；后者意为知识的呈现要符合学生认知发展水平，要以最能够促进学生理解的、最具有表现力的方式呈现出来。

第三，教学环节体现了教师对一堂课的结构化的设计，每节课甚至是每种课型都有其特定的教学环节以及教师对这些教学环节的个性化的展现。在观察一堂课的教学环节时，可以从其"流畅度"和"逻辑性"两个方面入手。"流畅度"是指一堂课的各个教学环节是否明朗以及各个教学环节之间的转换与衔接是否一气呵成，不生硬、不机械等。"逻辑性"是指各教学环节之间的关系，例如教师用于各个教学环节的时间是否安排合理，后面一个环节是否是前面一个环节的拓展和延伸，等等。

第四，观察课堂知识主要在于观察教师课前"预设"知识与学生课上"生成"知识之间的关系。前者是指教师课前准备的知识是否正确，是否与本节课课程内容相契合，以及是否符合学生当前的认知发展水平，等等；后者是指学生在课堂上是否能够基于已有知识和课堂所学进行拓展、延伸、创新，是否能够提出新的问题或值得思考的话题，等等。

第五，对目标达成的观察主要体现在对比目标的"预期"与"实现"。前者在于一堂课后学生是否达到了预期的目标，与预期目标相差或超越在哪里，等等，后者在于学生经过一节课的学习，其语言能力、文化意识、思维品质、学习能力是否提升到了一个崭新的高度。

3.2.5　开展课后研讨活动

1. 场地的确定

首先，最好的研讨场地是授课教室，因为在一节课结束后，教室的黑板上仍保留着教师的教学痕迹以及教学活动开展的痕迹,例如教师的板书、学生的展示等等,有助于研究小组回忆上课时的场景,可谓是"趁热打铁",从而使研讨活动更加快捷、高效。

但是,大多数情况下授课教室是学生日常生活中上课的教室,我们不可能要求学生在下课后离开,待研讨结束后再返回教室。在这种情况下,则需要研讨小组寻找专门的能够容纳所有研讨小组成员和执教者的研讨室,待课程结束后携带好上课所用的材料(包括纸质材料和电子材料)一起前往进行研讨。

2. 研讨的流程与规范

研讨环节应当有相应的流程与规范,例如先由主持人简要地拉开研讨序幕,再由执教者陈述自身教学意图及其教学中各个步骤的设计原因,接着是研讨小组成员各抒己见的自由发言时间,每人发言结束后,其他成员也可以对其发言提出疑问或做出评价,最后,待全员发言完毕后研究小组选 1 人进行总结,总结应主要是对教学形成的改进意见。

3. 责任的分配

在一次研讨会中,通常有主持人、执教者、评论员、总结人和记录员等角色。[1] 角色的分配应当在研讨之前做好,从而使研讨活动更加顺利、流畅地进行。

4. 研讨的原则[2]

第一,开放式、民主型的讨论,在讨论过程中研讨小组的各个成员无论其教龄的长短、年龄的长幼、职称的高低都应有平等的发言权。

第二,双向协商而不是单向建议,即研讨过程中执教者和研究小组应以协商为主,不应认为研究小组比执教者更加权威,执教者在听取意见后也应采取保留式改进的措施。

第三,有条理、集约型的记录,即记录员在记录研讨意见时应将意见归类整理后记录,而不是以碎片化的形式听一条记一条。

3.2.6 撰写课例研究报告

课例研究不是研讨过就结束,也不是研讨后形成研讨记录就结束,其最终应产生

---

① 安桂清. 课例研究[M]. 上海:华东师范大学出版社,2018:129.
② 胡庆芳. 课例研究,我们一起来:中小学教师指南(第二版)[M]. 北京:教育科学出版社,2016:48—49.

一个创造性的研究成果,即研究报告的生成。课例研究报告的撰写有助于执教者和研究小组的专业化发展,有助于形成新的、有价值的教学知识,并使这些知识得到推广和传播。撰写课例研究报告包括四个不可或缺的要素:课例研究主题、课例研究过程、相关案例支持和得出的结论①(参见本书实践篇)。

理论探讨

本节探讨了课例研究的六个基本步骤(包括明确课例研究主题、合作设计教学方案、开发课堂观察工具、确定分工观察任务、开展课后研讨活动和撰写课例研究报告),请结合自身教学或学习经历,谈谈各个环节在整个课例研究设计中的地位和作用。

3.3　英语教师课例研究素养

3.3.1　学习素养

教学即研究,课例研究将教学和研究融为一体,使得教学研究成为教师日常教学中一种常态化的活动。在课例研究过程中,教师立足一个或一系列教学问题或研究主题,在研究组中开展改进教学的一系列活动,既促进了教学的改进,也成就了自身学习的提升。因此,课例研究既是一种教师改进教学的研究方式,也是教师促进专业发展的学习方式,三者一起形成促进教师专业发展的"教、学、研"为一体的课例研究体系。基于三者之间的关系,从课例研究的视角看,教师要不断学习和研习,才能改进教学、完善教学,才能促进自身专业持续发展。因此,要开展课例研究,教师必须具备学习素养。学习素养可以解释为学会学习所需要的素养。学习素养是教师进行课例研究时所需要的知识、技能、方法、能力和态度等要素构成,是由知识素养、问题素养和创新素养三个维度整合形成的一个立体结构,②在教师开展课例研究中发挥着不可或缺的作用。

其中,知识素养是学习素养的发展基础,决定了学习素养的广度。在课例研究中,教师的知识素养包括政治理论知识、精深的学科专业知识、广博的科学文化知识和教

---

① 胡庆芳.课例研究,我们一起来:中小学教师指南(第二版)[M].北京:教育科学出版社,2016:49.
② 李笑非.基于核心素养的学习能力培养——课例研究[M].上海:华东师范大学出版社,2018:22—23.

学理论及实践性知识等。问题素养是学习素养的关键和质量保障，决定了学习素养的深度。在课例研究中，教师应具有问题意识和发现问题、分析解决问题的能力，以及自主、合作探究问题的能力和态度等。课例研究中，教师从日常教学活动中发现值得研究的问题，针对一个特定的研究问题逐步深入探寻解决方案，最终使问题得到合理解决，教学得到改进。创新素养是学习素养的外显形式，决定了学习素养的高度与学习者的高阶能力。在课例研究中，教师围绕着某一主题或问题，探寻解决这一问题的新的教学方法或途径，从而改进教学，即是围绕着问题的教学法知识的创造展开的。教师在课后将以往的教学数据与课中的研究数据加以组织，通过多轮相互比较和对照，从具体的案例中提炼经验，形成关于如何改进教学问题的观点或假设，实现教学法科学的创造。①

教师学习素养在知识素养、问题素养和创新素养三个维度上的发展共同决定了教师课例研究的整体质量和水平。

3.3.2　信息素养

在这个充满着"多媒体文化"和"网络文化"的信息社会中，不懂得信息技术的人犹如"文盲"。教师的信息素养的培养与提高是信息时代外语教学改革和外语教学质量提高的根本。教师的信息素养是指教师能够在纷繁复杂的信息中进行迅速且有效地筛选、创造性地加工与处理并最后将其运用于教学中的能力，②具体包括信息意识、信息知识、信息能力、信息和课程整合能力以及信息伦理。③ 在课例研究中，信息素养可以表现为英语教师利用网络资源为英语教学收集更多的真实语料，为英语教学创造一个尽可能真实的语言环境，优化英语教学环境。信息素养也可以表现为英语教师借助多媒体技术和网络技术呈现多模态的语言知识，组织更加丰富的学习活动，增加教学的直观性、活跃课堂氛围，激发学生学习的热情、参与度和主动性。信息素养还可以表现为教师学习并逐步掌握包括微课、翻转课堂、MOOCS、学习分析、自适应技术、虚拟

---

① 安桂清.课例研究[M].上海：华东师范大学出版社，2018：16.

② 谢徐萍.E时代英语教师信息素养探论[J].外语界，2005(4)：9—12，18.

③ 余丽，王建武，曾小珊.教师的信息素养——信息技术与外语课程整合的关键因素[J].外语电化教学，2009(5)：70—74.

现实等信息技术手段,为提升自己的专业发展能力,提升自己的教学研究资源搜索、分析与整合能力。

3.3.3 科学素养

国际上普遍将科学素养(Scientific Literacy)概括为三个组成部分,即了解科学知识、了解科学的研究过程和方法、了解科学技术对社会和个人所产生的影响。在教师方面,教师的科学素养主要包括三个方面:科学基本知识、科学探究的过程和方法、科学情感。教师科学素养的提高有助于将教学与研究相结合,并"让教学成为研究""让教师成为研究者",而"让教学成为研究"不仅包含着教师"引导学生去探究",还包括教师"研究自己的教学",其中就包括课例研究。[①] 课例研究是教育研究中的一种,属于科学研究范畴,自然需要教师具有良好的科学素养。

从课例研究的角度看,教师科学素养的有无和高低,影响着教师的专业发展以及发展的质量,同时也会影响和改变教师的教育教学观、价值观以及对很多教育教学问题的看法和行为。教师的任何与教育教学有关的决策和计划都要在教师和学生共同理解的基础上才能实现教育教学的教学育人功能。在课例研究中,良好的科学素养赋予教师一双发现研究问题的"慧眼",使教师在教学研究过程中始终保持科学、严谨的态度并自始至终对教学研究充满热情。科学方法是科学素养中重要的内容。对科学方法的掌握关乎到教师课例研究的综合素质。掌握课例研究的科学方法并运用这些方法不仅能解决自己教学中的各种问题,还能与其他教师一起构建"教、学、研"专业发展共同体,共同提升课例研究的素养。

理论探讨

结合英语核心素养和教师专业发展,谈谈英语教师课例研究素养与英语核心素养和教师专业发展之间的关系。

---

① 陆军."让教学成为研究"的历程[M].南京:东南大学出版社,2016:145.

实 践 篇

第4章　英语名师的主题式课例研究

课例1　基于思维导图提升读写能力的课例研究

——以 Posters 语篇阅读课为例

第一部分　教学预设

一、教学内容分析

1. 课标要求

《课标(2011 版)》指出：小学生的英语学习应特别强调对英语的感知能力和良好的语言学习习惯。这里强调的"对英语的感知能力"，应该是指学生对声音和文字两种媒介的感知能力，也就是听音辨义和识文断字理解文本的能力；而只会听、说，不会读、写的学生一定算不得具有"良好的语言学习习惯"。(张伊娜，2016)《课标(2011 版)》在语言技能分级标准中对"读"有着明确的要求：能在图片的帮助下读懂简单的小故事(一级)；能借助图片读懂简单的故事或小短文，并养成按意群阅读的习惯(二级)。无论是一级还是二级，都要求学生能借助图片的帮助"读懂"所提供的文本(小故事或小短文)，也就是要求学生能够理解其情节或意义。

写,既是使用语言的重要技能,也是学习语言的重要手段。关于"写",《课标(2011版)》中二级标准的要求是"能根据图片、词语或例句的提示,写出简短的描述"。实际上,在小学阶段,"写"不只是为了表达,更是一种不可或缺的习惯,是语言学习起始阶段的基本功和后续学习的重要基础。张伊娜教授(2016)对小学英语教学中"写"的教学提出了原则性建议:在培养学生正确书写习惯的同时,教师要给学生创造意义表达的情境与条件,激发他们真实表达的欲望,并逐步培养他们写的兴趣与能力。

同时,《课标(2017版)》提出的四个核心素养中,学习能力的培养是学生终身学习和发展的必要保障,自主学习、合作学习和探究学习构成学习能力的主要组成部分。学习能力也是小学英语教学追求的目标之一。而且《课标(2017版)》提出了英语活动观,体现在读写教学中,意指通过形式多样的英语读写活动,不仅可以提升学生的读写能力,还能培养学生的学习能力。

2. 教材分析

该课是六年级的一篇阅读文章,以海报的形式介绍了良好的生活及学习习惯。

第一份海报的作者 Mike 介绍了良好的睡眠习惯,提出了睡前不该做的事情,并建议要养成早睡早起的好习惯。

第二份海报的作者 Yang Ling 介绍了良好的用眼习惯,着重指出了在生活中不注意用眼卫生的现象,如不分场合读书以及用眼过度等。

第三份海报的作者 Liu Tao 介绍了良好的学习习惯,指出了在课上和课后两个时间段分别要做好的几件事情,提出了"今日事今日毕"的建议。

3. 重点与难点

教学重点:能正确地理解并朗读课文内容,在教师的引导和帮助下复述课文内容。

教学难点:能初步运用本课所学的词汇和日常交际用语谈论习惯,并仿照课文,以海报的形式提出建议。

4. 学情分析

(1)学生心智特征分析。本课是借班执教的江苏省小学英语优质课竞赛课,对象是六年级学生。据任课教师反映,该班同学平时上课比较活跃,敢于发表自己的观点,在公开课上尤其喜欢参与活动。

（2）学生已有知识经验分析。因本节课是竞赛课,所以执教教师课前与学生的交流时间是统一且有限的。从简短的交流中了解到:学生对于良好的睡眠、用眼习惯有一定的了解,但不全面;对于良好的学习习惯他们基本上都有自己的观点;虽然在生活中接触过海报,但他们对于海报的表现形式缺少深入的了解。

二、教学目标分析

1. 知识目标

（1）能听懂、会读、会说 poster、habit、finish、leave、never、do eye exercises、take notes、on time;

（2）能听懂、会读、会说日常交际用语... need to ... /... should ... 及 Do not ... /... should not ... 。

2. 能力目标

（1）能正确地理解并朗读文章内容,在教师的引导和帮助下复述课文内容;

（2）能初步运用本课所学的词汇和日常交际用语谈论习惯。能运用招贴宣传良好的习惯,并给出建议。

3. 情感价值观目标

明白良好习惯对于生活的重要性,形成正确的、良好的习惯意识,并在日常生活中改正坏习惯,养成好习惯。

三、思路、方法与资源

1. 整体思路

本节课设计理念为:站在儿童的立场,以童心童眼阅读文本,以童言童语创生文本。在教学流程上以"激活体验,走近阅读;激发思维,走进阅读;输出语言,走向语用"的顺序,帮助学生理清思路,掌握信息,训练思维,提高读写能力,养成良好的行为习惯。

主要教学环节如下:

Stage One：Pre-reading

Step 1：Free talk and lead-in

【设计意图】通过课前展示海报,激活学生的生活体验,以谈话交流的方式直接切入本课话题。本环节既营造了轻松、富有生活体验的课堂氛围,又激发了学生的学习兴趣,可以激活学生已有的知识储备,为文本的阅读做好铺垫。

Stage Two：While-reading

Step 2：Careful listening for the main ideas of the text

(要求学生听录音,选择阅读材料的主题是关于哪一方面的。)

【设计意图】学生通过听的形式首次接触文章,以选择的方式感知文章,了解文章大意,明确本课主题。

Step 3：Fast reading for the main ideas of the text

What habits are the posters about?

【设计意图】学生带着问题有目的地自读课文,从中寻找、获取有用信息,初步培养学生获取信息的能力,为细读文本做好铺垫。

Step 4：Careful reading for specific information of the text

What does Mike tell us? How do you sleep well?

【设计意图】教师带领学生细读文本第一段,获取具体信息。学生在此过程中,通过上下文语境及观察图画理解新单词,培养了学生的观察能力,促进思维发展。

Step 5：Group reading for cooperative learning

How do you take care of your eyes? What should you do in class and after class? Let's read，share and check.

【设计意图】《课标(2011 版)》鼓励学生在教师的指导下,通过体验、实践、参与、探究和合作等方式,发现语言规律,逐步掌握语言知识和技能,不断调整情感态度,形成有效的学习策略,发展自主学习能力。在此环节中,学生在个体学习的基础上进行小组交流,互相启发、相互沟通,学会倾听,互相学习。在分工、合作的过程中充分发挥学生的主体性,促进深度思考。

Stage Three：Post-reading

Step 6：Retelling the text by following the record

【设计意图】在跟读过程中学生能整体把握文章,为语言输出做好准备。通过复述,学生对于文章的理解更透彻,同时也训练了学生的语言表达能力。

Step 7：Game-playing

A game：Magic eyes

(坏习惯犹如树上害虫,通过该游戏活动,让学生用"火眼金睛"将坏习惯找出来。)

【设计意图】英语课程具有工具性和人文性的双重性质,这就要求教师注重学生在人格情感方面的协调发展,追寻有意义的人性教育。(吉桂凤,2015)本环节通过游戏,激发和培养学生的学习兴趣,使学生巩固对于课文内容的掌握,既能提高学生的语言运用能力,又可帮助学生形成良好的行为习惯。

Step 8：Poster-making

(Students make some posters and show their posters.)

【设计意图】同"Step 7"的"设计意图"。

2. 模式方法

当前,小学英语教学中普遍存在着重听说、轻读写的现象。然而,读写教学对于学生的英语习得同样有着不可忽视的作用。因此,听说可以阶段性领先,但读写必须跟上。只有这样方能确保学生综合语言能力的可持续发展。(张伊娜,2016)本课主要采用思维导图的模式,将传统的单向思维变成多维发散的思维,帮助学生训练思维,提高读写能力。

思维导图是由英国心理学家东尼·博赞于 20 世纪 60 年代提出的,它是基于放射性思维的有效图形工具,通过一幅幅形象的"图",直观呈现人类大脑的放射性思维过程,使大脑的思维可视化。应用思维导图展开教学,能充分运用思维导图的图形优势,最大程度发掘学习潜能,有效吸引学生的注意力,促进记忆、联想和创造,有利于全面提高学生综合运用语言的能力。(吉桂凤,2015)同时,思维导图将阅读和写作进行有机结合,让学生从可视化思维导图中获得语言、内容、结构方面的写作知识,进而完成写作任务,实现提高写作能力的目标。(李一李,徐杰,李岩,2018)

Pre-reading 阶段主要的任务有两个,一是背景知识的激活,二是提前学习新词。

(王笃勤,2002)在本节课的导入环节,教师和学生交流课前所观看的海报,开门见山地直接导入本课主题 Posters,并让学生结合"世界爱眼日"和"世界睡眠日"两幅海报,谈一谈在日常生活中自己是如何保护眼睛以及保证良好睡眠的,为学习做好了情境与知识的准备。

While-reading 阶段设计的活动除了让学生掌握文章信息,还要训练学生的阅读技能,发展学生的思维。围绕这一目标,本节课教师从扶到放,环环相扣,层层递进:整体感知内容;快速浏览文章,理清文章脉络;细读文章段落,获取细节信息;小组合作分工,提升学习能力。在此过程中,文章的关键词、各层级的关键词和信息以思维导图式板书逐级呈现,架构起文章脉络,学生的观察、理解、分析、运用等能力得到训练,思维得到发展,为语言输出做好了充分准备。

Post-reading 阶段的目的有两个,一是使学生根据阅读内容进行各种思维活动,二是鼓励学生将所阅读的内容与自己的经历、知识、兴趣和观点相联系。(王笃勤,2002)本节课以制作海报的形式,让学生"用英语做事情",进行带有创造性的书面表达,要求学生"写得正确""写得好看""写得有创意",同时发展了学生的思维和想象,促进正确行为习惯的养成和良好文化品格的形成。

3. 推荐资源

(1) 张伊娜. 当前小学英语读写教学的问题及建议[J]. 江苏教育,2016(17):23—25. 本文针对小学英语教学中普遍存在的重听说、轻读写的现象,主张听说可以阶段性领先,但读写必须跟上,以确保综合语言能力的可持续发展。文中阐述了读写教学的重要性,并分别对"读"教学和"写"教学提出了建议。

(2) 吉桂凤. 思维导图与小学英语教学[M]. 北京:教育科学出版社,2015. 本书从科学性、实用性、系统性等方面阐述了在小学英语教学中运用思维导图的可行性,书中既有理论支撑,又有大量鲜活的案例,内容涵盖了思维导图在小学英语语篇教学、词汇教学、综合板块教学、单元整体教学以及板书设计和家庭作业等各个环节中的具体做法和注意事项,内容全面系统、结构严谨有序,图文并茂,可操作性强,适合一线小学英语教师阅读。

(3) 李一李,徐杰,李岩. 思维导图在大学英语读写课堂"输入促成"环节中的应用[J]. 理论观察,2018(3):174—176. 本文基于产出导向法理论,该理论包括输出驱动、输入促成和评估三个环节。本文研究在读写课堂上,将思维导图引入到"输入促成"环节,同步提高学生阅读和写作能力,实现"以读促写"目标。

(4) 王笃勤. 英语教学策略论[M]. 北京:外语教学与研究出版社,2002. 本书从宏观和微观的角度论述了教学中的策略问题,既有总的教学原则,也包含一般的教学步骤,更不乏具体的教学技巧和实践内容,层层扩展,提供了大量的各种教学原则下具体的教学策略,具有较强的指导性、可操作性和实用性。

第二部分　精彩实录

授课地点:江苏省连云港市解放路小学。

授课时间:2018 年 9 月 21 日。

听课人员:江苏省教研室何锋书记,南京师范大学外国语学院教授、江苏省中小学外语专业委员会秘书长张伊娜教授,各市教研员以及教师代表共 350 名左右。

授课过程:

Stage One:Pre-reading

Step 1:Free talk and lead-in

T:Hello,boys and girls. Just now,I showed you some pictures. There are some pictures and words. What are they?

S:...(学生面露不知如何用英语表达的表情。)

T:You can speak in Chinese.

S:是海报。

T:Yes,they're posters.

(教学单词 poster。)

T:Look at these posters,what are the posters about?

S1:Eyes.

T:Right. The first topic is "Take care of our eyes".

(教读 Take care of our eyes。)

T:Look at this poster,the topic is ...?

S2：Sleep.

T：You're clever. The topic is "Sleep well".

（教读 Sleep well。）

T：From these posters，we know we should "Take care of our eyes" and "Sleep well". They're very important for everyone. How do we take care of our eyes? How do we sleep well? What should we do? What shouldn't we do?

S1：Get up early and go to bed early.

S2：做眼保健操。

T：Yes，we should do eye exercises.

S3：看绿色植物。

T：Right. We can look at some green plants.

S4：We shouldn't drink tea before bedtime.

T：Good. You shared some good habits. We can get some information from these posters.

Stage Two：While-reading

Step 2：Careful listening for the main ideas of the text

T：These are some posters from Mike's class. What are the posters about? Let's listen，choose and answer.

A. Food　B. Movies　C. Clothes　D. Habits

（教读并理解 Habits。学生认真听录音。）

S：Choose D. Habits.

Step 3：Fast reading for the main ideas of the text

T：Good.

S：These are some posters from Mike's class. They are all about good habits.（文中句子）

T：We know these posters are all about good habits. What habits are the posters about? Please skim the text and find them out.

（指导学生浏览课文后回答问题。）

S1：Sleep well.

T：Right. Who makes the poster?

S2：Mike.

T：Good. The next poster is about ... ?

S3：Take care of our eyes.

T：Good job.

（教读 Take care of our eyes。）

Who makes this poster?

S4：Yang Ling.

T：OK. The last poster is about ... ?

S5：In class and after class.

S6：Wang Bing makes the poster.

Step 4：Careful reading for specific information of the text

T：The posters are about different topics. Look at the first poster. Mike draws some interesting pictures. Look at the clock，what time does the boy go to bed?

S：It's a quarter to nine.

T：Oh，yes. It's early. What time does the boy get up?

S：It's half past six.

T：Early or late?

S：It's early.

T：Right. Boys and girls，how do we sleep well? What should we do? What shouldn't we do? Let's read the first poster. Please read and underline.

（学生认真阅读第一份海报，以横线划出应该做的事情,用波浪线划出不该做的事情。）

S1：We need to sleep well every day.

S2：We do not eat before bedtime.

S3：Do not drink too much water at night.

S4：Go to bed early and get up early.

（教师在此过程中适时板书关键词。）

Step 5：Group reading for cooperative learning

（1）T：We know how to sleep well. How do you take care of your eyes? What should you do in class and after class? Let's learn，share and report.

T：Step 1，learn. Choose one poster to learn and take notes. Do you know how to take notes?

（有学生面露不理解 take notes 的表情。）

T：When we read，we can circle some key words and sentences or write down some questions. Do you know now?

（学生点头，小声说：记笔记。）

T：Great. OK，if you have any new words，here's a tip for you. You can guess the meaning according to the contexts or pictures. You can also discuss in groups or ask me.

（两人一组，选择不同的海报学习，并在学习过程中做好笔记，用不同的符号划出应该做的事情和不该做的事情。教师在行间巡视，帮助个别学生。）

（2）T：Boys and girls，have you finished?

S：Yes.

T：Now，let's share in groups. Share your study notes，use the sentences … should/need to … Do not …/… shouldn't … Here's a new tip. Listen to your partner carefully. If you have any questions，you can ask.

（小组内交流自己的学习收获。通过交流，组内成员了解到两份海报的信息。）

Step 6：Practicing by following the teacher

T：Boys and girls，have you finished?

S：Yes.

T：OK，let's report in class. How do you take care of your eyes?

S1：We need to do eye exercises.

T：Read after me，do eye exercises. What does it mean? Can you do the action?

（做眼保健操的动作）

T：Great. Read after me, do eye exercises.

（学生跟读短语 do eye exercises。）

S2：Do not read on the bus, in bed or in the sun.

S3：We should not watch too much TV.

S4：We should not play computer games for hours.

T：We can play computer games for rest, but we should not play computer games for hours. Right?

S：Yes.

（教师随即板书关键词。）

T：Well done. What should you do in class and after class?

S1：We should listen to the teachers in class.

S2：Sometimes we need to take notes.

T：Right. Read after me, take notes.

（学生跟读短语 take notes。）

S3：Do my homework carefully.

S4：Finish it on time.

T：We should do my homework carefully and finish it on time. Please remember never leave today's work for tomorrow. Never means ... ?

S：从不。

T：I wish you can remember and do it. Read together.

S：Never leave today's work for tomorrow.

Stage Three：Post-reading

Step 7：Reading the text and retelling the text

T：Boys and girls, please read the text together, and pay attention to your pronunciation and intonation.

（学生阅读课文。）

T：Look at the blackboard, let's retell the text. Let's try.

（学生根据板书复述课文内容。）

Step 8：Playing a game and saying

T：Boys and girls，you know these good habits and bad habits. Oh，look at the tree. There are some apples on the tree. But the tree is unhappy. Why? Because there are some pests in it，let's help the tree. Find bad habits. Bad habits like pests，let's play a game，magic eyes，find and catch.

（同桌讨论哪些是坏习惯，进行游戏：火眼金睛捉害虫。）

S1：We shouldn't shout in the library.

S2：We shouldn't read in the sun.

S3：We shouldn't go to bed early.

T：Is it a pest?

S3：Sorry.

T：Don't worry，you can try again.

S3：We shouldn't watch too much TV.

T：The tree is happy now. You did a good job. Boys and girls，we should say goodbye to bad habits and make friends with good habits.

Step 9：Making a poster

T：Mike，Yang Ling and Wang Bing make these posters to introduce good habits. What about your good habits? Some of you study well，how do you do? Some of you are strong，how do you get stronger? Please make a poster to introduce your good habits.

For example，this is my poster. First，choose my topic. Then，write down my name. Finally，introduce my good habits.

（学生完成海报的书写。）

S1：In the library，we should read carefully. Do not speak loudly. We shouldn't eat or drink.

S2：Read books，we should read more books. We shouldn't read on the bus.

S3：Sleep well，we should drink some milk in the evening. We shouldn't drink too much water before bedtime.

T：Well done. Boys and girls，you have good habits. Please remember good habits make a wonderful life.

Step 10：Homework

1. Listen and read the text.

2. Finish your poster，introduce good habits.

板书设计

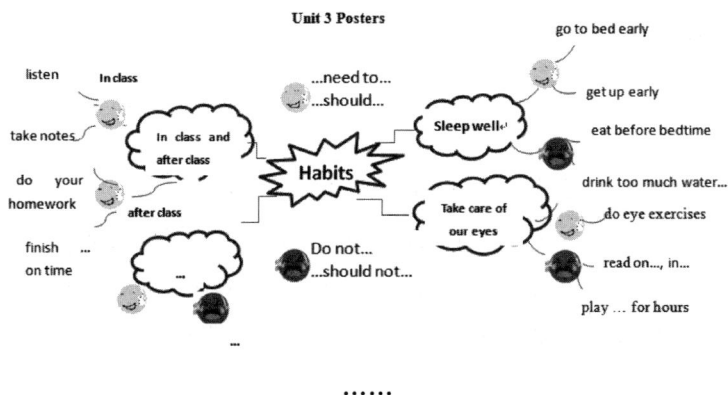

第三部分　课例评析

一、学生反响

学生 A：老师的板书很有趣，笑脸哭脸代表不同的态度，非常生动，我很喜欢。

学生 B：课堂上的活动挺多，有一些需要我们自己讨论完成，很需要动点脑筋。

二、同行声音

史明娟(泰州市城东中心小学)：王老师的课堂设计环节紧凑合理，师生互动和谐流畅，王老师以饱满的热情感染了学生、评委和听课老师，课后回答提问环节体现了其良好的教师基本功与理论积淀，值得我好好学习。

徐秀鸾(泰州市城东中心小学)：王老师的课堂体现了对于学生思维品质的关注

与培养。在对课文的理解、分析、感悟的过程中,学生的语言运用能力得到了进一步提升。

邢晓静(泰州市实验小学):王老师的教学设计体现了读写结合的特点,教学方法灵活,教学功底扎实,教态自然大方,口语纯正,课堂应变能力强,不愧是一等奖的获得者。

三、自我反思

1. 成功之处

(1) 扣住关键词,以思维导图模式促进思维品质提升

本节课抓住 habits 这一关键词,在富有逻辑关联的一系列问题推动下,学生由表及里,深入思考,从接触、理解、掌握到运用,在此过程中,学生的理解能力、想象能力、逻辑思维能力、创新能力等都得到了训练,做到了真正激发学生的思维,提升学生的思维品质。

(2) 找准兴趣点,以形式多样的活动激发、巩固、强化学习

本节课的授课对象是六年级的小学生,处于这个年龄段的孩子对新鲜的事物尤其感兴趣,因而在课堂中设计了多样的活动,以此达到激发兴趣、巩固运用语言知识的目的。比如,"火眼金睛捉害虫"这个游戏,将坏习惯比作害虫,帮助大树找出害虫。学生们兴致高涨,在游戏中巩固了所学语言。

(3) 基于生长点,以行为习惯教育渗透文化品格培养

课文以海报的形式介绍了良好的生活及学习习惯,是培养学生良好行为习惯、渗透文化品格的载体。课前通过简短的交流,对于学生已有的行为习惯以及关于一些习惯的判断有了一定的了解,寻求到了学生的生长点,合理定位情感价值观教学目标。学生通过学习海报,了解到了良好的行为习惯对于生活的重要性,制作海报的活动更是提升了其情感态度、文化品格。

(4) 借助可视化,以思维导图板书搭建阅读写作桥梁

思维导图式板书将抽象的思维可视化,以图文并茂的特点,将重要词汇和句型连接,形成多维度语言支架、文章结构支架,也为学生搭建了写作输出的支架。从文本学

习过渡到学生生活实际，制作属于自己的海报，这时的学生有话要写，有样可循，达到读写结合、读写促进的效果。

2. 不足之处

制作海报这一活动预留的时间不够充分，学生思考的时间不是很宽裕，因而学生所选择的主题与课文主题及老师的范例重合得较多。学生囿于时间的限制，未能完全激发其发散性思维。

四、专家点评

点评专家：姜建宇

英语学科的特点决定了学生读写能力培养的重要性。读是写的基础，写是读的再现。这节语篇阅读课，王莉老师抓住文本中三份 poster 的共同核心词 habits，按照"听懂"—"读懂"—"能说"—"能做"的顺序，逐层递进，在充分听说的基础上开展扎实的读写教学，训练学生的语言综合运用能力。文本中有三份海报，分别包含在睡眠、用眼和学习方面的 good habits 与 bad habits，信息量较大，王老师先扶后放，采用思维导图帮助学生提炼、记录关键信息，调动旧知、建构新知、修正完善、留白拓展，使繁杂的语言信息关系化、形象化，层级清晰，重点突出；板书呈现的主要句型为学生搭建了语言支架，再辅以直观醒目的笑脸、哭脸的标志，为学生复述文本、模仿运用降低了难度。在此过程中，老师组织学生开展小组合作，围绕思维导图展开交流讨论，充分理解文本，丰富语言运用，激发表达欲望，这时的学生不但不怕写，而且有词可用，有句可写，海报的书写制作便水到渠成，读写能力得到提升。

【点评专家简介】姜建宇，江苏省小学英语特级教师、高级教师，江苏省乡村骨干教师培育站学科指导专家、首届优秀培育站主持人，泰州市城乐中心小学校长。

【名师简介】

王莉：江苏省泰州市城东中心小学英语教师，泰州市英语学科带头人，泰州市海陵区小学英语名师工作室领衔人，海陵区小学英语名师培训班成员，海陵区督导室兼职督学。获得 2012 年江苏省小学英语优质课评比一等奖,被授予"第四届全国中小学英语教师名师"称号。参与、主持多项国家、省、市级课题研究,发表多篇论文。

课例 2　多模态视角下语用能力培养的故事阅读课例研究
——以 Pet Heroes 语篇阅读课为例

第一部分　教学预设

一、教学内容分析

1. 课标要求

《课标(2011 版)》明确指出:英语课程承担着培养学生基本英语素养和发展学生思维能力的任务。通过英语学习使学生形成初步的综合语言运用能力,促进心智发展,提高综合人文素养。课外阅读教学实践中,教师应分析文本特点,挖掘文本内在主线,促使学生在阅读中立足篇章整体,厘清文本脉络,挖掘深层内涵,促进综合语言运用能力的提升。

《课标(2017 版)》中提出英语语言技能为"听、说、读、看、写"。其中"看"作为一种新的英语语言技能,与传统的"听、说、读、写"技能一起构成了英语语言技能完整体系。在这一体系下,英语课堂教学必然要求教师设计的英语教学活动不仅要关注培养学生各项技能与能力,同时更要运用多种教学方法和教学手段实施综合技能教学,运用"多模态"教学方式开展阅读教学活动,培养学生语言的综合运用能力。

2. 教材分析

本材料选自《21 世纪报(小学版)》。就文本内容而言,该教学材料是一篇故事类题材的课外阅读短文,取材于真实的生活故事。以"宠物英雄"(Pet Heroes)为话题,以"总—分"的结构方式,围绕"一些宠物不仅是朋友,还是英雄"的中心句,分三段分别讲述不同宠物通过自身能力帮助自己或他人的故事。该语篇时态为一般现在时,每一段式均以"宠物姓名、所居住地和主要英雄事迹"为顺序展开介绍。

3. 重点与难点

教学重点:

(1)学生能在故事情境中理解生词意义,习得表达的准确性,读懂事件,并能按照故事发展顺序勾勒情节。

(2)学生能在阅读中通过观图、听音、猜测、想象等方式代入英雄事件,丰富具象感知,体验角色魅力,提升阅读能力。

教学难点:

(1)学生能在阅读中基于文本,再造想象,以文本语词为触媒,从中生发情境,以想象的情节填补和丰满文本。

(2)学生能在阅读后描述英雄事件,表达学后感悟,提升信息整合能力。

4. 学情分析

(1)学生心智特质分析。本课是借班执教的江苏省级赛课,对象是南京外国语学校仙林校区四年级学生。通过短短的赛前 20 分钟的"熟悉学生"环节,教师已经领略到他们的风采,小小年纪的他们大方、自信,活泼而不失规矩。

(2)学生已有知识经验分析。南京外国语学校仙林校区四年级学生具备较高的英语素养,从已有知识储备看,学生对常见动物能进行简单描述,如外貌特征、生活习性等,但对人与动物或动物与动物之间发生的事情(即动物事件)没有太多接触。从语言学习的角度看,该年段学生在语言技能上接近《课标(2011 版)》的二级要求,具备语言交流的基本能力和阅读基本技巧,如快速提取信息、概括信息等,同时他们已形成了一定的语言学习策略,如积极与他人合作,共同完成学习任务,能尝试阅读英语故事,并养成按意群朗读的习惯。从情感态度发展的角度看,他们敢于开口,不怕出错。基于他们的学习能力,为他们量身定制适合他们的阅读课尤为重要。"读前猜,读中品,读后议"将成为本节课的主线,成为引领他们课外"悦"读向前迈进一小步的"开胃小菜"。

二、教学目标分析

英语作为一种语言,是交际的工具、思维的展现和情感的表达。该课教学目标的定位直接指向英语核心素养,立足"儿童立场",基于多模态共现的语境,在学、思、议中达成提高学生多模态识读能力和通过故事育人的目标。具体教学目标如下:

1. 语言能力

(1) 能在语篇中读懂词汇,了解文本大意,明确英雄主题,理清事件脉络;

(2) 能运用目标语简单描述英雄事件。

2. 思维品质

(1) 能通过图片、声音提示进行合理推理、猜测;

(2) 能关注情节发展,深入理解角色,感悟事件意义。

3. 文化意识

(1) 能思辨英雄特质,树立正确的英雄观;

(2) 能树立"英雄不论成败""基于自身能力帮助他人"的价值观。

4. 学习能力

(1) 能根据图片内容提问和合作创编对话;

(2) 能借助思维导图处理文本信息,提炼英雄事迹;

(3) 能积极与同伴合作学习,主动分享读后启发,交流推荐其他英雄宠物。

三、思路、方法与资源

1. 整体思路

本节课采用 PWP 教学模式,即 Pre-reading(阅读前)、While-reading(阅读中)、Post-reading(阅读后)三段式教学思路。具体设计思路如下:

Stage One:Pre-reading(5 分钟)

Step 1:Free talk(赏图片,引话题)

T:Do you like these pets? Why?

【设计意图】视频是学生比较喜欢的模态之一。融合图像、声音、语言等多种手段和符号模态引出英雄话题,实现交际,继而引出中心句,创设英雄馆情景,推荐宠物英雄,引导学生进馆了解其英雄故事。

Stage Two：While-reading(25 分钟)

Step 2：Read and find(初感知,寻信息)

T：Who are they? Where do they live? Take out your files and read silently to get the information.

【设计意图】鼓励学生遇见 heroes,呈现文本,以跳读形式,获取姓名、生活居住地两处信息,使学生在简单任务中获得快乐初体验。

Step 3：Think and guess(观特长,猜事件)

T：What kind of cases are they involved in? You can guess based on their ability.

【设计意图】鼓励学生根据动物特征或自身能力,大胆设想其所参与的事件,使学生迫不及待地揭示谜底,走近英雄。

a. Jack

Step 4：Look and guess(识小偷,猜战略)

T：Who are they? What do they want to do? Why do they run away?

Step 5：Read and check(读故事,验猜想)

学生默读故事 1,找出赶贼妙招。

(教师出示鹦鹉玩偶,比划动作,使学生认读体会 peck 与 claw)

【设计意图】利用语言艺术、图像、动作来幽默地表达意义,吸引学生的注意力,使要表达的信息形象化。结合情节通过提问的方式,问在学生疑惑之处,问在故事转折之处,问在学生兴趣之处,使学生乐于猜想,并通过阅读验证猜测。

Step 6：Imagine and read(齐"悦"读,悟技巧)

T：Try to imagine the scene and read with eyes, ears, heart, mouth.

【设计意图】朗读作为阅读的一种方式,意在体会与品味,旨在启发学生,边读边想象画面,形成目视其文,口发其声,耳闻其音,心通其情的多模态语篇阅读。

b. Dotty

Step 7：Listen and imagine(听音效,猜事件)

T：Dotty is involved in?

T：As we know, Dotty is a hero, what happens on the farm? Do not read the files before guessing.

【设计意图】充分利用图片和声音资源,利用视觉和听觉模态激发学生兴趣,调动和活跃课堂气氛,引导学生根据猜测,大胆表达,按照事件起因、发展、高潮、结局的顺序小试牛刀,将故事初步勾勒。

Step 8：Read and find(赏原文,捋情节)

【设计意图】使学生在阅读中了解事件,梳理出故事脉络,在寻读中形成"关注事件发展顺序"的意识,为读后讲述自己的英雄故事作好铺垫。

Step 9：Read and act(忆情节,创对白)

T：You read the story well, can you act? To make the story vivid, we can add some words.

【设计意图】深入事件,在学生兴趣最高点搭建平台。恰当融合表演和想象的教学模态,引导学生在读、演、说中体会故事精妙,使其通过文字想象画面,再通过想象中的画面感悟语言文字。

c. Mila

Step 10：Watch and compare(知事件,解疑惑)

T：As we know, Jack saves with his beak and claws. Dotty saves with her feet. What does Mila save with?

【设计意图】利用三名宠物英雄的外部特征作对比,启发学生关注"基于宠物自身特长或外部特征"这一信息,引导学生带着问题去阅读,利用"一图胜千言"的优势,以直观的图文形式呈现文本中的情境、情节、角色等,通过多模态话语分析理论,化难为易,使学生简单勾勒故事脉络。

Step 11：Read and say(读文本,说过程)

T：Yang Yun is a trainer, she gets cramped. How to save her?

学生细读故事3,找出施救过程。

【设计意图】抓住重点,引导学生细细读,读出 Mila 的"情";继而细细思,思其文中的"意",体会字里行间丰富的内涵;继而水到渠成,鼓励学生细细悟,悟出 Mila 的

"义"。

Step 12：Think and say(借图式,识英雄)

T：(出示图式)That is her action. What does Mila say? How does Mila feel?

【设计意图】利用图式,呈现内涵,引导学生再造想象,深入思考,大胆表达,在想象中体验角色魅力,感悟角色风貌。

Stage Three：Post-reading(10 分钟)

Step 13：Watch the film(观影片,齐分享)

【设计意图】将文本赋予动态形式整体呈现于学生,利用动态符号资源,为学生搭建英语交流的真实场景,使学生更好地理解语言传达的知识及文化内涵,(张海燕,2017)给学生带来视觉冲击,启示影片的精彩源于英雄事件的精彩,激发学生深入思考,分享自己的深切感受,从中获得思想营养。

T：Recommend your stories of pet heroes. (寻英雄,乐推荐)

【设计意图】阅读教学的真谛即是来源于文本,超越于文本。在阅读中,学生既能从文本中汲取信息、习练语言,又能不断地向文本输出自己既有的经验和情感,使阅读充满活力。

Step 14：Homework

1. Scan and dub the film.

2. Send your stories of pet heroes to Tina. 48167209@qq.com

3. Make a mind map about one of three pet heroes and share with others.

4. Read more about heroes.

【设计意图】给学生布置一些多模态的课后作业,帮助学生独立探索,自主学习,注重对他们进行知识的拓展和技能的强化。

2. 模式方法

多模态理论主张：英语故事教学可以将图片、音频、视频、网络链接等多种符号模态引入教学过程,创设真实语境,调动学生运用多种感官参与学习,激发学习兴趣,提高学生对语言的输入、理解、探究、运用和输出。(张海燕,2017)本节课积极尝试在多模态视角下展开阅读前、阅读中以及阅读后故事教学,旨在培养学生语言能力、交际能力、思维能力,帮助学生在多模态环境下理解文本、建构认知、创造性学习,享受英语课外阅读的乐趣。

（1）读前运用多模态，营造主题情境

在阅读课学习文本之前进行一定的话题导入，有助于在短时间内抓住小学生的注意力，挖掘学生的已知并激发他们探索未知。阅读前的导入部分要做到夺人眼球，充分利用多模态话语分析理论就显得尤为重要。（张海燕，2017）为了吸引学生注意力，教师读前自制宠物电子相册，邀请学生欣赏宠物萌照，激发学生对宠物的兴趣，继而提问："Do you like pets? Why?"接着让学生观看关于小狗的视频，让学生借助"小狗救猫"故事图，描述狗的品质，引导学生得出"有些宠物不仅是朋友，还是英雄"的结论。学生短时间内进入了宠物英雄主题，主动了解其他宠物英雄。形象生动的图片和视频能够提供清晰的信息，将学生的注意力转移到话语交际上来，实现了图片模态、视频模态与语言模态的相互协调。

（2）读中借助多模态，丰富学习活动

读中活动要以学生阅读为主，主要借助任务型教学法，引导学生在完成一系列任务的同时深入解读文本，消化知识，获得相关体验。（张海燕，2017）在主办方提供的阅读材料包中，仅含有故事文本和音频。教师为了丰富学生的阅读体验，有效借助图片、视频、音频和文字模态融合的方式，给学生提供了丰富的语言材料，吸引他们的眼球。例如在 Jack 英雄出场时，直观呈现不同形态和神态的小偷、鹦鹉、鸟笼等大量与文字相关的图片，为学生提供视觉信息。同时尝试改变以往先整体呈现文本的形式，建议学生先不接触语言材料，而是选择先看图、猜情节，激发兴趣。在学习体会"put his hand in the case"与"peck and claw hard"时，教师分别利用课件与实物，结合声音与动作，恰如其分地演示出"伸手偷""狠狠抓"这两处细节，使学生加深了对小偷和鹦鹉的印象，准确揣摩出其心理活动，为下一环节表演式朗读作好铺垫。再如：在 Dotty 英雄出场时，教师大胆采用听音、看图猜测、创编故事等多模态学习方式，继续鼓励学生先不接触材料，听音猜义，保持对故事的新鲜感和好奇心。接着让学生走进文本，揭开故事面纱，观看图片，大胆想象，扩展语言，边说边演。图片模态与音频模态为新知识的学习提供了大量的材料，同时与动作模态相互交融，为学生在英雄情境中自主学习、预测故事、合理创编、角色体验等一系列主题任务做出有力支撑。

（3）读后借助多模态，提高思维品质

多模态教学即可以通过图像、视频、音频的展示和强调,突出阅读内容,营造宽松和谐的学习氛围,将外因转化为内因,也能够组织学生喜欢的自由探究、合作表演、分组讨论等多模态活动,这些多模态活动就如同发酵器皿,可以酝酿学生的学习热情。(张海燕,2017)多模态教学不仅关注多种模态的输入,还关注多种模态的输出。教师在教学故事中应充分考虑学生学情,设计教学时要尽可能将书本故事与学生生活联系起来,充分激活学生的生活经验与知识储备,促进学生情感与思维的发展。(周敏,2018)本节课的读后环节中,教师首先利用多媒体优势,自行制作视频,延续英雄情境,使学生整体观看英雄纪录片。浓浓英雄味的手绘视频带给学生视觉冲击,纪录片中生动、形象的图片刺激了学生的感官,他们仿佛置身英雄馆,对英雄充满敬意,自发形成对英雄的敬佩之情。这为学生下一环节的语言输出奠定了基础。接着教师趁势引导学生观察黑板上的思维导图,借助图示自由讨论,分享最触动心弦的英雄故事。清晰的思维导图具有直观性、关联性、发散性,学生的视觉模态与听觉模态组合起来,这一活动使他们理解更深刻,掌握更牢固。在故事教学中,教师应深入分析和把握故事板块的文体特征,从学生的兴趣和需求出发,引导学生在阅读活动中理解和内化文本的内涵及其语言特点,促使学生基于对文本的理解和自己的生活实际有条理地阐述和表达自己的观点,进而培养学生的综合语言运用能力。(沈国峰,2016)本节课结尾,当学生被邀请自主推荐其他宠物英雄时,学生善于使用本节课目标语和借助讲述故事的"起因、发展、高潮、结局"等方法,组织、整合、概括属于自己的故事;同时,在学生讲述之后,采取"听后反馈"的形式,自由表达观点,对新故事进行互动讨论,这种多模态活动符合交际的需要,同时又能促进学生思维的发展。

3. 推荐资源

(1)张海燕.小学英语阅读教学理论与实践[M].南京:译林出版社,2017.本书聚焦于小学英语阅读教学的特点和存在的问题,注重理论与实践的结合,以《"跟上兔子"小学英语分级绘本》研发及教学实例为主体,详细介绍了"小学英语'多模态'阅读教学模式"及评价体系。

(2)周敏.小学故事教学中的问题及对策[J].中小学外语教学(小学篇),2018(12):35—41.本文结合教学案例,具体分析了小学英语故事教学中存在重词句轻文本、重活动轻思维等问题,并提出通过立足故事语境、依托故事功能和巧设故事活动等方式引导学生建构知识体系,拓展思维情感,以提高故事教学的实效。

(3) 沈国峰.由一次磨课经历谈 Story Time 板块的教学活动设计[J].中小学外语教学(小学篇),2016(13):13—19.本文以一节 Story Time 板块阅读教学示范课的两次教学实践为例,分别对磨课试教和正式教学过程中的读前、读中和读后教学活动进行了对比与分析,旨在探讨如何优化 Story Time 板块的教学活动设计,以改善教学效果。

第二部分　精彩实录

授课地点:江苏省南京外国语学校仙林校区报告厅。

授课时间:2018 年 11 月 20 日。

听课人员:江苏省教育科学研究院英语教研员何锋教授、李娜老师,南京师范大学外国语学院张伊娜教授,各市、区教研员、骨干教师共 400 人左右。

授课过程:

Stage One:Pre-reading(5 分钟)

Step 1:Free talk

T:Do you like these pets? Why?

S1:Yes,because they are cute and they can play with me.

S2:Yes,I think some of them are beautiful.

T:(追问)Do you often play with your pet?

S2:Yes,my pet is clever,sometimes they are cute.

T:Pets may bring us a lot of joys because they are our friends. I would like to show you a video about a pet, it is a dog. Maybe he will bring us more.

Step 2:Watch and share

T:Do you like this dog?

S1:I like this dog, he helps the cat get out of the hole.

S2:I like this dog because I think he is clever and brave.

T:(追问) What do you think of this dog?

S3:I think it is brave, it likes his friend cat.

T：(小结)This dog is not only cute，but also kind and helpful，it is a super dog. (设计超人狗形象)Not only a friend，it is a hero. Here is a museum of heroes. There are three other pet heroes. Who are they?

Ss：Donkey, parrot, whale.

T：Do you want to meet them? Read the passwords loudly to open the door. "Not only a friend，it is a hero". (进入英雄馆通行密码)

Stage Two：While-reading(25 分钟)

Step 3：Read and find

T：Who are they? Where do they live? Take out your files and read silently to get the information.

S1：Jack is a parrot. He lives at a pet shop in the UK.

S2：Dotty is a donkey from the United Kingdom.

S3：Mila is a white whale in China.

T：(追问)Where does she live?

S4：She lives in a Polar Land Park.

Step 4：Think and guess

T：What kind of cases are they involved in? You can guess based on their ability.

a. Drowning Case　　b. Bulling Case　　c. Theft Case

S1：I think the white whale joins in Drowning Case because it can swim，it can help some people out of the water.

S2：I think Dotty joins in Bulling Case because Dotty is strong.

T：That is your imagination，but actually what kind of cases are they involved in?

a. Jack

Step 5：Look and guess

T：Who are they?

Ss：Three thieves.

T：What do they want to do?

S1：They want to go to the classroom to steal books?

T：（出示小偷伸手动作）Here comes a big hand and Jack is beside them at the pet shop.

S2：They want to steal some pets at the pet shop.

T：（出示贼逃跑图）Why do they run away? Who drives them away?

S1：Jack pecks and claws them with claws and beak.（边说边比划）

T：（继续启发）Any other ideas? What can parrot do?

S2：Maybe Jack says something and thieves are afraid.

S3：Maybe the policeman comes and thieves run away.

T：Maybe the owner comes. How to drive them away?

Step 6：Read and check

（学生默读故事 1，找出赶贼妙招。）

S1：One thief puts his hand into Jack's cage. Jack pecks and claws his hand very hard.

（教师出示鹦鹉玩偶，比划动作，使学生认读体会 peck 与 claw。）

T：Act and say, peck hard and claw hard.（启发被啄学生）You are the thief，are you afraid?

S1：（尖叫状）Oh! I am afraid.

T：Run away!（课堂气氛热起来了。）

Step 7：Imagine and read

T：Try to imagine the scene and read with eyes，ears，heart，mouth.

（教师启发：想象画面，做到目视其文，口发其声，耳闻其音，心通其意。）

Ss：边读边加动作（蹑手蹑脚、用力啄、抓、害怕，逃跑等）。

T：（总结）Why is Jack a hero? Jack fights against thieves and saves himself and other pets.

b. Dotty

Step 8：Listen and imagine

T：Dotty is involved in?

S1：Bullying Case. I hear the voice of a sheep and a dog. I think Dotty kicks the dog.

T：Who is bad in the story?

S1：A crazy dog.

T：Who is so weak?

S3：Sheep.

T：As we know, Dotty is a hero, what happens on the farm? Do not read the files before guessing.

S1：(大胆猜测)I think one day, a crazy dog runs to the farm and he catches the sheep. The donkey helps the sheep kick the dog. The dog is afraid and runs away.

T：Such a good storyteller. Actually, what happens? Try to read story 2, find the sentences according to the main line and number them.

Step 9：Read and find

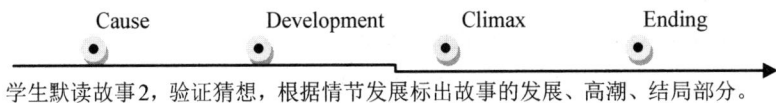

学生默读故事2，验证猜想，根据情节发展标出故事的发展、高潮、结局部分。

T：(Cause) One day, a crazy dog runs into the farm.

S1：(Development) The dog bites Stanley's body.

S2：(Climax) Dotty sees this. She runs to the dog. She kicks the dog with her feet.

S3：(Ending) The dog lets go of Stanley and runs away.

Step 10：Read and act

T：(加动作)I know you read them well. Can you act?

(起因、发展处——师生合作,想象表演:狗的咆哮声、咬声。)

(高潮、结局处——生生合作,想象表演:驴后踢腿,狗慌逃。)

(教师引导:Dotty is a donkey, she kicks backward. She kicks with hind feet.)

T：(编语言)To make the story vivid, we can add some words. What would you say if you were the crazy dog, the weak sheep or you were the hero?

(Cause)

S1：I am hungry. I want to eat you. (害怕状)

S2：What a fat sheep! I want to eat you. (比划胖子状)

S3：I am hungry. I must eat you.（凶恶状）

（Development）

T：Stanley is weak and afraid. What does he say?

S1：Why do you bite me?（疑惑状）

S2：Oh! I am so worried.（担心状）

S3：Please let go of me.（求饶状）

S4：Oh，my god! Who can help me? Help me?（求救状）

（Climax）

T：Dotty comes. he is a hero.

S1：Er，I will help my friend.

T：（启发）What will you say to the crazy dog?

S2：Crazy dog，run away. I will kick you.

S2：Crazy dog，if you do not go，I will kick you.

S3：Stanley，wait for a moment. I am coming!

（Ending）

S1：Oh，I must get out and find something to eat.

S2：Oh，I am hungry. I cannot eat the fat sheep. I will eat other cats.（教师启发：If you come again，maybe another hero will come!）

S3：I won't come to the farm again，I will go home to eat something.

T：（总结）Why is Dotty a hero?

Ss：Dotty fights against the dog and saves her animal friend.

T：（启发）If you were Dotty，would you save your friend?

Ss：Yes. I would.

T：Please choose the suitable way to protect them. Firstly we need to protect yourself and then protect others.

c. Mila.

Step 11：Watch and compare

T：As we know，Jack saves with his beak and claws. Dotty saves with her feet.

What does Mila save with?

Ss：Mouth.

Step 12：Read and say

T：Yang Yun is a trainer. she gets cramped. How to save?

（学生细读故事 3,找出施救过程。）

S1：Mila sees Yang and swims to her. She holds Yang lightly in her mouth. She pushes Yang out of the water.（教师引导：细细读,读出 Mila 的"情"。）

T：Why do we use lightly?（教师引导：细细思,思出词语的"意"。）

S1：When Mila holds hard，Yang will die.

T：Yes. they get along well. Mila does not want to hurt Yang.

Step 13：Think and say

T：（出示图式）That is her action. What does Mila say? How does Mila feel?

（学生同伴讨论,想 Mila 之所想、所说、所感。）

S1：（Thoughts）This is my best trainer. I must help her.

S2：（Words）Do not be afraid. I will help you.

S3：（Feeling）She feels afraid.

T：（补充）At first he feels worried. At last，she feels happy. She saves her trainer. she feels proud of herself.

T：From outside and inside of Mila，we can understand her well.

T：（总结）Why is Mila a hero?

Ss：She saves her human friend.

Stage Three：Post-reading(10 分钟)

Step 14：Watch the film

T：Here is a documentary about heroes.

（学生观看后,分享感悟。）

T：Which part of the story touches your heart? Let us share.

S1：I like white whale best. Because I think if she doesn't save her trainer, maybe Yang will die under the water. She is brave and clever.

S2：I like Jack. He helps the other pets out of the danger. He pecks and claws hard. He is brave and smart.

S3：I like Dotty. He is strong and clever. He kicks the crazy dog with her feet. If he does not kick，the dog will die.

T：(引导)For Stanley，Dotty is friendly and kind. How do we treat them? Will you be so friendly to them?

Ss：Yes.

T：We should treat them with love and respect.

T：(引导)To be a hero，we should be smart. If you are smart，but you are not brave，are you a hero?

Ss：No.

T：If you are smart and brave，but you are not kind and helpful，are you a hero?

Ss：No.

（Text to myself.）

Step 15：Recommend your stories of pet heroes

S1：This is a story I watched. The pet hero is a dog. It helps the cat. One day，a cat falls into the deep hole. It can't climb up. "Help, help!"it shouts. His friend dog comes there. He is smart. He pulls it out of the hole with a rope. The cat is happy. they play together again. The dog is kind and smart.

S1：(故事讲述者自主提问) How does the dog help the cat? What do you think of the dog?

S2：He gives the cat the rope and the cat catches it and climbs up.

S3：The dog is kind and smart.

T：(呈现 persistent)The dog tries hard to save the cat again and again. He never gives up. He is persistent.

T：(追问) Are they still heroes if the rescue fails?

S1：Yes，because I think heroes never give up. If the rescue fails，they will think about another way.

T：（引导）Hero means a person or a pet that is helping rather than a person or a pet that helped. 英雄，不论成败。Anyway，to be a hero，we should protect ourselves and base on our ability.（肯定获得勋章的同学）You are all my heroes in this class.

Step 16：Homework

1. Scan and dub the film.

2. Send your stories of pet heroes to Tina. 48167209@qq.com

3. Make a mind map about one of three pet heroes and share with others.

4. Read more about heroes.

板书设计

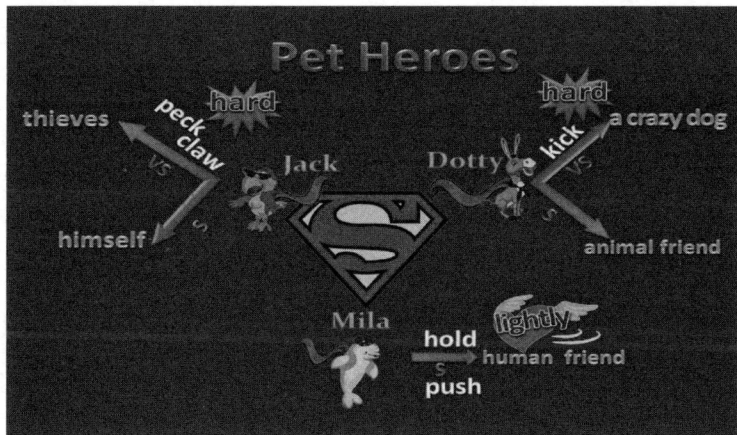

第三部分　课例评析

一、学生反响

学生 A：在英雄故事里，我们看图片、听音乐，边阅读、边想象，我还扮演了英雄 Dotty 呢，真是太过瘾啦！

学生 B：宠物不仅是我们的朋友，更是我们的英雄，我们应该善待他们！

二、同行声音

候燕(泰州市高港区英语教研员、高级教师):纵观课堂教学,封老师对教学内容有着较强的分析和把控能力,对故事阅读教学的设计别具匠心。她巧用文本,借学生的已有知识与对宠物英雄的好奇心,尝试凭借多种符号资源,丰富教学内容和教学形式,鼓励学生在故事情境中竞猜、想象、表演、感悟、思辨,课堂教学有层次、有逻辑、有新意,学生话语有内容、有空间、有深度。

史小进(泰州市高港口岸实验小学,高级教师):封老师在这节课中告诉学生,每段故事都有开始、发展、高潮、结局,而她的这节课何尝不是? 自然、简约的铺垫,步步为营的情节发展,扣人心弦的高潮,耐人寻味的结局。这是一节浓浓"英雄味"、浓浓"思维味"的课外阅读课。

周章红(泰州市高港实验小学,高级教师):本节课上,学生有话可说,有理可讲,有情可抒,动态的生成有模有样,可圈可点。这一切,源于教师层层铺垫、步步引导、因"模"施教。

三、自我反思

这一课,从区内选拔的第一次"登台"到省级竞赛台上的"亮相",共走过了一个月零两天。十次"打磨",十次"改课",不同的阶段,不同的教学观,如何改课? 改教学目标,改对教学内容的提炼,改课堂提问设计,等等。每一次的修改都是为了让课堂干脆利落地指向英语核心素养。

本节课努力尝试以多模态方式向学生呈现教学意图。在课堂上主要表现为多种视觉符号、听觉符号(如图片、音频、视频,口语交流、PPT,教师与学生手势、眼神、表情的交流等)的协同与配合,最大化地调动学生感官来参与课堂,感知语言。(张海燕,2017)

1. 情境贯穿,环环相扣

"什么样的文本,还他什么样的味道。"本节课体现着浓浓的"英雄味"。课堂伊始,通过观看小狗搭救玩伴视频,引出"宠物也可当英雄"的话题。借课件动感画面呈现"宠物英雄馆"这一情境,迅速点燃学生认识更多宠物英雄的学习热情,引导学生逐步完成走进英雄馆、看英雄榜、查英雄档案、知英雄事迹、赏英雄短片、讲英雄故事、推荐英雄入榜等主题系列活动,整节课形成了一个密切关联的有机整体,主题情境贯穿全过程,英雄情结萦绕其心间。

2. 亮明"文眼",层层推进

故事对小学生有着无比大的魔力,英雄故事,更是如此。"宠物英雄"即本课"文眼"。英雄是谁? 来自哪里? 为什么是英雄? 英雄做了什么? 你觉得英雄是什么样? 从英雄身上你学到了什么? 本节课力求做到紧扣文眼,以"英雄"为中心词,利用逻辑性的巧妙过渡,逐步发散学生思维。如:(1)快速默读英雄档案,寻找英雄姓名及居住地;(2)根据宠物自身特长推测英雄所参与事件;(3)看图、听音、读文,在多模态学习中走进英雄事件,证实最初推测;(4)朗读文字,构建故事画面,通过画面感悟英雄本色,继而展开想象,创编对话;(5)利用思维导图梳理、分享触动心弦的英雄事迹;(6)小组合作,自主推荐其他宠物英雄。本节课,教学活动从初步感知到分析理解,再到品读体悟、合作分享,步步深入,层层推进。在学、思、讲、演、评的主要活动中达成提高学生的语言能力和通过故事育人的目标,思维品质、文化意识和学习能力的培养已融合于学生语言能力。学生运用语言理解、表达,在理解和表达的过程中,不断遇见"英雄",读懂"作者",教会"自己"。

3. 节点提问,步步为营

"学起于思,思源于疑。"核心素养在英语课堂上的落地扎根依托于教师的精准提问。本节课,重在关注学生思维品质的培育,用问题切入学习内容,用问题推动教学流程,用问题搭建深入理解的"跳板",问于兴趣之处,问于故事情节转折之处,问于难点之处,满足学生"低阶思维",培养学生"高阶思维",浇灌学生的思维之花。

(1)以问激趣

课堂伊始,教师抓住该年龄段学生特点,开门见山,"你有宠物吗? 喜欢吗? 为什么?"简单的提问激发起学生对宠物话题的好奇心,纷纷带来不简单的回答。有学生喜欢宠物的可爱,有学生喜欢宠物的漂亮,有学生喜欢它们的聪明和乖巧。"宠物"的话匣子一经打开,跳出的是孩童的兴奋和迫不及待地分享。在这样轻松自如的氛围下,走进不一样的宠物世界,一切都显得如呼吸空气一样自在。

(2) 以猜导学

三位宠物英雄隆重登场后,教师并没有直接告知其英雄事迹,而是要求学生不看文本,大胆进行读前"三猜"。一猜英雄参与何种事件,二猜英雄搭救情节,三猜英雄内心独白。基于宠物自身特长的猜测是有抓手的;根据图片、音效提示的猜测是有底气的;理解故事,读懂英雄的猜测是走心的,也都是成功的。故事到底怎样?预测是否成功?学生们满心牵挂,热情不减,思维不止,直奔故事而去。强烈的阅读期待使学习水到渠成,学生主动阅读,解答自己的疑惑,促进思维能力的提高。读前猜,读中验,读后品,课堂上三位宠物英雄救人救己的图示自然生成,开放性的问题激发了主动思考的意识,为之后的英雄事迹梳理做足了铺垫。

(3) 以辩启思

从"走近"英雄到"走进"英雄,学生喜欢宠物的理由已经悄然变化。当询问"本节课是否有触动心弦的地方"时,学生的思维再次被激活,他们借助思维导图,梳理故事情节,提炼英雄品质,表达个人情感。图示的帮助让学习过程得以内化,学习能力得到发展,一切自信源于文本,又超越于文本。当询问"我们该如何对待宠物"时,课堂上回荡着这般响亮的回答,"Treat them with love and respect!""Be friendly to them!"当询问"如果英雄搭救行动失败,还是英雄吗?"时,课堂上又出现了独立的思考、辩证的观点。"或是,或不是",这一延伸性的提问,让学生的思维再次碰撞,"英雄不论成败",自主思辨让学生对故事的理解从显性意义走向隐性意义,达成了发展语言能力、思维能力和通过故事育人的多维目标。

4. 情感渗透,润物无声

(1) 读中悟

在遇见英雄的旅途中,必然少不了"朗读"。指导朗读就是指导感悟,体会英雄的情感世界,感悟英雄的品质,品味作者为什么这样写。例如,遇见鹦鹉英雄 Jack 之后,教师出示朗读技巧:目视其文,口发其声,耳闻其音,心通其意。其目的在于引导学生进行综合阅读。即:用读来揣摩文字,用朗读表现出贼的蹑手蹑脚、仓皇而逃以及鹦鹉的英勇斗贼,引导学生从读中塑造一正一邪,通过朗读无形中树立正确的是非观,表达出对"邪"的反感和对"正"的钦佩。在白鲸 Mila 的故事学习中,教师再次引导学生关注 Mila 营救驯养员朋友的过程,即"Mila sees Yang and swims to her. She holds Yang lightly in her mouth. She pushes Yang out of the water",引导学生细细读,读出 Mila 的"情"。同时,挖掘思维点:Why do we use "lightly" here? 建议学生细细思,思出词语的"意"。这一有心的设计提供了思考的空间,唤起了学生的情感共鸣。例如:"When Mila holds hard, Yang will die." "They are friends. Mila does not want to hurt her." "Mila is kind and brave."情有所感、理有所悟,学生的朗读与感悟是受到情节的感染的,是与文本的情感产生共鸣后感情的自然流露,也是本节课意在培养学生文化意识、进行情感教育的最好见证。

(2) 思中辨

学习 Dotty 驴的英雄故事后,教师与学生的互动如下:

T:If you were Dotty, would you save your friend?

Ss:Yes, I would.

T:Please choose the suitable way to protect them. Firstly we need to protect yourself and then protect others.

为师者,不仅教书,更要育人。通过角色体验学生意识到了"向困难中的朋友伸出救援之手"的意义,教师继而向学生渗透:选择最恰当的方式保护他人,同时保护自己。言语交谈中,将经典的力量、生存的守则转化为儿童成长的"生产力"。

四、专家点评

点评专家:姜建宇

封婷老师的这节语篇阅读课用精巧的设计、精练的语言、精当的板书激发学生强烈的求知欲,激活思维,成就学生精准的习得、精妙的表达、精心的演绎、精彩的成长,在语篇阅读教学中指向学生语言能力、思维品质、文化品格和学习能力等英语核心素养的培养。

该课基于多模态视角,将课程的设计、教学活动的开展、教学效果的评价均置于多模态特征的学习环境下进行,大量采用与语言文字内容高度关联的图像、动画、视频、音效、版式等多模态,并将它们进行有机融合、互补、协同,提供语境化的信息,让学生理解多模态共现的语境,强化了对文本信息的理解。在阅读的过程中,用多种模态相互配合来推断词义、预测情节、理解文章,辨析重点信息,训练逻辑思维,完成交际任务,恰当升华情感,提升了学生的阅读素养。

【名师简介】

封婷:江苏省泰州市高港实验小学英语教师,江苏省小学英语课程教材改革实验工作先进个人,泰州市教学能手,泰州市十佳辅导员,高港区师德模范,高港区优秀辅导员。2018 年 11 月获江苏省小学英语优质课评比一等奖,2018 年 5 月获泰州市小学英语写作课竞赛一等奖,2012 年获泰州市小学英语优质课评比一等奖,2014 年获泰州市教师基本功大赛一等奖,多次开设区级讲座,较好地发挥了示范辐射作用。

课例 3　基于思维导图培养写作能力的课例研究

——以 A healthy diet 写作教学课为例

第一部分　教学预设

一、教学内容分析

1. 课标要求

写作教学是小学高年级英语教学中的重点,也是难点。根据《课标(2011 版)》的要求,小学生写作能力的提高,应从养成良好的书写习惯、切实掌握分级要求的词汇和句型、拓宽阅读面、积累写作素材、循序渐进加强写作训练、培养写作兴趣等方面入手,多层面、立体式地进行写作教学,只有这样才能更加高效地提高小学生的写作能力。

2. 教材分析

本课是在对译林版《英语》六年级下册 Unit 3 A healthy diet 进行复习的基础上,从 What to eat? How many/much? How often? What's for? 等层面入手,了解饮食文

化,加深对 a healthy diet 的认识,借助思维导图来进行写作小练笔,训练思维,锻炼写作技巧,为后面的拓展写作奠定基础。

3. 重点与难点

本课的教学重点和难点是：准确理解和运用含有 a lot of,some,a little,a few 的句型来描述饮食比例,并能按总分结构,正确表述自己的健康饮食,拓展写作部分能按照总分总的结构来描述 How to keep healthy。

4. 学情分析

(1) 学生心智特征分析。本课是借班执教的一节市级比赛录像课,对象是六年级学生。据该班班任课教师反映,该班同学平时上课较为活跃,能够积极举手回答问题,课堂参与度较好,加上在录播教室,镜头给学生带来的刺激和兴奋,预计学生能够较好地参与到课堂学习活动中来。

(2) 学生已有知识经验分析。三年级是起点,经过将近四年的学习,学生的语言能力、学习能力、思维品质、文化品格等都有了初步基础。本课是在对课本内容复习的基础上来进行写作教学的,目标词汇对于学生来说难度不大,不少量词学生借助微视频教学能够更好地理解。但是从课前与该班学生交流中发现,学生对于食物更多地还是停留在个人喜好上,健康饮食的意识还比较淡薄,所以在课堂教学中要合理渗透健康饮食观,为后面的写作作好铺垫。

二、教学目标分析

根据对教学内容和学生情况的分析,本节课设定了以下教学目标,即经过本节课的学习,学生能够：

1. 在理解 diet 含义的基础上,进一步理解 a healthy diet 的含义;

2. 能根据思维导图,正确合理地写出"My healthy diet",并能按要求进行简单的检查和润色;

3. 从"健康饮食"的概念延展到"健康"这个大概念上进行讨论,并能按照总分总结构写一篇小短文。

三、思路、方法与资源

1. 整体思路

本节写作课在整体思路上遵循"以思维导图为抓手,积累素材理清脉络"的原则,注重训练学生的思维能力,提升学生崇尚健康的文化品格。在具体教学设计上主要有以下环节:欣赏"Nice food,wonderful world"。理解 diet,Discussion for writing,Skills for writing,Extended writing 等。主要教学环节如下:

Stage One:Pre-writing

Step 1:课件展示 Nice food,wonderful world

【设计意图】在进入新课之前,通过多图播放,让学生了解到在不同的国家、不同的节日等都具有不同的饮食文化,感受到生活中食物的丰富多样性。

Step 2:学习 food 的种类

【设计意图】了解食物的种类,并尽可能多地让学生来说出本课需要用到的一些目的语词汇,通过男孩体型的变化,让学生们知道食物是重要的,但一定要把握好食物的摄入量,从而渗透健康饮食的概念。

Step 3:理解 diet 的意义

【设计意图】饮食的含义是什么呢?引导学生对四个字母进行重新认识,"d"代表 day,"i"代表 I,"e"代表 eat,"t"代表 time,从而让学生理解 diet 的含义就是:Every day, the food I eat for breakfast,lunch and dinner on time.

Step 4:复习本单元 Story time 板块的主要内容

【设计意图】通过复习课本内容,了解 Mike 和 Yang Ling 的饮食状况,做出判断 Who has a healthy diet? 通过 Chant 来巩固,同时对 Mike 的不合理饮食提出自己的建议,为后面的写作积累素材。

Stage Two:While-writing

Step 5:Discussion for writing(可以从哪些细节来写我的健康饮食呢?)

1. What to eat?(吃什么?)

2. How much/many?(吃多少?)

3. How often?（吃的频率?）

4. What's for ... ?（一日三餐怎么安排?）

5. Where to eat?（在哪里吃?）

【设计意图】通过讨论,知道就餐的地点对健康饮食不是最重要的,关键是其他四个方面,逐一进行讨论,并借助微视频的讲解,让学生更多地了解一些语法细节,降低后面写作时的语法错误。

Step 6：Skills for writing(微视频播放写作指导)

【设计意图】通过微视频播放,图文结合、音视频结合更形象直观地对学生进行简单的写作指导,告诉学生可以采用的写作结构、写作素材、书写注意事项等,降低写作的难度。

Step 7：Writing and check

【设计意图】学生借助思维导图和提示词来写作,完成后根据老师提供的范例讲解,小组合作检查,再独自进行润色。

Stage Three：Post-writing

Step 8：Speech show

以演讲的形式展示个人的健康饮食。

【设计意图】既要让学生学会写,还要让学生学会讲,将书面语言内化,锻炼学生的思维和口头表达能力。

Step 9：Extended writing

在学生能够完成"My healthy diet"的基础上,将写作话题拓展到"How to keep healthy?"。讲解过程中完成板书"钻石"造型,并适当进行情感教育。由于课堂时间的限制,设计的时候主要让学生完成文章的开头和结尾。

【设计意图】健康饮食很重要,但要保持健康,我们还需要有良好的生活习惯,需要合理地安排运动,等等。话题的延展让学生由单向思维转向多维度思考,使学生围绕"健康"更客观真实地了解问题、分析问题、思考问题、解决问题,从而提升写作的深度,更具有现实意义。

Step 10：Homework

2. 模式方法

小学英语听、说、读、写四种能力的培养中,写作是最难培养的能力之一。在小学高年级阶段,学生写作水平两极分化非常严重,很多学生用英语表达简单的语言时总是力不从心,比较随意,不考虑整体构思和技巧,普遍存在着文体及格式错误、文章无重点、句子不完整、基本语言知识错误、缺乏逻辑性等问题,种种情况导致写作质量不高。

思维导图作为一种思维工具,主要使用线条、符号、词汇和图像等直观形象的方式来呈现思维的过程、表达知识结构和知识信息,有助于培养学习者的高阶思维技能和知识建构能力。

本节课多次利用思维导图,对 food 的种类进行归纳,有助于提高单词识记的数量和质量,为写作教学奠定坚实的词汇基础;借助食物金字塔,更形象直观地反映出食物摄入量的对比,强化学生对 a few/a little, some, a lot of 的正确使用;借助思维导图"What's for . . . ?"让学生能够对写作内容进行整体构思,使写作更有逻辑性;本节课最后形成的板书造型是一颗钻石,既是教学内容的集中展示,又更直观生动地表达了健康的重要性。小学生以形象思维为主,利用思维导图对写作布局能力的把握,恰好符合学生身心发展的特点,不仅能促进学生形象思维的发展,还能促进学生在思考过程中抽象逻辑思维的发展。

这节课将写作教学分为 pre-writing, while-writing 和 post-writing 三段式教学模式,三个阶段教学目标与教学活动有着各自的特点。

写作前(pre-writing)的核心任务就是为写作做前期认知和心理准备。通过欣赏"Nice food, wonderful world",引起学生对食物的兴趣,学生在感性认识的基础上来归纳食物的种类,再让学生说出自己喜欢的食物,从而对 diet 重新定义,并揭示本节课的主题 A healthy diet。复习课本 Story time 部分,了解 Mike 和 Yang Ling 的饮食,并追问:"Who has a healthy diet?",激起学生背景知识储备,直接切入主题,在引起学生表达欲望的同时,也为后面的写作打下基础。

写作中(while-writing)是写作教学的核心。此环节从健康饮食的四个方面进一步细化学生的写作素材,借助微视频讲解写作结构和简单的写作技巧,最后让学生借助思维导图来写作,并根据老师提供的范例分析,以小组合作学习的方式来相互检查,然后独立对习作进行修改和润色。

写作后(post-writing)侧重写作内容的口头语言表达和综合提升。演讲展示既可以检查学生的书面完成情况,也可以反映学生的语言口头表达情况,提升学生的思维品质。而将话题进一步拓展到 How to keep healthy,更加锻炼了学生综合运用语言的能力。

3. 推荐资源

(1) 吉桂凤. 思维导图与小学英语教学[M]. 北京:教育科学出版社,2015.该书主张运用思维导图来改善小学英语教学,其学理源于脑科学、心理学和教育学的相关理论,其实践价值获得了大量教学实践的验证和肯定。

(2) 吉桂凤. 思维导图在小学英语写作教学中的应用[J]. 中小学外语教学(小学篇),2019(4):7—13.本文建议运用思维导图来提高小学英语课堂教学质量,并就其学理进行了探讨,如脑科学、心理学和教育学的相关理论,同时提出了具体的使用方式。

第二部分　精彩实录

授课地点:江苏省泰州市城东中心小学经东校区录播教室。

授课时间:2018 年 4 月 18 日。

听课人员:泰州市、各市(区)教师发展中心教研员,专家代表,各小学英语教师代表共 60 人。

授课过程:

Stage One:Pre-writing

Step 1:课件展示 Nice food,wonderful world

T:Now let's enjoy some pictures about food.

Step 2:学习 food 的种类

T:We have enjoyed some pictures about food before class. Do you like food?

Ss:Yes!

T:Me too. Food all comes from plants and animals. It includes grain, ...

Ss:fruit, vegetables, ...

T:What food do you like? Speak more. The pictures will be clearer and clearer.

S1：Meat.

S2：Snacks.

...

T：Food is important. But eating too much food is ...

Ss：... bad for our health.

T：So what do we need?

S1：We need a healthy diet.

（教师板书课题，并明确这是一节写作课。）

Step 3：理解 diet 的意义

T：Do you know the meaning of the word "diet"?

Ss：饮食。

T：It's about the food. The letter "d" means "every day", the letter "i" means "I","e" means ...

Ss：eat.

T：Good. Eat for breakfast，lunch and dinner，and "t" means ...

S1："today".

T：About the time，on time. So diet means ... Let's read together.

Ss：Every day，the food I eat for breakfast，lunch and dinner on time.

T：So，remember?

Ss：Yes.

Step 4：Let's review

T：How about their diets? Let's say together. Mike likes ...

Ss：Mike likes ...

T：How about Yang Ling?

Ss：Yang Ling likes ...

T：Who has a healthy diet?

Ss：Yang Ling.

T：Let's chant "Yang Ling's diet".

Ss：Yang Ling has a healthy diet. A lot of noodles for breakfast. She sometimes eats an egg for lunch and for dinner some vegetables，some meat. She only eats a little rice. Sweet food，also likes. Every day，eats some fruit. A healthy diet，isn't it?

（通过拍手来打节奏，让学生的 chant 更有律动感，并通过加快节奏达到熟练化。）

T：Who has an unhealthy diet?

Ss：Mike.

T：Can you give him some suggestions. You can use：To keep healthy，... should/shouldn't ...（教师板书该句型结构。）

S1：To keep healthy，he should eat some fruit.

S2：To keep healthy，he should eat some vegetables.

S3：To keep healthy，he shouldn't eat too much sweet food.

...

Stage Two：While-writing

Step 5：理解 healthy

T：But in our daily life，many people have unhealthy diets. Just like Bill，Jill，Hill. In order to set a good example，we should write a passage about a healthy diet. But what details can we write about "healthy"? Please discuss with your partner first.

（学生小组讨论。）

T：Now let's choose.

S1：What to eat?

S2：How much/many?

S3：How often?

S4：What's for ...?

T：Where to eat? It doesn't matter. So the word "healthy" contains the four parts：What to eat? How much/many to eat? How often? What's for ...?

① Part 1：What to eat?

T：Now let's know the first detail. What to eat? In our meals, there is a lot of food. Can you make a sentence like this：In a healthy diet, there is/are ...（教师板书

该句型结构。)

S1：In a healthy diet，there are a lot of fruit and some vegetables.

S2：In a healthy diet，there are a few eggs and a lot of noodles.

S3：In a healthy diet，there is some fish and some meat.

...

T：Please remember tip 1：写作时要注意区分可数名词和不可数名词、单数和复数。

② Part 2：How much/many?

T：But in different countries，different people like eating different food. No matter who you are，Chinese people or western people，no matter what you eat，vegetables or salad，I think how much/many to eat is the key. Let's look at the food pyramid. At the bottom，noodles，rice，bread，we can eat ...

Ss：A lot of.

Ss：We eat a lot of noodles，rice and bread.

依次引出 some，a little，a few 并正确表达。

T：These words are quantifiers. Please pay attention to them. Now read and fill in tip 2.

Ss：写作时我们应该准确运用量词。some 和 a lot of 后面都可以跟可数名词或者不可数名词。

T：Let's learn more about "a few" and "a little".

（通过微视频教学，正确区分 a few 和 a little。大约 2 分 30 秒。）

T：Now let's play a game. Please stand up quickly and say it loudly：I eat/drink a little/a few ... Ready ... go!

Ss：I eat a few hamburgers.

Ss：I drink a little coffee.

...

T：Do you like eating these food?

Ss：Yes.

T：How often to eat these food? Every day? Sometimes? I think you shouldn't eat too much.

（通过练习让学生明白,对于一些食物,特别是甜食、碳酸饮料等,一定要注意适量。）

③ Part 3：How often?

Tip 3：写作时,正确运用频度副词(always, usually, often, sometimes 等)和表示频度的名词短语(every day, every week 等),更能体现某种饮食习惯的程度。

T：So when we write our healthy diets, we should use these words correctly, such as always, usually, often, sometimes ... every day, every week. Please choose these words to make sentences about Su Hai's diet.

你能选用频度副词来说一说 Su Hai 的日常饮食吗? For ... , Su Hai ... eats ...

S1：For breakfast, Su Hai often eats a lot of noodles. Sometimes she eats a cake.

S2：For lunch, Su Hai always eats a little rice, some meat, some fish, and ...

S3：For dinner, Su Hai usually eats some vegetables, a little rice, and ...

④ Part 4：What's for ... ?

（教师出示思维导图。）

T：How about your diet? What do you eat for breakfast/lunch/dinner? （引导学生说。）

Ss：For my breakfast/lunch/dinner, I ... eat ....

（一名学生说 eat a lot of rice,教师及时指出 Don't eat too much rice. ）

Step 6：Skills for writing

T：We have known four details about writing a healthy diet, but how to write? Let's learn after the video.

（微视频播放写作指导,大约 2 分 30 秒。）

Step 7：Writing and check

① Writing

T：Are you ready? Let's write down your healthy diet. Please finish it in 5 minutes according to the mind-map. Pay attention to your handwriting.

（播放非常轻缓的背景音乐 5 分钟。教师行间巡视了解写作完成情况，对于个别学生进行指导。）

② An example

（切换到视频展台。）

T：Please look at the screen. I have an example. Can you read and find some mistakes?

S1："Diet" is wrong. The correct spelling is "diet".

S2："A few meat" is wrong. The correct answer is "a little meat".

S3："Porridges" is wrong. The correct spelling is "porridge".

S4："it's" is wrong. The correct spelling is "It's".

（根据学生的回答，教师圈出错误部分，并写出正确答案。）

③ Check

T：Change your notes with your partners, check for him/her. If you find the mistakes，you can circle or underline, or ask me for help.

（同桌相互检查，找出错误，时间大约 1 分钟。）

④ Revise your passage

T：According to the checking results, please revise your passage.

（学生对于写作中的错误进行订正，时间大约 1 分钟。）

⑤ Show

（选择一位学生，展示一下修改好的文章。）

Stage Three：Post-writing

Step 8：Speech show

T：Let's have a speech show. Tell us your healthy diet. Maybe you can do some actions. Maybe you can tell us without the note. 大胆地说出自己的日常饮食习惯，演讲时可以适当做动作，如果能脱稿演讲就更棒了！准备一下吧！（学生准备时间大约 1 分钟。）

Step 9：Enjoy the show

（教师适时鼓励，对于三位学生中一位脱稿的及时 A big hand for her。）

Step 10：Discuss

T：You have healthy diets. Su Hai has a healthy diet too. Look at her，she looks so ...

Ss：so sunny, so slim, so graceful, so healthy.

T：So how to keep healthy? What do we need?（教师画出钻石造型。）

S1：We need to do sports.

S2：We need good habits.

S3：We need a healthy diet.

T：We need happy feelings. We should be happy every day. It's very very important.

Step 11：Extended writing

T：So let's try to write something about "How to keep healthy?". We can something about "a healthy diet". We can something about "good habits". We can something about "sports".（出示范文的主体部分。）Is this a whole passage? What's missing? We need a beginning and an end. How to write? An example about beginning：Health is the most important thing. An example about ending：Health is wealth. To keep healthy，let's do all three.

T：Health is wealth! Just like a diamond, it's valuable.（教师对学生进行情感教育。画出钻石光芒，为最后张贴学生作品做板书准备。）

（学生完成"How to keep healthy?"的开头和结尾，一到两名学生示范朗读。教师行间引导学生在黑板张贴部分学生作品。）

Step 12：Assignments

1. Try to read your passage or give a speech to your parents and friends. 朗读或把你的习作演讲给父母和朋友听。

2. 从 Bill、Gill、Hill 三人中选择一人，为他量身定制一份健康饮食表。

板书设计

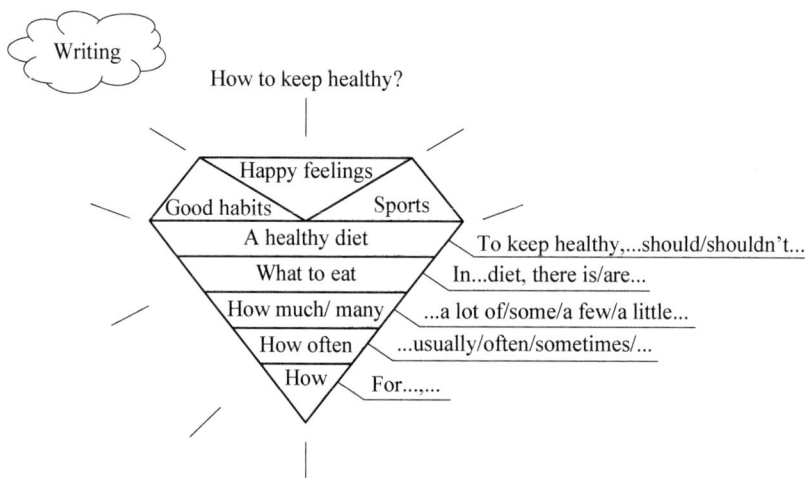

第三部分　课例评析

一、学生反响

学生 A：肖老师上课很洒脱，也很幽默，自编的 chant 打起节拍说起来朗朗上口，特别是对于 diet 的理解让我印象深刻。

学生 B：活动多，很有意思，比如动画大嘴吃食物，形象生动。不过写作时有点尴尬，我感觉语言不够用，有的单词平时只会说不会写，演讲时脱稿感觉有点难度，所以有点紧张。

二、同行声音

王莉（泰州市城东中心小学）：肖老师的教学设计环环相扣，教学思路清晰，注重思维训练，由浅入深，活动设计丰富有效，亮点多，比如对 diet 的解释让人耳目一新，Chant 语言简练，节奏欢快，对 healthy 的分析层次分明，紧抓要点，写作环节层层递进,由易到难,书面口头语言得到锻炼的同时,思维品质也获得了进一步的提升。

郭晓莉(泰州市城东中心小学):肖老师的课很好地发挥了思维导图在写作教学中的作用,从开始的 food 的种类,到食物金字塔复习可数、不可数名词,并结合 a few、a little、a lot of 进行整合巩固,到写作 My healthy diet,有助于培养学生的思维品质,提高写作的效率。

三、自我反思

本节写作课采用 PWP 三段式教学模式,注重在分析写作话题的基础上训练学生思维能力,培养学生思维品质。

1. 本节课的成功之处

(1) 教学活动的设计错落有致,效果明显

课始的图片欣赏"Nice food, wonderful world"一下子就吸引了学生们的注意力,很轻松地就突出了今天写作的主要词汇基础,通过对 food 词汇的举例,图片中男孩的体型由瘦变胖,很直观地用图片语言告诉学生,Eating too much food is bad for our health。复习课文内容之后,及时通过 Chant 对课本内容进行了归纳总结,既为学生提炼出写作时需要的语言精华,又通过欢快的拍手节奏,很好地调节了课堂氛围。在学生学习了解了 a few 和 a little 的区别之后,通过一个简单游戏"大嘴吃食物"来及时巩固,学生很感兴趣。写作之后的 Speech show 和 Writing show,轻松欢快地消除了学生的胆怯,让他们勇于站出来展示自己。每一个活动的设计和完成都为后面的活动做好了认知的铺垫和思维的准备。从教学效果来看,整节课学生的课堂专注度和参与度都很高,较好地达成了预设的教学目标。

(2) 注重写作思路的分析,培养学生思维品质

在学生对比知道 Mike has an unhealthy diet 后,及时地回归到写作的中心话题 My healthy diet 上,并对关键词 healthy 进行讨论思考,引导学生分析出我们饮食要做到 healthy,重点从四个方面来体现:吃什么(What to eat?)、吃多少(How much/many to eat?)、吃的频率(How often?)、如何安排(What's for ...?),这样做既兼顾到面,也

突出了细节注意的点,帮助学生分析、理解、整理和加工信息,训练了思维,使学生一直处于积极、主动的学习之中。

(3)注重写作策略的指导,帮助学生获得写作的成就感

本节课借助了两节微视频,既学习了正确区分词汇 a few 和 a little,也讲解了围绕主题来写作的基本技巧。在学生初步尝试写作时,提供层次鲜明的思维导图,给学生提供了策略和抓手,让学生知道写什么、怎么写,不至于跑偏主题。初稿完成后,先示范告诉学生要注意哪些问题,再利用小组合作学习的方式,相互检查,查遗补缺,订正润色。在拓展写作部分,借助范文的主体来分析写作时应该采用的简单结构总—分—总,这样文章的结构才能更加完整。通过 Speech show 和 Writing show,把学生的写作成果生动形象地展现出来,获得成功的喜悦。

2. 本节课需要改进之处

课的开头部分还留有传统阅读教学的影子,写作主题的出现略微晚点了,课始导入以后可以直接切入写作主题,然后再根据主题来学习相关的写作素材、写作策略指导等。此外对学生的评价可以更多元化一些。由于考虑到时间限制和追求录像课形式上的完整和流畅,导致在回答问题、游戏、演讲等方面不能涉及更多的学生,课堂活动的参与度还需提高。教师对课堂的驾驭能力和信息处理能力也还要进一步提升。

四、专家点评

点评专家:姜建宇

写作教学在小学高年级英语教学中有着举足轻重的地位,同时也是一致公认的薄弱环节和教学难点,学生怕写,老师怕教。这节课上,肖兴华老师聚焦 A healthy diet 这一中心话题,借助思维导图具化思维过程,条分缕析地理顺了与话题相关的四个问题,用直观而精巧的图式,在学生的头脑中勾勒出简明清晰的知识框架和写作框架,培养了阅读和写作的"整体"观。同时借助微视频向学生讲解了语法细节和写作策略,突破本课的难点,形成一定的语篇意识。整节课中,肖老师将语言输入与语言运用、口头表达与书面表达紧密地联系在一起,训练了思维的清晰性、开阔性、批判性和创新性,提高学生的写作能力。肖老师轻松潇洒的教学风格,更是拉近了师生距离,消

除了畏难心理,增添了写作趣味,激发了写作热情,为今后的英语学习打下了良好基础。

【名师简介】

　　肖兴华:泰州市小学英语名师工作室成员。多年来,时刻关注着英语课堂教学的发展变化,通过参与省市级多项课题的研究,不断更新自身的教育理念,形成自己的教学风格,并经常执教公开课向同事同行展示自己对课堂的不同诠释。在各类教学竞赛中多次荣获市级一等奖、一次省级三等奖,有多篇论文和知识短文获奖或公开发表,多次指导青年英语教师参加各级各类教学竞赛,并获得优异成绩。

课例 4　基于"微课"促进思维品质提升的课例研究

——以 Seeing the doctor 单元复习课为例

第一部分　教学预设

一、教学内容分析

1. 课标要求

英语学科的学习离不开语言、文化和思维,因此,修订后的《课标(2017 版)》将语言能力、文化品格、思维品质和学习能力列为英语学科的四大核心素养。《课标(2011版)》也明确指出,"语言既是交流的工具,也是思维的工具。所以学习和使用语言的过程与发展思维能力有密切的联系。学习一门新的语言能够进一步促进人的心智发展,有助于学习者从多角度理解世界的多样性,提高分析能力与认知水平"。由此可见,英语课程承担着发展学生语言运用能力和思维能力的双重任务。

2. 教材分析

本课是五年级下册 Unit 4 Seeing the doctor 的单元复习课,教学内容是表示建议类情态动词 should 及其否定形式 shouldn't 的用法,以及有关询问和描述病情的句型

What's wrong with you/...？ I/He/She/... have/has a headache/... 等。本单元的目标词汇还有 take medicine、have a rest 等短语,在教学中可以让学生尝试活用动词组成更多的动宾短语,丰富语言表达。

该单元包含以下八个板块:

Story time:分别讲述了 Su Hai 发烧去看医生和 Mike 牙疼去看牙医的故事,对话内容为关于病人描述病情和医生提供建议等。

Grammar time:讲解情态动词 should 的用法以及医生如何询问病情 What's wrong with ...？ 及其答句 I/He/She have/has a(n) ...。

Fun time:采用对话形式角色扮演,一名学生扮演病人,另一名学生扮演医生。病人描述症状,医生用 should/shouldn't 提供建议。

Sound time:了解字母组合 ch 在单词中的发音之一—[t∫]。

Culture time:介绍了摄氏度和华氏度的区别。

Cartoon time:描述了小动物们去医院看病,涉及到的重点句型 What's wrong with you 和 You should ...,并引入了 How do you feel now? My ... hurt(s)等与单元主题相关的句型。

Checkout time:通过听、写两个活动检测学生对单元知识的掌握情况。

Ticking time:学生通过自评的方式检测自己对单元具体内容的熟悉程度。

这节复习课是本单元的最后一个课时,主要内容是复习前面各版块,完成 Checkout time 和 Ticking time 的教学。

3. 重点与难点

本课的重点与难点是学生能够正确使用关于看病的日常交际用语,如用 What's wrong with you? 来询问病情,用 I have a ... 句型来回答,用情态动词 should 和 shouldn't 给建议,需要注意的是有部分短语的语音需要加强,如 medicine, brush 等。字母组合 ch 在单词中的读音也是复习重点之一。

4. 学情分析

(1)学生心智特征分析

本节课是借班执教的一节市级公开课,研讨主题是"泰微课"在学科教学中的应用,授课对象是五年级学生。由于"泰微课"在泰州地区已推行多年,学生对微课比较熟悉,且具有一定的信息获取和整合能力。课前在查看自主学习任务单的完成情况时,教师就已感觉到该班学生自主学习能力较强,思维比较活跃。正式上课的地点在录播教室,面向全市中小学教师现场同步直播。学生对此次直播充满好奇和兴奋,课堂参与的积极性更高于平常。

（2）学生已有知识经验分析

五年级英语在小学英语教学中起着承上启下的作用,它既是中年级的延伸,又是高年级的开始。本单元的话题是看病,在四年级下册 Unit 7 What's the matter? 中,学生已经初步学习了 hungry,ill,sad 等表示感受的形容词,以及关心他人的句型 What's the matter(with you)?;四年级下册 Unit 8 How are you? 中又出现过疾病类词汇 cold,cough,fever,headache 等。因此,学生对该话题并不太陌生,且有一定的知识基础。

二、教学目标分析

根据对教学内容和学生情况的分析,本节课设定了以下教学目标,即经过本节课的学习,学生能够:

1. 自主复习课文,与他人合作交流;

2. 小组合作,谈论已学过的疾病类单词;

3. 联系生活,用 should 和 shouldn't 给别人提供建议;

4. 了解字母组合 ch 在单词中的发音。

三、思路、方法与资源

1. 整体思路

本节课教师通过 Word puzzle 引出 WeChat,将本单元各板块有机串联起来,内容编排顺序为 Story time→Sound time→Checkout time→Culture time→Cartoon time,其中教学重点是 Checkout time,Ticking time 贯穿在复习的过程中。由 WeChat 中 Tim 的朋友圈,完成了 Checkout time 的练习。再从朋友们在朋友圈中的评论过渡到对如何询问别人身体状况句型的讨论,用微课对上述句型进行梳理和拓展,重点强化单元目的语的学习。接着通过 Yang Ling 的朋友圈呈现华氏度的表达,再用一节微课讲解华氏度与摄氏度的区别及换算方法,突破难点,巩固 Culture time 中的相关文化知识。在拓展运用版块,小组合作续编绘本 *Help Floppy* 就医的情节,再引导学生回到 Cartoon time 中的场景,仿写受伤的小动物们就医的病例,活用本单元所学知识。

Step 1：Choose the revision aims

T：Boys and girls! We're having a revision lesson today. Which are the aims for Unit 4?

【设计意图】课前,教师将通常的直接呈现本课学习目标改为由学生自主选择目标,激活了学生对单元旧知的回忆,学生在回顾中甄别已学内容,排除干扰项,去伪存真,锻炼思维的清晰性和准确性。

Step 2：Let's retell the story

【设计意图】先让学生选择一段进行复述,再集体讲述。分层次地进行复习,将课堂的选择权交给学生。

Step 3：Magic eyes

T：There are some words in the cross-word puzzle. Can you find the illnesses you know? Let's have a competition.

【设计意图】通过小组竞赛的形式有效激发了组内合作与组际竞争的意识,在观察、记忆、比较的过程中快速、批量地复习同一类单词,训练了学生思维的敏捷性,提高了课堂学习效率。从这些单词中归纳出字母组合 ch 的发音/k/,再由字谜中暗藏的 WeChat 一词,带出 ch 的另一个发音/tʃ/。

Step 4：Let's choose

T：Here's a WeChat about Tim，let's look.

【设计意图】通过字谜中的 WeChat 引入微信主题,接着呈现出 Tim 发的微信朋友圈"I want to fly kites，but ..."，这欲言又止的一句话既引起了微信好友 Wang Bing 的关注,也激发了学生的好奇心。

Step 5：Let's summarize

T：Look at the sentences. When can we use them? Feel well or not well?

【设计意图】复习课上对同一类知识点的总结归纳很重要。通过播放微课,让学生了解更多询问别人身体状况的句型,从书上的一种句型扩充为七种,拓展学生的知识面。

Step 6：Let's say

【设计意图】通过看朋友圈里 Yang Ling 发热的度数,播放微课,进一步了解华氏度与摄氏度的换算,了解中西方文化差异。指导学生如何向生病的朋友提建议,表示关切。

Step 7：Write and check

T：Who wants to be teachers? (拿一学生的书到展台前批改。)

【设计意图】通过让学生到前面进行批改的形式,充分体现了学生在英语课堂中的主体地位,将课堂真正还给学生。

Step 8：Help Floppy

T：When someone is not well, you can help him. Now let's help Floppy.

【设计意图】学生语言能力和思维品质的训练都需要适时强化,在高年级复习课上更要加强听说读写的综合训练,引导和帮助学生对语言材料进行归纳和整理,提炼出其中带有规律性的东西,加深对语言的理解,熟练对语言的运用。在拓展环节中,教师让学生根据绘本续编故事,引导学生注意语言表达的严密性和话轮的转换,严谨表达、有序表达,以及有理有据地表达,训练思维的逻辑性。小组讨论时,学生的思路从 Floppy is not well 拓展开去,结合种种身体不适的可能性,发挥想象创编对话,并提出了相应的可行性建议;汇报时,各组的答案是丰富而开放的,只要存在合理性,教师都予以了充分肯定,鼓励学生大胆想象、勇于表达,训练学生思维的开放性和创造性。

Step 9：Assignments

【设计意图】充分挖掘、激活教材中的语言资源,选择 Cartoon time 中的场景作为创作素材进行课后仿写练习,有助于建构单元各板块间的联系,不但能够更牢固地复习单词句型,组句成篇,提高书面表达技能,而且能让学生尽情发挥想象,培养思维的创造性,在文本再构的过程中体会创作的乐趣。

2. 模式方法

"微课"这一概念最早出现于美国,是一种以建构主义为指导思想,以在线学习或移动学习为目的,以某个简要明确的主题或关键概念为教学内容,通过音频或视频影像录制的短时课程。微课的载体是微视频,内容是教师对某个知识点的专项讲解,一般为3—5分钟,可用作课前自主预习,课中强化讲解,以及课后的巩固拓展。"泰微课"是泰州市教育局开发的自主学习平台,汇集了全市名师制作的近13万节微课资源,涵盖小学三年级到高中三年级的全部学科,为广大教师和学生提供了海量教学资源。

英语复习课,是英语教学活动中不可或缺的环节,对学生学好语言、运用语言、培养思维能力极为重要。与以语言信息输入为主的新授课相比,英语复习课以语言信息输出为主,如果遇到输出障碍,则需要再次输入语言信息以备重新提取、整合、输出,更具有针对性、综合性、系统性和灵活性。因此,复习课并不是简单重复学习已学的内容,而是要把平时所学的分散的、局部的、零碎的知识通过纵横联系横成链、竖成串,进而系统化、结构化,在再现和回顾旧知的过程中温故知新,重新认识一些遗漏的知识,生成新知,提升知识综合运用能力。有效的复习课应该是师生互动、生生互动的过程,教师要精心设计有趣、有效、有意义的复习课教学活动,促进学生思维品质的发展。本节单元复习课中,微课的恰当使用起到了积极的作用,有利于促进学生思维品质的提升。

一用微课,突出重点。

思维品质的相关性、灵活性与语言表达的得体性、丰富性有着密切关联。小学英语课本总体来说语料比较单薄,词汇量少,句式简单而较少变化。例如译林版小学英语课本中关于"询问他人身体状况"的句子仅有4句:How are you? /What's the matter? /What's wrong with ...? /How do/does ... feel now? 在复习课上,教师不能拘泥于教材所学的内容,要适当拓展与超越,适时补充新鲜语料,尤其是英美国家日常生活中的惯常用语,逐步丰盈学生的语言表达。围绕核心句型,教师从"泰微课"平台中遴选了一节与本单元配套的微课"如何询问他人的身体状况",以旧带新,由易到难,先激发学生已有的知识经验,再引导学生带着问题观看微课,记住还有哪些新课本上没有的新句型,看完后进行归纳和拓展,训练了学生的专注力和记忆力。微课呈现的方式不仅强化了本单元重点语言的学习,而且丰富了课堂呈现形式,激发了学生学习的热情,调动了他们参与的积极性,使课堂活跃起来。

二用微课,突破难点。

微课时间短,切口小,讲解透,能够有针对性地解决学生在学习中所遇到的疑难问题。本单元的 Culture time 介绍了华氏度与摄氏度,举的例子是 39℃等于 102 ℉,但并未对两者之间的关系进行说明。华氏度离我们的生活距离较远,学生普遍感到陌生。于是,老师设计了杨玲发热 104 华氏度的情境,学生急于想知道这个温度究竟等于多少摄氏度,激起了强烈的好奇心。那么,两者之间有着怎样的等量关系呢? 学生带着浓厚的求知欲观看了一节 3 分钟的"泰微课"——"华氏度与摄氏度",了解了华氏度与摄氏度的起源,记住了两者之间的换算公式,并通过计算得出了正确的答案是40℃。这样,体现了数学与英语学科的完美融合。这节微课,不仅突破了难点,而且拓宽了学生的知识面,让学生了解到不仅仅是课本上所提到的美国在日常生活中多采用华氏度测量体温,还有缅甸和利比亚等国家也如此,同时培养了学生的国际意识和跨文化交际能力。

三用微课,巩固拓展。

除了课堂上呈现了两节微课以外,教师还将"观看第 4 单元相关泰微课"列入家庭作业,鼓励学生课后根据自己的学习需要,查漏补缺,巩固拓展,自主选择所需微课开展自定进度的学习,巩固所学知识技能,拓宽文化视野。

3. 推荐资源

(1) 鲁子问. 英语教育促进思维品质发展的内涵与可能[J]. 英语教师,2016(5):6—12. 该文章强调语言可以促进思维发展,英语更是有助于促进中国学生发展与汉语有着显著差异的一些思维品质。由此可知,思维品质应该成为英语学科核心素养的基本组成部分。在探讨英语学科应发展学生思维品质内涵的基础上,结合案例说明在英语教育中如何促进学生思维品质的发展。

(2) 姜建宇. 例谈小学英语复习课中思维品质的培养[J]. 南京晓庄学院学报,2019(2):28—33. 该文认为思维品质是最贴近小学生核心素养个体个性发展的维度,必须在小学英语课堂教学中予以足够的重视。文章以一节五年级复习课为例,结合多轮磨课的经历,探讨小学英语复习课中思维品质培养的内涵与策略。

第二部分　精彩实录

授课地点：泰州市实验小学录播教室。

授课时间：2017 年 5 月 25 日。

听课人员：泰州市、各市(区)教师发展中心教研员,专家代表,各小学英语教师代表共 100 人。

授课过程：

Step 1：Choose the revision aims

T：Boys and girls! We're having a revision lesson today. What are the aims of Unit 4?

(The computer presents the teaching aims.)

Step 2：Let's retell the story

(The students work in four and choose one part to tell, trying their best to be the best story teller.)

T：Now, let's tell the whole story together.

(先让学生选择一段进行讲述,再集体讲述。分层次地进行复习,将课堂的选择权交给学生。)

Step 3：Magic eyes

T：There are some words in the cross-word puzzle. Can you find the illnesses you know? Let's find.

S1：Eye ache.

S2：Headache.

. . .

(The teacher writes the words on the blackboard.)

T：In these words, ch is pronounced?

S：/k/.

T：Here's another word. Listen to me, "WeChat". In this word, ch is pronounced?

Ss：/tʃ/.

T：Can you say words that are pronounced/tʃ/?

S：Chair . . .

Step 4: Let's choose

T: Here's a WeChat about Tim, let's look. Tim says I want to fly kites, but...
Here's a remark from Wang Bing. What's up? What's the meaning of "What's up"?
Let's choose.

S: What's the matter? What's wrong with you?

Step 5: Listen and choose

T: What's wrong with you, Tim? Here are two more questions.

Ss: How does he feel? What should he do?

Step 6: Let's summarize

T: Look at the sentences, when can we use them? Feel well or not well?

S: Not well.

T: What sentences do you know? Let's work in four.

Ss: How are you?

...

T: You know many sentences. And here are two more. Let's watch the micro-
lecture and find out.

Ss: What's the trouble with you? How are you feeling now?

Step 7: Let's say

T: Mum tells Tim he should have a rest. What shouldn't he do?

Ss: He shouldn't...

T: I believe that with your help, Tim will be better soon. Here's another one,
Yang Ling is ill. And she says "I have a fever, my temperature is 104 ℉." It equals to
...? Let's watch a micro-lecture and think about the answer.

Ss: 40℃.

T: Here are some remarks from his friends. What should they say? What
shouldn't they say? Let's judge.

Step 8: Write and check

（老师拿一学生的书到展台前批改。）

T：Who wants to be teachers?

Ss：Let me try.

（The students read the pictures together.）

Step 9：Help Floppy

T：When someone is not well, you can help him. Now let's help Floppy. Listen to the story please. Boys and girls, just now, we read the picture book about the dog Floppy. Why does the writer say "Poor Floppy"?

S1：Because he is ill.

T：Excuse me. Who is ill? the writer or Floppy?

S1：Ha-ha, Floppy is ill.

T：I think so. I'm sorry to hear that. But how do you know that?

S1：It says "Floppy is not well. He lays on his bed."

T：OK. What else?

S2："Kipper is sad. Mum takes Floppy to the vet."

T：Do you know "vet"? What does a vet do?

S：兽医, Animals' doctor.

T：Yes! A vet is the doctor for the animals. If your pet is ill, you should take it to...

S：See a doctor. Oh, see a vet!

T：Wow, good thinkers! Floppy is not well. What's wrong with him? How does he feel? What can't he do? Can you imagine? And if you are the vet, what's your advice for floppy? Make a dialogue between them, and then complete the case of illness for Floppy, OK?

S：OK.（Discuss in groups then write down.）

T：The vet is very busy. Do you know why? Look! Here comes some patients. What's wrong with them?

Ss：The giraffe's neck hurts. The monkey's arm hurts. The rabbit's ear hurts. The elephant's nose hurts.

Step 10：Assignments

T：Please write a case of illness for them. Here's another one. Watch the other micro-lectures about Unit 4. These are your homework. 1. Watch the Micro-lectures about Unit 4；2. Write the cases of illness for other animals in the hospital.

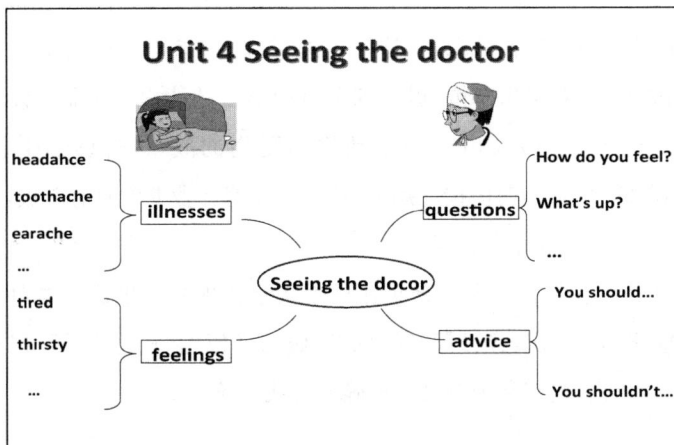

板书设计

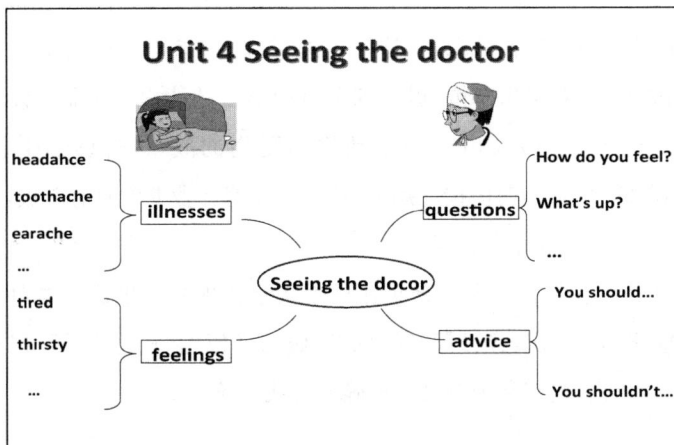

第三部分　课例评析

一、学生反响

学生 A：这节课让我更好地检测了自己的学习情况。看两节泰微课，我知道了怎样把华氏度换算成摄氏度，还知道除了书上讲的关心别人的句型以外还有哪些句型可以用，增加了好多知识。

学生 B：微信的出现很好玩，有人发朋友圈，还有人留言，特别贴近生活，也让我很有兴趣去了解 Tim 到底发生了什么事。字谜游戏也很有趣，在寻找疾病类单词的过程中，我还学会了许多新的单词呢！

二、同行声音

王素玫（泰州市实验小学）：复习课不仅仅是对本单元所有内容的复现与强化，还是对知识的延伸。这节课非常注重对学生进行思维训练，很费脑子。我最欣赏本节课的拓展环节，借用绘本 *Help Floppy* 让学生通过体验、参与、合作、实践完成这项任务，发挥合理的想象用英语做事情，提高综合运用语言的能力。作业设计也与 Floppy 就医一脉相承，融合 Cartoon time 中小动物们受伤的故事，告诉学生它们也到了 Floppy 所在的医院，请你当兽医撰写病例，这样的家庭作业非常具有开放性和挑战性，对于学生来说完成的积极性会更高。

翟静（泰州市实验小学）：课的开头让学生从干扰项中选出适合本单元的教学目标，然后逐一检测达成情况，经过仔细的思考，做出谨慎判断，这样既可以让学生了解本单元自己要学什么，也有利于对自己正确的自我评价。

三、自我反思

本节课通过设计"微信朋友圈"这一主线,将各个环节有机地整合起来。每一个环节的设计,充分尊重学生的主体地位,及其知识经验。所设计的任务都是学生可以完成的,在拓展方面是源于文本,但又别于文本。在 Help Floppy 这一环节中,充分利用绘本激发学生学习英语的兴趣。在板书上,老师通过思维导图的形式,让学生对本节课所复习的内容有清楚的了解。内容分为四个板块:illnesses, feelings, advice, questions。让学生清楚地认识到复习课要复习哪几个面,以此为切入口,复习所涵盖的内容。板书的完成也是在学生的帮助下进行的。学生通过思维导图的复习清楚地将所学知识进行系统化的整理。

四、专家点评

点评专家:姜建宇

在英语复习课上,教师不能仅仅满足于温习、巩固已学的语言知识,强化语言技能,还要创设新颖的、真实或模拟真实的语境,让学生学会思考,学会运用,促进综合语用能力和学科核心素养的提高。在朱映月老师的这节单元复习课上,教师设计了微信朋友圈的交际情境,将各板块内容进行了有趣、有机、有效的统整,引导和帮助学生对凌乱琐碎的语言材料进行归纳、整理、提炼,尤其是课中插入的两节微课,指向对重点知识的强化,对书本知识的拓展和对难点知识的解析,加深了对语言和文化的理解和运用,加强了听、说、读、写、看的综合训练,学生语言能力和思维品质得到了同步提升。

【名师简介】

朱映月:江苏省泰州市实验小学英语教师,海陵区 213 人才培养对象,海陵区小学英语教师骨干班成员。获得 2019 年泰州市小学英语教师基本功比赛一等奖,获得 2017 年海陵区优质课评比一等奖,多次面向全市开设基于泰微课的英语研究课,注重培养学生的信息综合能力。

课例 5　语法教学中情境创设及语言能力培养的课例研究

第一部分　教学预设

一、教学内容分析

1. 课标要求

（1）关于语言能力

《课标(2017 版)》提出：语言能力目标为具有一定的语言意识和英语语感,在常见的具体语境中整合性地运用已有语言知识,理解口头和书面语篇所表达的意义,识别其恰当表意所采用的手段,有效地使用口语和书面语表达意义和进行人际交流。

语言技能是语言运用能力的重要组成部分。发展学生英语语言技能,培养学生语言能力,就是使学生能够通过听、说、读、看、写等活动,理解口头和书面语篇所传递的信息、观点、情感和态度等;并能利用所学语言知识、文化知识等,根据不同目的和受众,通过口头和书面等形式创造新语篇。学生应通过大量的专项和综合性语言实践活动,发展语言技能,为真实语言交际打基础。

（2）关于语法教学

英语语法教学的目标是使学生在进一步巩固和扩展已有的语法知识的基础上,在具体语境中恰当地运用所学语法知识来理解和表达意义,进一步增强英语语法意识。课标所倡导的英语教学语法观,是以语言运用为导向的"形式—意义—使用"三维动态语法观。语法参与传递语篇的基本意义,语法形式的选择取决于具体语境中所表达的语用意义。教学中教师应重视在语境中呈现新的语法知识,在语境中指导学生观察所学语法项目的使用场合、表达形式、基本意义和语用功能,并通过课内外和信息化环境下的练习和活动,巩固所学语法知识,在语境中带领学生学会应用语法知识理解和表达意义,引导学生不断加强准确、恰当、得体地使用语言形式的意识;在练习和活动的选择和设计上，教师应根据学生实际需求，围绕"形式—意义—使用"采用和设计不同类型的学习实践活动，以既有层次又强调整合的多种教学活动来引导学生发展英语语法意识和能力。

（3）关于主题语境

主题语境不仅规约着语言知识和文化知识的学习范围，还为语言学习提供意义语境，并有机渗透情感、态度和价值观。教师要认识到，学生对主题语境和语篇理解的深度，直接影响学生的思维发展水平和语言学习成效。英语课程应该把对主题意义的探究视为教与学的核心任务，并以此整合学习内容，引领学生语言能力、文化意识、思维品质和学习能力的融合发展。

在以主题意义为引领的课堂上，教师要通过创设与主题意义密切相关的语境，充分挖掘特定主题所承载的文化信息和发展学生思维品质的关键点。基于对主题意义的探究，以解决问题为目的，整合语言知识和语言技能的学习与发展，将特定主题与学生的生活建立密切关联，鼓励学生学习和运用语言，开展对语言、意义和文化内涵的探究，特别是通过对不同观点的讨论，提高学生的鉴别和评判能力；同时，通过中外文化比较，培养学生的逻辑思维和批判性思维，引导学生建构多元文化视角。在主题探究活动的设计上，要注意激发学生参与活动的兴趣，调动学生已有的基于该主题的经验，帮助学生建构和完善新的知识结构，深化对该主题的理解和认识。通过一系列具有综合性、关联性特点的语言学习和思维活动，培养学生语言理解和表达的能力，推动学生对主题的深度学习，帮助他们建构新概念，体验不同的生活，丰富人生阅历和思维方式，树立正确的世界观、人生观和价值观，实现知行合一。

2. 教材分析

本节课教学内容为译林出版社《英语》（2011 版）八年级上册 Unit 6 Birdwatchers 的语法板块——动词不定式作目的状语和宾语补足语的用法，没有生词。A 部分用 Comic Strip 和 Reading 中的例句呈现目标语言，完成"在扎龙自然保护区人们可以做什么"的句子配对，练习动词不定式表示目的（也可用 in order to，语气更正式）的用法；B 部分为动词不定式作宾语补足语的用法，Sandy 描述了自己的观鸟见闻，用动词的适当形式帮她补全句子。

3. 重点与难点

教学重点：灵活运用动词不定式来描述图片、讲述经历和表达自己的观点。

教学难点：能正确运用动词不定式谈论观鸟计划，区别带 to 和不带 to 动词不定式作宾语补足语的用法。

4. 学情分析

学生在之前的学习中已经多次遇到含有动词不定式的句子，在上一单元的语法板块学习了动词不定式作宾语的用法。但动词不定式是英语特有的语言现象，学生受汉语思维的干扰，运用时容易犯语言形式的错误（to do/do 的误用）。机械记忆和操练的方式有助于学生巩固语言形式，但不利于学生把握目标语言的功能和意义并在情境中灵活、准确运用。

二、教学目标分析

基于教材、学情的分析和语法教学的要求，笔者制定了如下教学目标：

1. 学习、总结归纳动词不定式作目的状语和宾语补足语的用法，灵活运用动词不定式来描述图片、讲述经历和表达自己的观点。

2. 能运用动词不定式谈论观鸟计划。

3. 写一篇文章介绍自己的观鸟计划（尽可能多地使用动词不定式）。

4. 更多地了解鸟类及它们所遇到的问题，激发爱鸟之情和保护鸟的愿望。

三、思路、方法和资源

1. 整体思路

根据意义形式兼顾的教学理念，笔者确定本节课的教学思路为：将知识学习和语言能力发展融入主题、语境、语篇和语用之中，让学生在情境中感知语法形式的同时领悟其语法意义（聚焦意义），引导学生归纳总结语法规则（聚焦形式），进而在新情境灵活运用语法项目（聚焦形式和意义）。在此基础上，笔者以"观鸟"为话题和主线索，以"设计观鸟计划"任务驱动学习，设计"去哪里观鸟—观鸟时带什么—邀请谁一起去—父母会叮嘱什么—我们能为鸟做什么"的情境链，在真实的情境中引导学生学习和总结归纳动词不定式的用法，并运用动词不定式谈论观鸟计划。

意义形式兼顾的语法教学模式赋予静态的语法知识以动态的激发,学生学习语法知识的过程不只是对语法知识的加工和认知,也是面对新的情境整合运用语法知识进行师生、生生对话交流,产生情感和思维共鸣的过程,达到知行合一。

2. 模式与方法

（1）情境教学法

情境教学法是指在教学过程中,教师有目的地引入或创设具有一定情绪色彩的、以形象为主体的生动具体的场景,以引起学生一定的态度体验,从而帮助学生理解教材,并使学生的心理机能得到发展的教学方法。情境教学法的核心在于激发学生的情感。

美国哲学家杜威最早在教育学意义上运用"情境"一词,他提出"思维起于直接经验的情境",并把情境列为教学法的首要因素。教师在教学过程中必须创设情境,依据教学情境确立目的,制定教学计划,利用教学情境引起学生的学习动机,实施教学计划和评价教学成果。杜威认为所谓好的教学必须要能唤起学生的思维,因此,学校必须要提供可以引起思维的经验情境。

学生学习的过程不是被动地接受信息,而是获取信息、理解加工信息、内化建构知识、创新运用知识的过程。语言的学习过程是一个迁移运用的过程,即将从一个情境中学到的知识,迁移运用到一个新的情境。古希腊教育家苏格拉底从事教学,经常会为学生创设一定的问题情境,叫做"产婆术",进而引导学生主动思索,探究并获得问题的解决;借创设问题情境启迪学生,激励学生主动求知。

（2）三维语法教学理念

Larsen-Freeman(2007)将语法（技能）界定为语言形成图式的动态过程之一,人们可以用它来表达适合语境的语意;并指出语法不仅是一种语言知识,更应被视为一种与听、说、读、写并行的技能,一种动态的、有意义的系统。在此基础上,Larsen-Freeman 提出了语法的三维体系,即形式、意义和用法。

语法是一个动态的过程,语法教学首先应帮助学习者建构三维语法意识,不仅要让学习者注意或理解语法结构,而且还要训练他们有意义地、恰当地使用语法结构,以实现语法运用的自如化。（Larsen-Freeman, 2009）教师可通过意识增强活动、输出练习及反馈策略等的运用对目标语的形式、意义和用法进行充分的外显教学。在此基础上,应随时界定学习难点(形式、意义或用法),有所侧重地教,在互动交流中教给学生探究语言的工具,从而发展其语法技能。"自由运用是语言的产出活动,是大量语言输入之后的自然输出,是学生在一定语境中的自由表达"(林立,2012),学生"把课堂语言学习和自然环境或交际中的语言接触结合起来,对语言的形式和意义同时关注,他们的语言能力提高得更快"(阮金菊,2003)。

3. 推荐资源

(1) 李宝荣. 提升中学生英语语法知识运用能力的实践策略[J]. 中小学外语教学(中学篇),2014(5):1—5. 该文章指出语法能帮助学生准确、恰当地理解语言和使用语言。中学阶段英语语法教学的目的是提升学生运用语法知识进行交际的能力,即运用语法知识在交际中准确、规范地进行意义表达,并准确理解他人的语言表达。为此,教师要引导学生在语言实践中正确运用语法规则,从而提高学生的语言能力。

(2) 黄雪祥. 基于语言能力发展的初中英语阅读课例探究[J]. 中小学外语教学(中学篇),2016(9):47—52. 该文章以一节基于语言能力发展的阅读课为例,分析了各项活动对语言能力发展的指向意义,并提出了基于语言能力发展的阅读教学策略。

(3) 周华. 指向核心素养的初中英语语法教学[J]. 江苏教育,2019(2):68—73. 该文章基于一节语法公开课,阐述如何在主题情境引领下,依托语篇,以不同认知层次的活动为途径,引导学生学习语言知识、发展语言技能、理解文化内容和内涵,提升学生语言能力,发展提高学生的核心素养。

(4) 周华. 意义形式兼顾的初中英语语法教学[J]. 基础外语教育,2017(4):37—42. 该文章针对当前初中英语语法教学的存在问题,结合具体的教学案例,探讨如何创设情境,引导学生操练和运用语法知识,在真实的情境中提高学生的语用意识和综合运用语言的能力。

第二部分　精彩实录

授课地点:苏州木渎实验中学图书馆四楼。

授课时间:2018 年 11 月 20 日,时长 45 分钟。

听课人员:江苏省"教海探航杯"论文比赛获奖者、参会代表、木渎区各校听课代表约 100 人。

授课过程：

Stage One：Preparation

Step 1：Lead-in

在"Song of Irish Whistle"轻扬的音乐声中,学生欣赏由各种各样美丽的鸟的图片制作的视频,不时发出惊叹声。

【设计意图】观看鸟的图片、视频能帮助学生更多地了解鸟,激发学生爱鸟之情和观鸟的兴趣,激发学生的学习兴趣和参与课堂的热情,自然导入新课。

Stage Two：Presentation

Step 2：Talk about plans for birdwatching（Where to watch the birds?）

T：Hello，boys and girls. Do you like the birds? Do you want to go bird-watching? Where can we watch the birds in Suzhou?

S1：We can watch the birds on Tianping Mountain.

S2：We can watch the birds by the Tai Lake.

S3：We can watch the birds in the park.

T：（Showing some pictures of Qinghai Lake）I will go to Qinghai Lake to watch the birds and see the sights. What about you?

S4：I will go to the nature reserve to watch the birds.

S5：I will go to the East Mountain to watch the birds.

T：（Showing the sentences "I will go to Qinghai Lake to watch the birds and see the sights. /She will go to Zhalong to take photos of the cranes. /The boy will go to Yangcheng to see the cranes and do something for the birds."）Now read the sentences together.

T：Can you work out the rule?

S6：We can use "to" infinitives to express purpose.

T：Good. Now read the passage and fill in the blanks.

Every year，many tourists go to Qinghai Lake _____ （watch）the birds. They take cameras _____ （take）photos. The lake is so beautiful. People often get up early in the morning _____ （enjoy）the sunrise. They also like to ride around the lake _____ (see) more birds.

T：Ready? Now check your answers in groups.

T：Let's check the answers together.

Step 3：What to take with you when going bird-watching?

T：The tourists go to Qinghai Lake to watch the birds. They take cameras to take photos. What will you take with you if you go bird-watching there? Why?

S7：I'll take sunglasses to protect my eyes from the sun.

S8：I will take an umbrella to keep away from the sun and the rain.

S9：I will take a book to read on the way.

S10：I will take a coat to keep warm and a notebook to write down my travelling diaries.

S11：I will take a mobile phone to take photos and keep in touch with my family and friends on Wechat.

T：(Showing the sentences)I will take a camera with me in order to take photos. In order to take photos，I will take a photo with me. Can you work out the rules?

S12：We can use in order to express purpose.

T：Yes. It can be put in front of the sentence or at the end of it. The negative form is "in order not to do sth. ".

T：Many people like to go traveling during the holiday. But sometimes the traffic is so heavy. Look at the pictures. What did they do in order to enjoy themselves?

S13：They had square dances to pass the time.

S14：The man walked his dog to enjoy himself.

S15：The children had snowball fights to enjoy themselves.

T：Good. Everyone had a good time. Now open your books and finish the exercises on page 73.

T：Now let's check the answers.

Step 4：Who will you invite to go bird-watching with you?

T：The Bird-watching Society goes to study the birds in the wetlands. They invite more people to join them? Why?

S16：They invite people to help them.

S17：They need more people to count and describe the birds.

T：（Showing the sentences "They invite people to help them. They need more people to count and describe the birds."）Here we use "to" infinitives as object complements. Do you know other verbs like "invite/need"?

S18：Tell, ask, would like, teach, want, wish.

S19：Order, encourage, warn …

T：If you go bird-watching, will you go alone or with your parents and friends? For me, I will invite my friend Betty to go bird-watching with me. I need her to take photos for me and have fun together. What about you?

S20：I will invite my friend Lily to go bird-watching with me. I need her to chat with me all the way.

S21：I will invite my cousin Tony to go bird-watching with me. I want her to teach me to take photos of the birds.

Step 5：What will your parents say?

T：If you go bird-watching without your parents, what will they tell/ask/advise you to do?

S22：They will tell me to be careful and take good care of myself. They will also tell me not to go out alone at night.

S23：They will advise me to take a coat in order not to catch cold and a hat to keep away from the sun.

T：Let's watch a video by Nick Vujicic. What does he encourage you to do or not to do?

S24：He encourages us not to give up.

S25：He tells us to dream big.

S26：He wants us to be patient and thankful.

S27：He encourages us not to be afraid of difficulties.

S28：He encourages us to try our best to do everything.

S29：He encourages us to face the problems and difficulties bravely.

T：It's amazing for Nick Vujicic to enjoy his life so much though he is disabled. I also have some amazing birds for you. Let's watch the video. What can you see/hear the birds do in the video?

S30：I can see a parrot dance to music. I can also hear a bird make different sounds.

S31：I can hear a parrot sing songs. I can hear a parrot speak English.

T：(Showing the sentences) Some verbs can be followed by "to" infinitives without "to". Do you know such verbs?

S32：Let, make, see, hear, watch, listen to ...

T：And also "have, notice, find ..." Do you want to keep an interesting pet like this? Does your mother let you keep one?

S33：I want to keep a dog, but my mother doesn't let me keep one.

T：Just like this. Work in pairs.

S34：What pet do you want to have at home?

S35：I want to keep a cat.

S34：Do your parents let you have one?

S35：No, they don't.

T：Now let's play a game "Talk big". One student say "If I have a dog, I will teach it to dance." The other student will say "If I have a dog, I will teach it to play football." Try to talk big and make your pet better than your partners. Now work in pairs.

S36：If I have a parrot, I will hear it play the piano.

S37：If I have a parrot, I will hear it play the erhu and dizi.

S38：If I have a dog, I will teach it to get newspapers for me.

S39：If I have a dog, I will teach it to play all kinds of tricks.

S38：I will watch it walk upright just like us.

S39：I will watch it dance disco and play basketball.

T：Now open your books at page 74. Complete the sentences.

T：Let's check the answers.

Step 6：What problems do the birds have? What can we do for them?

T：Birds are so cute and lovely. Yesterday I went to Tianping Mountain to enjoy the beauty of the maple leaves. But I saw something unpleasant and it made me sad. Now let's watch the video.

T：Do you feel sad when watching the video.

Ss：Yes.

T：Birds are facing serious problems. Do you know what problems they have?

S40：People make the wetlands smaller to build farms and buildings.

S41：Fishermen keep fishing in their living places. As a result, birds do not have enough food to eat.

S42：Hunters catch them and sell them at the market.

S43：People drop lots of litter carelessly. When birds eat litter, they get ill and some of them die.

T：What can we do to protect the birds?

S44：We should build more reserves for them.

T：And I think the government should encourage people to leave the reserves.

S45：The government should make laws to protect the birds.

S46：People who catch or hurt birds should be punished or fined.

T：If you find people hurt birds or catch birds, you should call the police.

S47：We can tell more people to join us and protect the birds.

T：How can let more people know about the birds' problems?

S48：We can write letters to newspapers or magazines.

Stage Three：Production

Step 7：Writing

T：OK. So we can do a lot for birds. Now write down your plan for watching birds. The following table may help you. Or you write a letter to *Suzhou Daily* to ask more people to help birds.

Where to go?	go/fly/ride to ... to ...
What to take?	in order to ... , ... ; to ... ,
Who to invite? Why?	invite/tell/ask/need/... sb. to do sth.
Your parents' words	tell/ask/advise/... sb. (not) to do sth.
What to do to protect birds?	tell/ask/advise/encourage/wish ... sb. (not) to do sth.

T：Ready? Show your passage to us. (学生展示文章,其余学生和教师点评。)

Step 8：Homework

1. Surf the Internet to learn more about birds.

2. Write an article in the voice of a crane(以鹤的口吻)and tell people about their lives，problems and needs.

第三部分 课例评析

一、学生反响

学生 A：这节语法课让我觉得很新鲜,老师与我们谈论观鸟计划,每一个问题我都感兴趣。如:你打算去哪里观鸟? 和谁一起去? 如果你和好朋友一起去观鸟,妈妈会叮嘱什么? 这些问题让我觉得英语表达不是那么难,我不需要想太多,就能表达自己的想法。

学生 B：我喜欢老师课上的 Nick Vujicic 的视频,他是一个残疾人,却积极乐观地生活。老师让我们用动词不定式转述视频中胡哲的话,我们很自然就能用 tell/ask/encourage/advise 来表达。

二、同行声音

尤亚琴(苏州吴中区木渎实验学校,一级教师):这堂课周老师创设了很多生活化情境,引导学生在真实的情境中感悟、理解、运用所学的语法项目去表达和交流,学生课堂的参与度很高,课堂语言表达和生成很精彩。这样的课不像是语法课,而像是老师在和学生拉家常,在轻松愉悦的氛围中达成教学目标。

陆淑华(苏州吴中区木渎高级中学,一级教师):这堂课是一节非常精彩的语法教学课,周老师将情境创设与语言能力培养有机结合,将语法的显性讲解和隐性操练相结合,将聚焦语言形式和语言意义相结合,学生很轻松地就能运用语法知识去看图说话、表达观点和想法、自然交流、评判,课堂开放度很高,教学效果很好。

张小林(扬州高邮市赞化学校,一级教师):学生学习动词不定式的易错点之一是带 to 和不带 to 的动词不定式作宾语补足语。周老师通过创设父母亲对孩子观鸟叮嘱的情境,专门练习 tell sb. to do sth. 的用法,学生在对话中思考外出旅游应照料好自己,也自然体会到父母的关爱,语言活动关注目标语法的形式,也兼顾了意义。在此基础上提供励志视频、鸟的视频,引导学生在语言输出中验证和使用目标语法项目。Nick Vujicic 的视频有教育性,很能激励学生,一个没有手臂没有腿的残疾人,在生活中那么开朗、乐观、自信,并且成为世界有名的演讲家,学生观看视频以及运用英语交流的同时,能够接受隐性的情感教育,起到"润物细无声"的效果。借用视频中能唱歌、跳舞、会口技的鸟帮助学生更多地了解鸟,喜欢鸟,谈论鸟,在情境中运用不带 to 的动词不定式,突破难点。

三、自我反思

目前初中英语语法教学中存在两种误区:一些教师固守原来的语法教学模式,课堂中花费很多时间和精力讲解语法规则,加以"题海"训练,学生缺少在真实情境中应用语法项目的机会,课堂气氛沉闷;还有一些教师认为课程改革后语法教学中不应该再讲语法规则,语法课仅仅设计交际性任务,这导致学生对于语法项目的形式、意义和用法理解模糊,在交际运用时混淆不清。

意义形式兼顾的语法教学模式改变了传统语法教学课堂的单调、机械化、枯燥和沉闷。以话题为引领,以主情境为教学线索,以若干子情境将整节课教学内容自然衔接,保持了课堂教学的生动有趣、连贯自然、条理清晰、简洁高效。教师和学生在宽松的环境中,怀着轻松愉快的情感,以克服困难的意志,在言语情景中围绕语言功能对话,对话之中操练语言结构,点破归纳语法规则。(章兼中,2001,转引自田式国,2001)"英语教师不仅要让学生大量接触语言,还要让他们分析语法结构,反复使用所学会的知识;要为学生提供系统的、严格的语法训练,使学生的语言能力全面提高"。(Swain,2006,转引自汤燕霞,2016)

1. 本节课的可取之处

(1)师生自由会话中引出包含语法项目的例句

笔者以学生为课堂主体,营造轻松的课堂学习氛围,师生自由交流会话,激活学生的知识体系中与语法项目相关的部分,引出目标语法,为后续的归纳语法规则和自由运用表达和交际做准备。

(2)聚焦形式,学生归纳总结语法规则

学生只有理解和领会了语法规则,才能准确、得体地运用语法项目。需要注意的是,教师不能过分强调语言的交际功能而忽视对语法规则的纲要式提炼。(朱兰英,2012)笔者采取小组合作的形式,引导学生观察例句,小组讨论归纳语法规则,充分发挥学生的主体性地位。

(3)创设真实情境,引导学生进行有意义的语言实践

学生只有在动态的交际运用中才能自觉地把语法的形式、意义和用法有机结合起来,通过自身的知识结构重组,使语法技能发展成为运用语法进行交流的能力。(朱兰英,2012)笔者以"观鸟"话题为线索,创设若干符合学生年龄特点和生活实际的有趣的情境,引导学生在真实情境中师生、生生对话和交流,运用所学语法内容表达自己的观点和见解。不但保持了整节课的连贯性,而且学生在故事情境中不断整合、内化和运用所学语法知识,在鲜活的情境中学习和运用"活"的语法知识,保持学习语法的兴趣。

(4)以语篇为载体,综合运用语法知识

语法知识的练习和训练不能只局限于句子层面,还要有语篇层面的运用。笔者将

目标语法与语篇情境相结合,与听、说、读、写技能训练相结合,学生在对话和语篇写作训练中将语法的形式、意义和用法结合起来,更好地理解和运用语法知识,不断提高运用语法项目交际的能力和综合语言运用能力。

2. 本节课的不足之处

(1) 因为是借班上课,学生课堂参与度和默契度不够,因为设计的活动较多,后面学生写作和展示作文的时间偏少,整节课有点前松后紧。

(2) 活动的开放度还不够,学生的精彩生成有限。应给予学生更多的两两对话、小组讨论交流的时间和机会。

四、专家点评

点评专家:冒晓飞

英语课程改革的重点就是要改变英语课程过分重视语法和词汇知识的讲解与传授、忽略对学生实际语言运用能力的培养的倾向,强调课程从学生的学习兴趣、生活经验和认知水平出发,倡导体验、实践、参与、合作与交流的学习方式和任务型的教学途径,发展学生的综合语言运用能力。语法教学应从语法的形式、意义和语用三个维度进行,使学生能够自如地运用语法表达和交流,达成交际的目的。因此语法教学要兼顾形式和意义。

本节课中,周华老师善于引导学生在有意义的语言活动中感知、归纳、操练、运用语言形式,同时理解、体会语言形式表达的意义和功能,进而在交际性任务中提升语用能力。这节课主要具备以下几个特点:

第一,创设真实的情境,激发学生参与课堂和用英语表达的兴趣。周老师在本节课以观鸟为主情境,创设了若干子情境,形成情境链。整节课条理清晰。课前借用由各种鸟类的精美图片构成的视频、美丽的青海湖及湖边鸟的图片、有特殊能力的鸟类的视频、尼克胡哲的励志视频,整节课从头至尾时时激发学生的无意注意,学生愉快交流,自如表达。学生在真实的情境中感知、归纳、操练、运用语法项目,同时理解、体会语法项目表达的意义和功能,并在贴近自己生活实际的交际性任务中运用目标语法,提升语言运用能力。

第二,基于学生认知的多样性活动,促进学生语言能力的提升。本节课中学习理解、应用实践、迁移创新这三个层次的英语活动穿插进行,依托学生感兴趣的"观鸟"主情境,循序渐进。学生谈论去哪里观鸟、观鸟时带什么、邀请谁一起去观鸟、父母亲会叮嘱什么、"吹牛大比拼"游戏,谈论鸟类所面临的问题,以及我们能为鸟类做什么。

第三,设计开放性问题,引导学生发散思维,提高语言表达的多样性。周老师设计了"去哪里观鸟?观鸟时带什么?父母会叮嘱什么?鸟类面临哪些问题?我们能为鸟类做点什么?"等开放性问题,培养学生思维的开放性、发散性、逻辑性和创新性。学生课堂语言表达很丰富,产生了很多意想不到的精彩生成。

【点评专家简介】冒晓飞,教育硕士,正高级教师,江苏省初中英语特级教师,南通市英语学科专家组成员,江苏省教科研先进个人,南通市"226"高层次人才培养对象。

【名师简介】

周华:江苏省如皋市外国语学校教研组长,教育硕士,教授级高级教师,江苏省特级教师,南通市英语学科专家组成员,南通市学科带头人,南通市"226"、省"333"高层次人才工程培养对象,全国中小学外语教师园丁奖获得者。担任多所高校"国培项目"专家,江苏教育学会名师培养工程徐州新沂项目导师,江苏省第一届乡村骨干教师培育站导师,第三届乡村骨干教师培育站主持人,两次在中国教育学会外语专业委员会年会做主旨发言,多次参加省教育厅"名师送培"、省教师培训中心网络培训课程录制和江苏省各县市教材培训项目,在省内外开设公开课和讲座60多场;主持、参与多项省、市课题研究。参与发表论文30多篇,其中近20篇论文发表于国家级核心期刊,4篇被人大复印资料中心全文转载,多篇被索引。辅导学生参与竞赛,多人次获国家、省、市奖。

课例 6　初中英语主题复习课例研究

第一部分　教学预设

一、教学内容分析

1. 课标要求

主题语境不仅规约着语言知识和文化知识的学习范围,还为语言学习提供意义语境,并有机渗透情感、态度和价值观。教师要认识到,学生对主题语境和语篇理解的深度,直接影响学生的思维发展水平和语言学习成效。英语课程应该把对主题意义的探究视为教与学的核心任务,并以此整合学习内容,引领学生语言能力、文化意识、思维品质和学习能力的融合发展。

在以主题意义为引领的课堂上,教师要通过创设与主题意义密切相关的语境,充分挖掘特定主题所承载的文化信息和发展学生思维品质的关键点,基于对主题意义的探究,以解决问题为目的,整合语言知识和语言技能的学习与发展,将特定主题与学生的生活建立密切关联,鼓励学生学习和运用语言,开展对语言、意义和文化内涵的探究,特别是通过对不同观点的讨论,提高学生的鉴别和评判能力;同时,通过中外文化比较,培养学生的逻辑思维和批判性思维,引导学生建构多元文化视角。在主题探究活动的设计上,要注意激发学生参与活动的兴趣,调动学生已有的基于该主题的经验,帮助学生建构和完善新的知识结构,深化对该主题的理解和认识。通过一系列具有综合性、关联性特点的语言学习和思维活动,培养学生语言理解和表达的能力,推动学生对主题的深度学习,帮助他们建构新概念,体验不同的生活,丰富人生阅历和思维方式,树立正确的世界观、人生观和价值观,实现知行合一。

2. 教材分析

本节课教学内容为译林出版社《英语》(2011 版)九年级下册 Unit 3 Robots 的单元

117

主题复习课。本单元主题语境是 Robots。在 Comic 部分,Eddie 写了一封投诉信,向机器人商店投诉 Hobo,但是 Hobo 不会替他寄信;Welcome to the unit 部分,谈论机器人能为人类做什么,导入单元教学;Reading 部分讲述了江先生的经历,江先生是一位公司经理,因为太忙所以购买机器人,刚开始机器人让他很满意,替他做完了所有的家务,江先生也有了更多的空余时间,但是机器人中毒后,犯了一系列的错误,最后江先生无可奈何,只能退货;Grammar 部分是简单句与复合句之间的转换;Integrated skills 部分是关于机器人的一个国际展览;Task 部分围绕理想的机器人展开,包含问卷调查、投诉信和商家回信。

这节单元主题复习课主要复习单元主要单词、短语和句式,回顾课文内容,引导学生发挥想象,谈论自己想要设计的机器人。

3. 重点与难点

教学重点:激活学生已有知识和技能,促进新旧知识的融合和迁移。

教学难点:学生发挥想象,运用单元所学内容介绍自己设计的机器人;谈论机器人未来的发展以及是否会代替人类。

4. 学情分析

本节课是本地中考复习研讨会的一节公开课,学生为教者本班学生。学生基础知识掌握尚可,但是不能在新情境中灵活运用;九年级的学生与七、八年级的学生相比,学习更内敛,课堂发言不够活跃;语言输出想象力不够,课堂生成较少。

二、教学目标分析

教学目标	认知层次	核心素养
1. 头脑风暴,复习有关形状、能力、缺点的短语和句式	学习理解	语言能力 学习能力
2. 发挥想象,与同伴谈论你设计的机器人	应用实践 迁移创新	语言能力 学习能力 文化意识 思维品质

教学目标	认知层次	核心素养
3. 正确运用宾语从句谈论一个机器人大赛获奖者,归纳总结宾语从句的语法规则	学习理解 应用实践	语言能力 思维品质 学习能力
4. 阅读语篇回答问题,讨论未来机器人的特点,观看视频,讨论机器人将来是否会替代人类	应用实践 迁移创新	语言文化思维 学习能力
5. 写一篇短文,介绍机器人的优缺点,描述你所设计的机器人,并发表你对机器人的看法	应用实践 迁移创新	语言文化思维 学习能力

三、思路、方法和资源

1. 整体思路

单元主题复习课是以单元主题为线索,将单元内容及其他活动进行整合,帮助学生梳理、复习、整合、内化、活用各课时内容,发展学生的听、说、读、看、写能力,提高学生的能力和素养。本节课依托主题语境,通过对教材内容的解构和文本再构,实现对已学知识的内化和灵活运用。

具体思路如下:

(1)谈论机器人。由谈论机器人外貌→机器人能为人类做什么→听语篇选择,更多地了解不同的机器人→设计你最喜欢的机器人(形状、能力等)。

(2)谈论机器人设计大赛获奖者,复习宾语从句。

(3)阅读语篇,更多地了解机器人,并讨论:未来的机器人将会是怎样的?机器人是否会代替人类?

(4)语篇写作。

2. 模式与方法

(1)主题教学

清华大学附属小学的窦桂梅校长根据西方统整课程理论,联想比较文学中的母题研究,从儿童自身特点、学习现状、课程单元、教材等出发,提炼教材的"主题词"——以

"积累、感悟、创造"为形式,由这一主题"牵一发","动"教材知识能力体系的"全身",把这些散乱的"珍珠"串联起来,统整成一个"集成块",由个及类,由类及理,个性与共性相融,形成立体的主题教学效果。从而站在哲学的高度,从生命的层次,重新全面认识课堂教学,着力于文与人、语言与精神的同构,整体构建课堂教学的一种体系。

孙铁玲指出主题阅读是指根据教材中的主题,选出与学生的语言水平相适应的多篇相同主题的文本,将提取、对比、联想、归纳和评价等阅读策略运用在阅读课堂教学中的一种教学方法。这是一种以学生为主体,以学生自主阅读为主、课堂讨论为辅的教学方法。它不仅能够丰富阅读教学内容,拓展学生的阅读视野,还能让学生掌握同一主题的大量词汇,对相同主题的文本的结构和内涵有更好的把握,从而提高学生的阅读理解水平。

(2) 连接主义理论

语言输入的每一个形式在大脑中就是一个信息节点,各个节点之间由路径(pathway)相连,形成网络结构。两个节点共同被激活的次数多,则它们之间的路径就被加强;两个节点共同被激活的次数少,则它们之间的路径就被削弱。随着两个节点间路径的加强,学习者就能够在两者之间建立联系。两个节点共同被激活的次数越多,则两者之间的联系就越紧密。按照这种观点,在语言学习的过程中,若有某些内容重复出现,则学习者在这些内容之间所建立的联系就会被加强,从而形成模式。这些模式因反复被激活而得到了强化,最终导致语言习得。

(3) 整体语言教学法

整体语言教学是关于语言、语言学习、语言教学、课程内容和社团学习的一整套教育哲理。整体语言教学围绕主题进行教学,能够使一个主题概念多角度多层次地反复出现,使学生有机会把过去的知识和经验与现在的学习任务结合起来,使新旧知识在头脑里形成网络记忆、网络联想,使英语学习产生质的飞跃。

3. 推荐资源

(1) 冒晓飞. 中考英语话题复习的实践与思考[J]. 中学外语教与学,2013(2):41—47. 该文章分析了中考英语复习存在的问题,阐述了话题复习的思路:围绕话题整合教材、在真实情境中通过活动板块复习知识、训练技能,提升语篇表达能力。同时探讨了复习课激趣促思、提高学生参与度的策略与方法,从而提高英语中考复习课的效率。

（2）顾雪丹. 初中英语主题阅读实践探究——以 2018 年江苏省初中英语主题阅读研讨会课例为例［J］. 中小学外语教学（中学篇），2019(2)：13—18. 该文章分析了阅读教学中存在的问题和困境，解读了主题阅读的定义和相关理论依据，并提出了选择恰当的拓展阅读素材、设计综合性阅读活动、实现阅读素养的正向迁移和同步提升、构建课堂内外的交融和互通等实施主题阅读的路径。

（3）孙铁玲. 深化主题阅读　提升核心素养［J］. 北京教育，2018(9)：46—47,44. 该文章指出主题阅读不仅能够丰富阅读教学内容，拓展学生的阅读视野，还能让学生掌握同一主题的大量词汇，对相同主题的文本的结构和内涵有更好的把握，从而提高学生的阅读理解水平。

（4）胡久华. 指向"深度学习"的化学教学实践改进［J］. 课程·教材·教法，2017(3)：92—98. 该文章探讨了基于主题的深度学习：教师引领下，学生围绕具有挑战性的学习主题，全身心参与、体验成功、获得发展的有意义的学习过程。指出基于深度学习的主题教学能促进学生学习方式的转变，对课程改革有效推进具有重要意义，是发展学生核心素养的有效途径。

第二部分　精彩实录

授课地点：江苏省如皋市外国语学校视频教室 1。

授课时间：2018 年 4 月。

听课人员：如皋市各校听课代表约 100 人。

授课过程：

Stage One：Lead-in

Step 1：Watch a video about the birds

T：Hello, boys and girls. What's the video about?

Ss：Robots.

T：Do you want to have a robot at home?

Ss：Yes.

Stage Two: Talk about robots

Step 2: Talk about a robot exhibition

T: There is a robot exhibition at Sunshine Square. Would you like to have a look?

Ss: Yes.

(The teacher asks the students to talk about robots' shapes and different parts of them.)

T: What do robots usually look like?

S1: They look like us humans.

T: (showing some pictures) Yes. Robots usually look like humans. What parts do they usually have?

S2: Head, eyes.

T: Yes. And their eyes can take photos of whatever they see.

S3: Arms, hands, chest, legs, knee and feet.

T: And they have wheels to move around. There are also some other robots. Look at the pictures. What do they look like?

S4: They look like animals, such as snakes, worms, insects and dogs.

T: And these robots look like big machines. They can help doctors do operations. Millie went to the robot exhibition and saw many different kinds of robots. Now listen carefully and choose the correct answer.

T: What do the robots made in India look like?

S5: They look like snakes.

T: What are they used to do?

S5: They are used to look for victims after the earthquakes.

(Then the teacher asks the students to talk about housework robots can do.)

T: What housework can robots do?

S6: They can do the laundry. They wash the clothes and then iron them.

S7: They can go shopping at the supermarket.

S8: They can look after children and play with them.

S9：They can also look after the elderly.

S10：They can clean the flat, such as sweeping the floor and mopping it up.

T：What else can robots do? Try to be imaginative.

S11：They can explore dangerous places.

S12：They can help put out fire.

S13：They can look for victims after natural disasters.

S14：They can do the difficult, dangerous or heavy jobs.

S15：They can help doctors do operations.

Step 3：Design a robot yourself

T：There is going to be a robot designing competition in Rugao. Would you like to take part in it?

Ss：Yes.

T：What kind of robot would you like to design?

S16：I'd like to design a robot to help me with my homework.

S17：I'd like to design a robot to help Mum with my housework.

S18：I'd like to design a robot to help firemen put out the fire.

S19：I'd like to design a robot to play chess with my grandfather.

T：Why?

S19：Because when I go to school and my parents go to work, my grandfather is alone at home and feels lonely. I want to design a robot to play chess with him.

T：You all have creative designs. Now work in pairs and talk about what kind of robot you want to design and try to explain the reasons.

T：Are you ready?

S20：What robot are you going to design?

S21：I'm going to design a robot to help look for victims after natural disasters. What robot are you going to design?

S22：I want to design a robot to help our teachers so that they can have more free time. When we have problems, it can explain them to us patiently. It can also listen to our worries and give us some useful advice.

T: Thank you for your wonderful design. I will be very happy because I will have more time to relax.

S23: What robot are you going to design?

S24: I'm going to design a robot to look after my two-year-old sister. Mum has always been busy and tired since my younger sister was born. What about you?

S23: I want to design a robot so that workers needn't do the dirty and dangerous work.

T: Wonderful ideas.

Step 4: Talk about Mr. Jiang's robot

T: Do you remember Mr. Jiang's robot?

Ss: Yes.

T: Why did Mr. Jiang want to buy a robot?

S24: In order to have more free time.

T: Where did he order the robot?

S24: He ordered it from a robot shop.

T: Was he satisfied with the robot?

S25: Yes.

T: How do you know?

S25: The robot satisfied his needs in general.

T: How did the robot help Mr. Jiang in the morning?

S26: When Mr. Jiang got up in the morning, breakfast was made, his business suit was smoothly ironed, and his lunch box was already prepared.

T: What happened a few weeks later?

S27: The robot caught a virus and no longer worked properly.

T: What mistakes did the robot make?

S28: When Mr. Jiang got home, he would find his flat in a complete mess: food was laid on the bed; milk was stored in the rubbish bin; coins, bills and his private papers were spread all over the floor.

T: So robots can help people a lot, but they can be too much trouble.

T: Now read the passage and fill in the blanks.

T: Are you ready. Check your answers in groups.

(changes, while/when, also, dried, swept, caused, machine, dustbin, mess)

Step 5: Read a passage about robots

T: Robots have both advantages and disadvantages. Now let's read a passage about robots and answer the questions.

T: Ready? OK. Question 1: Why do people need robots to do the simple jobs instead of human beings?

S29: Because the jobs are boring and robots will never get bored.

T: How long will it take to have more robots in the future?

S30: It may take hundreds of years.

T: What do you need to do in order to prevent the robot from breaking down?

S31: I need to give it some oil every month and change the batteries every two months. I also need to check it every 6 months.

T: What might happen if a robot catches a virus?

S32: They may make a mess and even cause a lot of problems.

T: What will robots be like in the future?

S33: I think robots in the future will think like us. Maybe they can do everything like us.

S34: I think robots will look like us and think like us.

T: Do you think robots will take the place of humans? Let's watch a video first.

T: Will robots take the place of humans? Why?

S35: Yes.

T: Why do you think so?

S35: Because some robots are clever and can do better than humans.

T: What about you?

S36：I don't think so because we have brains and can do everything better than robots.

Stage Three：Talk about a robot designer

Step 6：Ask a question you want to know about him first

T：Look at the picture. The boy, Lu Tao was a winner at the 12th International Robot Competition. Do you want to know more about him? You can ask questions like "I want to know when he became interested in robots."

S37：I want to know how many times he took part in robot competition.

S38：I want to know how he learnt to design robots.

S39：I want to know who taught him how to design robots.

S40：I want to know whether he would study robots in college.

S41：I wonder if anybody helped him to design the robot.

T：Now discuss in groups and work out the rules of object clause.

Stage Four：Write about robots

T：Robots have brought a lot of changes to our lives. The Robot Club wants to do a survey about robots. Please write an article according to the questions.

T：Are you ready? Who'd like to show your article?

T：Do you like his article?

Ss：Yes.

T：What do you like about his article?

S42：I like the robot he designs. It can help us solve problems and explain to us.

S43：I like the sentences "Each coin has two sides. Robots can also be too much trouble."

Step 7：Assignments

1. Search the Internet and try to find more information about robots.

2. Make a small piece of newspaper using the pictures and find in newspapers, magazines or the Internet and tell us about your designs.

第三部分　课例评析

一、学生反响

学生 A：今天这节课老师让我们设计自己喜欢的机器人，设计出形状和功能。我们都很感兴趣，我们小组的成员积极讨论，设计了不同的机器人，我的同桌设计的机器人能救火，我设计的机器人能照顾老人。

学生 B：机器人是我们感兴趣的话题，今天的课围绕"机器人"复习了整个单元的内容，我们谈论机器人，设计机器人，阅读有关机器人的文章，观看机器人视频。我和周围的几个同学都特别兴奋。

二、同行声音

汪泓（如皋外国语学校，一级教师）：这节课给我的感觉是灵活。学生不是简单地复习单词短语，而是在听说读写中不断地用英语交流和表达。整节课围绕"机器人"这个主题，让学生通过谈论机器人，谈论机器人设计者，最终写一篇关于机器人的文章，目标明确，教学效果很好。

施琴（如皋市搬经初级中学，一级教师）：复习课我们通常是让学生读背本单元单词短语，然后默写，很少像周老师这样，围绕一个主题，设计多种多样的活动，帮助学生在活动中运用知识。在这样的课堂上，学生不断用英语回答问题和两两对话，学生的思维是活跃的，学生的语言是不断生成的。

黄晓燕（如皋初级中学，一级教师）：周老师上的这节单元主题阅读课，让我们学到很多。例如，复习课应该围绕主题设计活动，整节课基于主题情境，借助于几个子情境展开，衔接自然，层层推进；语言输入与语言输出紧密结合。本节课的最终目的是学生能用英语写一篇文章，周老师在写作前为学生搭建了支架，降低了学生写作的难度。

三、自我反思

单元主题复习课是与传统复习课不同的一种教学尝试,反思本节课,我认为可取之处在于:

1. 把握课程要求,设置多层目标。我根据单元内容确定多层教学目标。在确定目标时注意根据学生的水平差异,采用分层设计,让不同层次的学生都能有所收获。(1)基于教材高于教材,课内向课外拓展。学困生的重点为掌握课本主题词汇及基本句式,学优生则要灵活运用。(2)设计活动时考虑伸缩性,可以照顾各取所需。

2. 整合教材内容,设计主题活动。本节课紧扣"Robots"主题,充分利用生活中真实的素材创设情境,设计真实的活动,激发学生参与课堂的兴趣;循序渐进,每一个活动都为下一个活动搭好支架,学生参与活动比较主动。

3. 基于学生认知,发挥学生主体作用。主题复习课不是对旧知识的简单重复,而是学生认识的继续、深化和提高。本节课充分发挥学生的主体作用,以再现、整理、归纳的方式建立知识之间的联系,使学生对所学知识加深理解、系统掌握、查缺补漏,在贯穿始终的活动中掌握语言知识、发展语言技能,激发学生英语学习的内驱力。

4. 联系学生生活,迁移创新运用。本节课联系学生生活,设计交际性强的语言活动,引导学生进行有意义的表达和交流,促进知识的迁移创新和运用,不断提高学生的语言运用能力。

5. 链接主题语篇,促进深度学习。语篇是教学的最小单位。本节课中,我将Reading改编为新语篇,设置短文填词练习;选用课外阅读语篇,引导学生阅读语篇,回答问题,思考未来的机器人将会是什么样,机器人将来是否会代替人类,不断激活学生的思维,培养学生的思维品质和语言能力。

本节课的不足之处:开放性问题有一定难度,问题提出后出现冷场。我采用小组讨论的形式,引导学生智慧碰撞,才化解了课堂的气氛,学生的表达还不错;在阅读关于机器人语篇后再过渡到谈论机器人设计大赛获奖者,过渡不够自然,有些生硬。

四、专家点评

点评专家：冒晓飞

单元主题复习课注重激活学生已有知识和技能，促进学生知识的重构和能力的提升，促进新旧知识技能的互动、连接、融合。周华老师的这节课充分体现了她对教材、课标、课程的理解，依托主题语境设计活动，实现对单元的系统化复习，体现了她较强的教学能力、灵活运用教学资源的能力、依托教材进行文本再构的能力。这节课的优点主要体现在以下几个方面：

第一，教学设计有创意。周华老师在本节课以单元话题为主线，整合复习单元内容，超越教材提升学生能力和素养。整节课设计具有系统性、整合性、开放性和创新性。

第二，活动设计有梯度。本节课周老师设计了不同层次的活动，面向班级不同英语基础的学生。如：(1)学习理解类活动，包括头脑风暴(复习有关机器人外貌、能力、缺点的短语和用法)、阅读语篇回答问题、观看机器人视频。(2)应用实践类活动，包括正确运用宾语从句谈论一个机器人设计大赛的获奖者，并归纳总结宾语从句的语法规则。(3)迁移创新类活动，包括发挥想象，与同桌谈论你设计的机器人(包括形状、能力等)；谈论未来机器人的特点；讨论机器人是否将会替代人类；写一篇短文介绍机器人的优缺点，并发表你对于机器人的看法，介绍你设计的机器人。

第三，课堂教学有深度。本节课周老师避免了脱离语境和语用的机械式讲解和记忆，而是联系学生生活，设计交际性强的语言活动，引导学生进行有意义的表达和交流，促进知识的迁移创新运用。这节课实现了教材主题与生活实际的融合，语境、语义和语用的融合，语言、思维、文化的融合，语言输入与语言输出的融合，复习教学与情感教育的融合。周老师在本节课中，以引导者的角色，引导学生自主梳理、讨论交流、合作探究、归纳总结，学生通过观察、比较、分析、概括等活动获取、强化、运用学习策略，掌握学习的主动权。

主题复习课对教师的要求很高，教师需要更新理念，钻研课标和教材，依托主题和语篇，整合教材中的词汇、语法、话题、功能和情境，精心设计复习课任务，帮助学生由

"学语言"转变为"用语言",由"机械识记"到"灵活运用",由"注重知识"到"能力提升和素养提升",由"学习理解"到"实践应用"和"迁移创新",不断提高学生的学习能力、思维能力和语言能力,指向学生核心素养的培养和提高。

【名师简介】

周华:江苏省如皋市外国语学校教研组长,教育硕士,教授级高级教师,江苏省特级教师,南通市英语学科专家组成员,南通市学科带头人,南通市"226"、省"333"高层次人才工程培养对象,全国中小学外语教师园丁奖获得者。担任多所高校"国培项目"专家,江苏教育学会名师培养工程徐州新沂项目导师,江苏省第一届乡村骨干教师培育站导师,第三届乡村骨干教师培育站主持人,两次在中国教育学会外语专业委员会年会作主旨发言,多次参加省教育厅"名师送培"、省教师培训中心网络培训课程录制和江苏省各县市教材培训项目,在省内外开设公开课和讲座60多场;主持、参与多项省、市课题研究。参与发表论文30多篇,其中近20篇论文发表于国家级核心期刊,4篇被人大复印资料中心全文转载,多篇被索引。辅导学生参与竞赛,多人次获国家、省、市奖。

课例 7　基于文化意识培养的初中英语阅读教学课例研究

第一部分　教学预设

一、教学内容分析

1. 课标要求

文化意识指对中外文化的理解和对优秀文化的认同,是学生在全球化背景下表现出的跨文化认知、态度和行为取向。文化意识体现英语学科核心素养的价值取向。文化意识的培育有助于学生增强国家认同和家国情怀,坚定文化自信,树立人类命运共同体意识,学会做人做事,成长为有文明素养和社会责任感的人。《课标(2017版)》指出,文化意识的目标是帮助学生"获得文化知识,理解文化内涵,比较文化异同,汲取文化精华,形成正确的价值观,坚定文化自信,形成自尊、自信、自强的良好品格,具备一定的跨文化沟通和传播中华文化的能力"。

教师应通过创设有意义的语境,恰当利用信息技术,基于语篇所承载的文化知识,引导学生挖掘其意义与内涵,帮助学生在语言练习和运用的各种活动中学习和内化语言知识和文化知识;通过感知、比较、分析和鉴赏,加深对文化异同的理解,提高对文化差异的敏感度和处理文化差异的灵活性,帮助学生坚定文化自信,增强国家意识。学生学习文化知识,形成文化意识一般要经过"感知中外文化知识——分析与比较;认同优秀文化——赏析与汲取;加深文化理解——认知与内化;形成文明素养——行为与表征"的过程。

2. 教材分析

主题语境:人与社会——英国礼仪。

语篇类型:采访稿。

授课时长:45分钟。

文本分析:

本节课教学内容为译林出版社(2011版)牛津初中英语教材八年级下册 Unit 5 Good Manners 的阅读板块,课题为 When in Rome,这是一篇关于英国礼仪的采访稿。Daniel 主持本周学校电台,他采访刚从英国回来的九年级学生 Jenny 以了解关于英国的礼仪。采访稿中包含了大量的文化知识,可分为四个部分的内容:英国人如何互相问候、如何对话交谈(经常谈论的话题和避免谈论的话题)、在公共场所的礼仪以及在家里的礼仪。

3. 重点与难点

教学重点:在适当的情境中得体地运用本课所学到的文化知识。

教学难点:能运用本课所学词汇向外国朋友介绍中国礼仪,弘扬祖国的礼仪文化。

4. 学情分析

本节课是在南京雨花台区马辉名师工作室"聚焦核心素养"研讨会上开设的一节

同课异构的公开课。本节课是借班上课,与该班级学生见面交流后发现,班级学生英语基础较好,学习积极性高,学习态度较认真。该班英语教师告诉我:该班学生具备在阅读中获取细节信息的能力,一部分学生能用英语表达自己的观点;但是多数学生在逻辑推理、批判评价、灵活运用语用知识进行得体交流方面仍比较欠缺。

二、教学目标分析

基于教材、学情的分析和语篇教学的要求,笔者制定了如下教学目标,即在本课学习结束时,学生能够:

1. 学习和掌握关于英国文化礼仪的生词和短语:greet,shake,proper,properly,conversation,avoid,behave,push in,push past,touch,bump into,in one's way 等,培养学生在语境中猜测 avoid,proper,in one's way 等词汇的意思;

2. 以问题牵引阅读,培养学生的思维品质;

3. 阅读关于英国礼仪的采访稿,了解英国礼仪,在英语情境中得体地运用所学到的文化知识;

4. 能运用本课所学词汇向外国朋友介绍中国礼仪,弘扬祖国礼仪文化。

三、思路、方法和资源

1. 整体思路

本节课采用常见的 Pre-reading,While-reading,Post-reading 三阶段教学模式,教学中以"以学致用"作为教学活动设计的原则,不断引导学生阅读文本,理解文化知识,并创设真实情境引导学生运用文化知识去判断、推理、比较、思考和对话交流,旨在培养学生在情境中获取文化知识、理解文化内涵、欣赏西方文化和比较中西方文化异同的能力,形成一定的语用能力和乐于传播我国优秀文化的意识和习惯。具体思路如下:

阅读前的活动:师生自由会话中导入生词。生词导入紧扣本节课主题"礼仪文化"。

阅读中的活动：

（1）Read about the main idea

引导学生归纳文章大意，思考是关于英国礼仪还是罗马礼仪。指导学生通过略读首尾段、关注标题、看插图等方法来获取文章大意。

（2）Read and analyze the structure

以填空的形式引导学生梳理文章结构，归纳 Daniel 采访用的问题。帮助学生整体把握文章结构和大意。

（3）Read and answer

学生阅读采访稿，回答问题，学生需要根据短文中的文化知识进行推理和判断。该活动旨在发展学生的思维能力，培养学生在语境中运用文化知识的能力。

（4）Watch a viedo

学生观看英国礼仪专家 William Hanson 的视频，借助录像和名人名言给学生更多接触英语文化知识的机会，帮助学生在英语语境中理解文化知识。

（5）Read and use

设计开放性任务：Kate 是来自英国的新朋友，你如何向她问好？如何与她进行对话交流？以真实的情境引导学生运用文本中的文化知识进行交流，开放性的任务有助于培养学生得体运用英语进行交际的能力。

（6）Read and answer

学生阅读文本，理解语篇，在语篇中复现和运用文本中的主题词汇，并在上下文语境中猜测词义，进一步了解和感知文化知识。

（7）Further thinking

创设真实的语境，引导学生展开思考和想象，在语境中比较中西方文化的异同，学习和欣赏西方优秀文化。

（8）Read and learn

学生阅读短文，了解英国人在家里的礼仪。

阅读后的活动：

（1）Further thinking

提出开放性问题，引导学生思考：我们中国人是否有必要在家里说"Please"和

"Thank you"？学生经过对比和思考，表达自己的观点和见解。

（2）Discussion

阅读初预留问题：整个采访是关于英国的礼仪的，为什么作者选用标题"When in Rome"？阅读后学生经小组讨论找出文章末尾的谚语"When in Rome，do as the Romans do"。该谚语是本课的主题，引导学生思考和理解该谚语的含义：只有"入乡随俗"，才能更好地融入当地文化。

（3）Discussion

设计开放性任务：你的一个朋友暑假将要去英国。你能给他一些建议吗？引导学生综合、灵活运用文化知识进行交际，培养学生跨文化交际的能力。

（4）Pair work

设计开放性任务：你的朋友 Kate 将要来参观中国。她想要了解关于中国的礼仪。请两人一组，谈论关于中国的礼仪。

2. 模式与方法

英语文化意识作为英语学科核心素养的重要组成部分，融合了文化意识和情感态度价值观两个要素的内容，指"对中外文化的理解和对优秀文化的认知，是学生在全球化背景下表现出的知识素质、人文素养和行为品质"。（周大明，2016）教师在英语教学过程中应培养学生的文化理解、欣赏能力和包容异国文化的能力，（周大明，2016）帮助学生"获得文化知识，理解文化内涵，比较文化异同，吸收文化精华，形成正确的价值观和道德情感，自信、自尊、自强，具备一定的跨文化沟通和传播中华优秀文化的能力"（程晓堂，赵思奇，2016），培养学生的全球视野、开放精神，以及乐于学习和借鉴其他文化中更有优势的文化因素、积极的文化传播态度。英语教学中如何基于教材帮助学生形成文化意识是我们一线教师应该思考和探索的一个课题。

文化意识有利于正确地理解语言和得体地使用语言。改版后的(译林版)牛津初中英语教材增加了很多关于中西方文化的语料，有助于学生学习和了解中外文化知识，"关注中外文化异同，加深对中国文化的理解"。目前我国的英语文化教学存在两种错误的倾向，"一是语言学习被置于边缘地位，教学目的脱离语言教学，偏重文化行为规范；二是以西方文化和价值观为准绳，忽视本土文化"。（李永大，2014）教师进行英语文化教学，要遵循以下几个原则：

（1）关联性原则。不同的阅读文本所蕴含的文化元素是不同的。（周智忠，2015）文化意识的培养应从深度剖析文本的文化内涵入手，以此丰富英语教学。（刘林峰，王俊，2013）首先教师要善于解读文本，分析和提炼文化教学的内容，设计相关的具有针对性的文化教学活动，帮助学生体验文化教学的价值和意义，激发学生学习的动机和兴趣。其次，教师所教学的文化内容必须与学生的生活和年龄水平密切相关。只有这样，才能使教学贴近学生的生活实际，符合学生的年龄特征，不断提高学生对于中外文化异同的敏感和鉴别能力。

（2）应用性原则。学习语言的最终目标是运用，文化知识也是如此。教师要创设真实的情境，引导学生在情境中理解和运用文化知识。在英语教学中，很多学生发现学习内容距离日常生活很远。如果学到的词汇可以用来表达日常生活中的所见所闻，表达中国文化，他们就会觉得学习英语和日常生活是紧密结合在一起的。（程晓堂，2010）

（3）渗透性原则。学生英语文化意识的形成，需要一个循序渐进、潜移默化的过程。英语课程具有工具性和人文性双重特性。教师要根据教材中的以话题为主线的中外文化知识，制定文化意识目标，引导和帮助学生了解和理解中外文化差异，提高学生对中外文化异同的敏感性和鉴别能力，提高跨文化交际能力。需要注意的是：文化知识教学要避免贴标签的行为，不能生搬硬套；不是每一节课都要进行文化知识教学渗透。

（4）思辨性原则。语言的学习与思维训练是密不可分的。教师要注意不仅要对学生渗透文化知识，还要有意识培养学生独立思考和判断的能力。教师要让学生明白"文化是平等的，不同文化之间存在某些共性"，要提醒学生注意"学习西方文化，绝不是否定中国文化"，要学会吸收不同文化的精华，增进跨文化理解和跨文化交际的能力。

3. 推荐资源

（1）周大明. 基于核心素养的高中英语 RISE 教学模式探究[J]. 中小学外语教学（中学篇），2016（10）：17—22. 该文章梳理了英语学科核心素养的概念内涵，并根据阅读促素养的原理，构建了体现学思结合的语言输入—语言内化—语言输出同期互动的高中英语阅读 RISE 教学模式；同时，通过该教学模式指导下的教学实例，诠释了体现核心素养的英语阅读课的教学程序及其操作应用。

（2）周智忠. 如何在初中英语教学中实施文化教学[J]. 中小学外语教学（中学篇），2015（11）：1—7. 该文章基于在初中英语阅读课中实施文化教学的课例研究，从微观角度描述了文化教学中出现的问题及其改进过程，并从教师的文化意识及能力、文化教学的内容及原则等方面提出了在初中英语阅读课中实施文化教学的建议。

（3）李永大. 英语教学和文化相结合的问题[J]. 基础教育外语教学研究，2014（8）：10—16. 该文章针对近年来跨文化能力和跨文化交际能力的研究和发展，指出跨文化教育的一个认识误区是英语教学目的从语言能力转向跨文化交际能力。文章建议，英语教学首先要关注学生的语言基础知识和基本技能，避免单方面接受异国文化而忽略本土文化和价值观，努力做到文化素材和语言内容高度关联，以促进语言教学。

第二部分　课堂实录

授课地点：江苏省南京市雨花台中学阶梯教室。

授课时间：2015 年 5 月 11 日。

听课人员：南京市江宁区、鼓楼区、建邺区部分教师，南京市雨花台区马辉工作室全体成员。

授课过程：

Stage one：Pre-reading

T：Boys and girls, just now we said "good morning" to each other, that is, we greeted each other. （板书 greet，带读）How do we usually greet each other?

S1：We say "hi" or "hello".

T：And after that we shake hands with each other. （板书 shake，带读）Do we Chinese greet each other with a kiss?

Ss：No.

T：It's not proper. （板书 proper，带读）Western people usually greet each other with a kiss. We Chinese don't greet each other with a kiss. We should greet people properly. （板书 properly，带读）

T：Also we should behave properly in public. （呈现插队图片）Do they behave properly?

Ss：No.

T：It's very important to have good manners in public. Today we'll read an article about manners. Now open your books at page 57.

Stage Two：While-reading

Step 1：阅读了解文章大意

T：What type of text is it?

A. A diary. B. News. C. An interview. D. A report.

S2：An interview.

T：What is it about，manners in Rome or manners in the UK?

S3：Manners in the UK.

T：How do you know the answer?

S3：From line 2.

S4：From line 23.

S5：The passage uses "British people" many times.

T：So when we read，we can get the main idea from the first or the last paragraph. We can also get the main idea from the picture and the title.

T：What's the title of the interview?

S6：When in Rome.

T：Do you have any questions?

S6：The interview is about manners in the UK. But the title of the interview is "When in Rome". Why?

T：Good question. We'll discuss the question later.

Step 2：阅读分析文章结构

T：Now read carefully. Pay attention to Daniel's questions. What does Daniel want to know about manners in the UK? Finish the questions.

S7: How do British people greet each other?

S8: How do British people start a conversation?

S9: How do British people behave in public ?

S10: How do British people behave at home?

Step 3:阅读理解文本,迁移创新运用

T: Good. So first how do British people greet each other?

S11: British people usually say "hello" or "Nice to meet you." and shake your hand when they meet you for the first time.

T: Do they greet everyone with a kiss?

S12: No. They only greet their friends or relatives with a kiss.

T: What do British people do after greeting?

S13: They start a conversation.

T: Good. A conversation means "a small talk". How do they start a conversation?

S14: They talk about the weather, holidays, music or something else.

T: Do they talk about subjects like age, weight or money?

S14: No.

T: How do you know?

S14: They avoid subjects like age, weight or money.

T: What does "avoid" mean in this sentence?

S14: It means "try not to do sth.".

T: How do you know?

S14: They talk about . . . But . . .

T: Right. So we can guess the meaning of a new word from the context. British people avoid talking about age, weight or money. Pay attention to "avoid doing sth.".

Step 4:观看视频,了解英国礼仪文化

T: Now let's watch a video by William Hanson. And then tell me what he asks us to avoid doing.

S15：He asks us to avoid talking about money.

S16：He asks us to avoid asking about how much his cost and how much that cost.

T：(呈现 Dorothy Nevill 名言,学生齐读)The real art of conversation is not only to say the right thing at the right place，but to leave unsaid the wrong thing at the improper moment.

Step 5：交际应用,拓展延伸

T：Kate is your new friend from the UK. What will you say to her?

S17：Hi，Kate. Nice to meet you.

S18：Nice to meet you.

S17：Welcome to Nanjing. Did you have a nice journey?

S18：Yes，I did.

S17：Nice. Let me show you around Nanjing，OK?

S18：It's so nice of you.

S19：Hello，Kate.

S20：Hello，Sara. Nice to meet you.

S19：Nice to meet you.

S20：Nice weather today，isn't it?

S19：Yes. It's really warm and pleasant weather here in spring.

T：What did they talk about?

S21：They talked about weather and trip.

T：Why do British people like to talk about weather?

S21：Because Britain is an island country and weather changes often.

S22：Because weather in the USA is really changeable.

T：Because the weather changes all the time in the UK. It can be warm and sunny in the morning，but cold and windy in the afternoon.

Step 6：阅读文本,欣赏文化

T：Now read carefully and answer some True or False questions. British people think it's not proper to push in before others.

S23：True.

T：They'll say nothing if they bump into people.

S24：False. They'll say sorry if they bump into people.

T：They will push past you if you are in their way.

S25：False. They won't push past you if you are in their way.

T：They often talk loudly on the bus.

S26：False. They always keep their voice down in public.

T：Now please fill in the blanks according to the passage.

British people think it is rude to _____ before others. They always _____. They say "sorry" if they _____ you in the street. If you are in their way, they won't touch or _____ you. They'll say "excuse me" and be polite enough to wait till you move. They do not like to shout or laugh loudly _____.

S27：push in, queue, bump into, push past, in public.

T：If you're in their way, they won't touch you or push past you. They'll say "excuse me" and be polite enough to wait till you move. What does "in their way" mean?

A. You're on the way and they want you to go together.

B. You're in front of them and they can't move forward. Which one is right?

S28：B.

T：Further thinking. If someone is in your way, what will you do?

S29：I will say "excuse me".

T：What will you do if you bump into someone?

S30：I will say "sorry".

T：Will you say sorry if you are bumped into?

S31：Nothing.

T：British people even say "sorry" if you bump into them or stand on their feet! Do they behave politely at home?

S32：Yes. They say "please" and "thank you" all the time.

Stage Three：Post-reading

Step 7：对比鉴赏，辩证思维

T：Do we need to say "please" and "thank you" at home? Why or why not?

S33：Yes. Our parents have done so much for us. They spend all their time looking after us. If we say "Thanks" to them, they will be very happy.

S34：No. I think we needn't say "please" or "thank you" because in our Chinese culture, we do not need to do so. We seldom say "thank you" even when people have helped us a lot. Maybe that is what "大恩不言谢" really means.

S35：No. Because we are a family and if we say "please" or "thank you" all the time, it seems that we are not so close to each other. There is something between us.

S36：Yes. I think it's polite of us to say "please" and "thanks".

Step 8：小组讨论，点明主题

T：We have one question left at the beginning of this lesson. The main idea of the passage is "Manners in the UK". But the title is "When in Rome". Why?

S37：Because just as the saying goes, "When in Rome, do as the Romans do."

T：What does it mean?

S37：When we are in a strange place, do as the local people do. We should have good manners and follow local customs.

T：When we are in the UK, we should do as the British people do.

Step 9：小组合作，学以致用

T：Suppose one of your friends is going to the UK this summer holiday. Can you give him/her some advice?

S38：You should behave properly.

S39：Don't push in before others or push past others.

S40：If someone is in your way, you should say "excuse me". If you bump into others, you should say "sorry".

S41：Don't talk about age, money or weight. You can start a conversation by talking about weather，music，books，holidays or something else.

S42：When you see someone for the first time，you should say "hello" or "Nice to meet you. ".

Step 10：两两对话，中西合璧

T：Your British friend Kate is coming to visit China. She wants to know about manners in China. （or you can design some questions yourself. ）

Kate：How do people greet each other?

You：...

K：How do people start a conversation?

Y：...

K：How do people behave in public?

Y：...

K：How do people behave at home?

Y：...

（略）

T：Let's improve ourselves to make our country a better place to live in.

Step 11：Homework

Read the interview loudly and fluently；Write something about manners in China；Search the Internet and find more about manners in different countries.

第三部分　课例评析

一、学生反响

学生 A：周老师这节课让我们学到很多英国的礼仪，英国礼仪专家的视频让我们加深对如何交谈的理解，后面补充的名人名言都很好。整节课问题和活动很多，很有意思。

学生 B：我喜欢那个问题"英国人在家里总是说'请'和'谢谢'，我们有必要在家里也说'请'和'谢谢'吗?"很多同学说需要,我的答案是不需要,因为我们中国的文化不同,我们通常"大恩不言谢",如果经常这么说,感觉我们和家人之间疏远了。

二、同行声音

崔云强(南京市雨花台中学春江分校,中学高级教师):这篇文章是一个采访稿,谈论有关英国的礼仪。周老师的这节课充分解读文本中的文化知识的特点,引导学生一边阅读一边学以致用,并引导学生对比中西方文化差异,取得了很好的教学效果。

戴琳(南京市板桥中学,中学一级教师):在这堂课中,学生的学习热情被充分激发出来。无论是对话表演,还是小组讨论,师生互动、生生互动、生本互动贯穿其中,整节课层层推进,自然生成。

刘浏(南京市雨花台中学,中学一级教师):整节课可以用一个"活"字来概括,活学文化知识,活用文化知识,灵活思考,灵活讨论,灵活表演,学生始终积极主动参与到多样性的课堂活动之中。整节课与传统阅读课完全不同。周老师引导学生从语篇中学习理解文化知识,再在真实的情境中灵活运用,真正促进学生语言运用能力和文化意识的形成,学生的思维能力也能获得提升。

三、自我反思

本节课的可取之处:

1. 交际应用,拓展延伸

笔者设计开放性任务:Kate is your new friend from the UK. What will you say to her? Kate 是来自英国的新朋友,你如何向她问好并与她进行对话交流? 以真实的情境引导学生运用文本中的文化知识进行交流,培养学生得体运用英语进行交际的能力。然后笔者以问题"Why do British people like to talk about weather?"进行拓展延伸,介绍英国人喜欢谈论天气的原因是因为英国天气多变(Because the weather changes all the time in the UK. It can be warm and sunny in the morning, but cold and windy in the afternoon.），帮助学生了解更多的关于英国的文化背景知识。

2. 阅读文本，欣赏文化

学生理解语篇后，笔者设计以下问题，引导学生展开思考和想象：如果有人挡了你的道，你会怎么做？如果有人撞到你，你会怎么做？如果你被撞了，你会说 sorry 吗？学生在语境中比较中西方文化的异同，学习和欣赏西方优秀文化。在此基础上再进行文化知识的拓展和延伸：British people even say "sorry" if you bump into them or stand on their feet! 英国人即使你被撞或者被人踩到也会说"sorry"。

3. 对比鉴赏，辩证思维

在英国，人们不仅在公共场所表现得很礼貌，而且在家里也是如此，总是"请"和"谢谢"说个不停。笔者设计开放性问题，引导学生思考，即我们中国人是否有必要在家里说"please"和"thank you"？学生经过对比和思考，表达自己的观点和见解。此环节的开放性问题没有标准答案，旨在引导学生比较中西方文化的区别，引导学生独立思考，用英语发表自己独特的观点。在国际交往中，我们不仅要尊重和接纳异国文化，而且要保留和传播本国文化。（周智忠，2015）进行中西方文化差异的对比是文化教学的重要内容，有助于学生更为深刻地理解目标语文化和母语文化。（李振环，2013）学生在思考问题和回答问题时，思维和语言能力得到训练。面对西方优秀文化，我们不应该一味地模仿、赞扬和吹捧，而是应该经过对比，发现和传播中华民族优秀文化，并保持对于本国文化的自尊、自信和自强，形成积极的文化传播意识和能力。

本节课的不足之处：

1. 因生词较多，加上是借班上课，师生互动默契度不够。学生课堂互动范围偏小，对于一些开放性问题、思辨性问题，回答集中在少部分学生身上。

2. 学生对于文本内容迁移运用能力不强，在"你的好朋友要去英国旅游，请给他提出一些建议"和"两两对话，谈论中国的礼仪"这两个交际性活动中，学生尚不能灵活运用，只能打开书本找寻答案，与笔者预期的学习效果相差不少。

3. 学生的语篇意识不强，习惯于逐字阅读语篇。在阅读全文分析篇章结构活动中耗时过多。学生不能快速浏览语篇，获取语篇中四个主要问题：How do British people greet each other? How do British people start a conversation? How do British people behave in public? How do British people behave at home?

四、专家点评

点评专家：马辉

周华老师今天给我们展示了如何在阅读教学中培养学生的文化意识。整节课以学以致用为设计原则，引导学生边阅读边运用所学文化知识进行对话交流，给我们今后的英语阅读教学很多启发和收获。

第一，教学设计构思巧妙。本节课以阅读—理解—运用作为整节课的教学流程，侧重于培养学生获取文化信息，理解内化运用文化知识，比较鉴赏文化差异。目前我们的阅读教学仍然存在模式化、应试化的倾向，很多教师固守阅读教学模式，不能引导学生充分阅读文本，培养学生在语境中运用语言知识的能力。

第二，基于教材超越教材。周老师本节课并不是照着教材教学，而是结合视频、名人名言、问题设计等帮助学生更多地了解英国文化。如英国礼仪专家 William Hanson 的视频，Dorothy Nevill 关于礼仪的名言，问题"为什么英国人见面时喜欢谈论天气？"，以及开放性任务"Kate 是来自英国的新朋友，你如何向她问好并与她进行对话交流？"，以真实的情境引导学生交流，培养学生得体运用英语进行交际的能力。

第三，文化意识培养到位。本节课真正激活了学生的思维，学生或阅读文本获取文化知识，或在情境中运用文化知识，或在小组讨论中比较文化异同。学生的思维活跃，语言生成丰富精彩。周老师流利的口语和课堂驾驭能力也是本节课成功的因素之一。

【点评专家简介】马辉，南京市雨花台中学教师发展处、学术委员会主任，江苏省特级教师，教授级高级教师。

【名师简介】

周华，江苏省如皋市外国语学校教研组长，教育硕士，教授级高级教师，江苏省特级教师，南通市英语学科专家组成员，南通市学科带头人，南通市"226"、省"333"高层次人才工程培养对象，全国中小学外语教师园丁奖获得者。担任多所高校"国培项目"专家，江苏教育学会名师培养工程徐州新沂项目导师，江苏省第一届乡村骨干教师培育站导师,第三届乡村骨干教师培育站主持人,两次在中国教育学会外语专业委员会年会作主旨发言,多次参加省教育厅"名师送培"、省教师培训中心网络培训课程录制和江苏省各县市教材培训项目,在省内外开设公开课和讲座60多场;主持、参与多项省、市课题研究。参与发表论文30多篇,其中近20篇论文发表于国家级核心期刊,4篇被人大复印资料中心全文转载,多篇被索引。辅导学生参与竞赛,多人次获国家、省、市奖。

课例8 基于深度学习的应用文阅读教学课例研究

第一部分 教学预设

一、教学内容分析

1. 课标要求

(1)语篇教学

语言教学中的语篇通常以多模态形式呈现,既包括口头的和书面的,也包括音频的和视频的,并以不同的文体形式呈现。语篇承载语言知识和文化知识,传递文化内涵、价值取向和思维方式。不同的语篇类型为学生接触真实社会生活中丰富的语篇形式提供了机会,也为教师组织多样的课堂学习活动提供了素材。

接触和学习不同类型的语篇,熟悉生活中常见的语篇形式,把握不同语篇的特定结构、文体特征和表达方式,不仅有助于学生加深对语篇意义的理解,还有助于他们使用不同类型的语篇进行有效的表达与交流。因此,开展对主题意义探究的活动中,语篇不仅为学生发展语言技能和形成学习策略提供语言和文化素材,还为学生形成正确的价值观提供平台。教师在教学时要认真研读和分析语篇,在引导学生把握主题的活动中,要整合语言知识学习、语言技能发展、文化意识形成和学习策略运用,落实培养学生英语学科核心素养的目标。

（2）六要素整合的英语学习活动观

六要素整合的英语学习活动观是指学生在主题意义引领下，通过学习理解、应用实践、迁移创新等一系列体现综合性、关联性和实践性等特点的英语学习活动，使学生基于已有的知识，依托不同类型的语篇，在分析问题和解决问题的过程中，促进自身语言知识学习、语言技能发展、文化内涵理解、多元思维发展、价值取向判断和学习策略运用。这一过程既是语言知识与语言技能整合发展的过程，也是思维品质不断提升、文化意识不断增强、学习能力不断提高的过程。

2. 教材分析

本课例教学内容为译林版《英语》九年级上册 Unit 6 Reading　A TV guide 第一课时。该单元主题为"电视节目"（TV Programmes），与学生生活紧密联系，包含了解电视节目类型、阅读电视指南、谈论看电视习惯、创作你自己喜欢的电视剧脚本和故事等板块。

阅读文本为介绍周六的四个电视节目的电视指南，体裁为应用文。学生需要阅读四个电视指南，了解更多的与电视节目相关的词汇和短语句式，了解电视指南这种应用文的语言特点。

3. 重点与难点

教学重点：指导学生学会阅读电视指南，了解电视指南这种应用文的语言特征，并学习如何运用恰当的语言推荐电视节目以吸引观众。

教学难点：学生向朋友或家人推荐一个电视节目，要使自己的介绍吸引对方。

4. 学情分析

本节课是江苏省教师培训中心"名师送培（扬州）"活动中的一节公开课。本课为借班上课，通过在课前与学生接触，了解到该班学生英语基础较好，英语学习积极性较高，但是灵活性不够，在新情境中迁移运用语言的能力不够强。

二、教学目标分析

在本节课结束时，学生能够：

1. 通过阅读一份电视指南(TV guide),获取节目播放的时间、内容及观看建议等信息;

2. 通过阅读选择自己感兴趣的节目,说明理由;

3. 学会在语境中理解生词,通过细节深入阅读,学习电视指南吸引观众的方法;

4. 尝试向朋友或家人推荐一个电视节目。

三、思路、方法和资源

1. 整体思路

本课按照"生活—语篇—生活"的原则解读、分析语篇,基于"真实""交往"理念设计阅读活动,指导学生理解语篇大意,体会语言特点,并将所学知识迁移到新情境仿写一则电视指南,实现应用体裁语篇的深度学习。具体思路如下:

阅读前阶段:谈论学生最喜欢的电视节目——猜测游戏(学生描述最喜欢的节目,其他同学猜测;教师描述家人最喜欢的电视节目,学生猜测,描述过程中导入生词)。

阅读中阶段:根据图片预测电视节目内容→阅读检验预测→阅读获取更多信息→阅读赏析应用文写作特点(吸引观众观看,并给出观看建议)。

阅读后阶段:为 Millie 等选择合适的电视节目——模仿文本特点,向家人或朋友推荐一个电视节目。

2. 模式与方法

深度学习最初是机器学习领域的一个术语,本是指机器学习领域中一系列试图使用多重非线性变换对数据进行多层抽象的算法。根据美国研究院最新的研究成果,深度学习是学生对核心课程知识的深度理解以及在真实的问题和情境中应用这种理解的能力。此处的能力有三种:一是认知能力,即深度理解内容知识、批判性思维与复杂的问题解决能力;二是人际能力,即协作与交流;三是内省能力,即学会学习以及学术信念。我国学者何玲、黎加厚(2005)认为深度学习是指在理解的基础上,学习者能够批判地学习新思想和事实,并将它们融入原有的认知结构中,能够在众多思想中做出决策和解决问题。郭华教授认为,深度学习是指在教师引领下,学生围绕具有挑战性的学习主题,全身心积极参与体验成功、获得发展的有意义的学习过程。深度学习并不能自然发生,需要促发条件。其中,先决条件是教师的自觉引导。此外,至少还要依赖以下条件:第一,学生思考和操作的学习对象,必须是经过教师精心设计、具有教学意图的结构化教学材料;第二,教学过程必须有预先设计的方案,要在有限的时空下,有计划、有序地实现丰富而复杂的教学目的。

深度学习的主要特征:(1)批判性思维。深度学习是基于学习者认知和理解的学习,学习者将新学知识批判性地接收,纳入原有的知识结构,建立多元连接。(2)信息整合。学生建立多种信息和知识间的连接,包括多学科知识融合和新旧知识之间的连接;形成知识内容整合的认知策略和元认知策略,并存储于长时记忆。(3)建构反思。学习者通过新旧知识之间的联系实现知识的同化和顺应,调整原有认知结构,并对建构产生的结果进行审视、认知和调整。(4)迁移运用。深度学习与浅层学习的区别是能否将所学知识迁移到新情境中去解决问题。

3. 推荐资源

(1) 张晓玲,殷刚魁. 基于深度学习的中学英语写作教学策略[J]. 基础教育外语教学研究,2018(4):14—19. 该文章以深度学习为基础,结合中学英语写作教学的现状,探索基于深度学习的写作教学原则及教学策略。

(2) 黄雪祥. 促进学习能力发展的深度教学课例探究——以一节英语阅读课为例[J]. 教学月刊(中学版),2018(7/8):68—73. 该文章以一节阅读课为例,分析如何结合语篇开展深度教学,引导学生深度学习,并通过学习监控,发展学生的学习能力。

(3) 王丽菲. 英语深层阅读的渐进性教学策略[J]. 教学与管理(理论版),2017(3):113—115. 该文章结合学生的阅读学习规律,探索循序渐进的深层阅读教学策略,从培养阅读耐性、提高语篇分析能力以及细节掌握能力入手,通过分解突破、以问促思、品味语言等方式进行训练,强化学生的深层阅读能力。

第二部分　课堂实录

授课地点:江苏省扬州市邗江实验学校报告厅。

授课时间:2017 年 11 月。

听课人员：扬州市各县区听课代表约 300 人。

授课过程：

Stage One：Pre-reading

Step 1：Enjoy some pictures of different kinds of programmes

Step2：Talk about the students' favourite TV programme

T：OK. Boys and girls, just now we enjoyed some pictures of different kinds of TV programmes. What kind of programme do you like best? And why?

S1：I like documentaries best because I can learn a lot about nature, history and real-life events.

S2：I like chat shows because there are always many famous people there talking about their life. I can always learn a lot from them.

S3：I like game shows because I hope one day I can take part in one of them, answer all the questions and win a big prize.

S4：I like cartoons because they are funny and make me relaxed.

Step 3：Play a guessing game

T：OK. I can see you like different programmes. Now let's play a game. Choose one of your favourite programmes. Describe it in detail and let others guess. What information should be included?

S5：The type of programme.

S6：The names of the TV stations.

S7：The time of the programme.

S8：The reason why you like it best.

T：Now you describe and let others guess.

S9：It's a game show on Jiangsu TV. I watch it every Monday. People take part in the show and answer questions. If someone answers the question incorrectly, he will fall down.

S10：*Who is Still Standing*？（一站到底）

S11：It's also on Jiangsu TV. Many famous people such as film stars or singers take part in the show. They usually have a game together.

S12：*Running Man*.

Step 4：Talk about what the teacher's family like best

T：Now try to guess my family's favourite programmes. First, my son's. It's on CCTV. It covers many ball games. Sometimes he has to get up at night to watch the games because they are often covered live. Which TV channel is it? (板书生词 cover, live)

S13：CCTV - 5.

T：Yes. My son is a sports fan.

T：And my wife's favourite. It's on Zhejiang TV every Friday. She can enjoy many beautiful voices. Also, their courage. The singers encourage my wife a lot because they practice hard to try out for the best voice. She often votes for them. (板书生词 vote)

S14：*The Voice of China*.

T：Do you like watching *The Voice of China*?

Ss：Yes.

T：What about me? It's a kind of films. I often get scared when someone is found dead, murdered in the film. That means I feel afraid when someone is killed. But I'm curious. Who is the murderer? I wonder. (板书生词 scared, murder, murderer)

S15：Horror films.

T：What do you want to watch this Saturday? Let's read a TV guide online.

Stage Two：While-reading

Step 5：Read for some basic information

T：What programme will be on TV this Saturday? Do you need to read the article?

Ss：No.

T：Try to get the information as quickly as possible.

S16：*Sports World* will be on Sunshine TV from 10 a. m. to 11：30 a. m. *Beijing Music Awards* will be on Sunshine TV from 8 p. m. to 10 p. m.

S17：*Murder in a Country House* will be on Golden TV from 7 p. m. to 9:30 p. m..
Tiger Watch will be on Golden TV from 10:30 p. m. to 11:30 p. m..

Step 6：Read for main information

T：Look at the pictures, predict what you can watch this week.

S18：In *Sports World*, I think I can watch football games.

S19：In *Beijing Music Awards* I think I can see some famous singers and some of them will get awards.

T：Read the TV guide and try to find the answers. What can you watch this week?

S20：A number of interviews with famous players and a report on the coming World Cup.

T：Who can you see in *Beijing Music Awards*?

S21：Many Asian pop stars.

T：When can we know the result?

S21：During the show.

T：Why?

S21：Because the programme will be covered live.

T：OK. Look at the pictures, predict what you can watch in *Murder in a Country House*.

S22：In *Murder in a Country House*, I guess we can see a horror film.

T：Look at the knife, who is murdered?

S22：I don't know.

T：Where does the tiger live?

S23：Maybe in Asia or Africa.

T：Why is it sad?

S23：Maybe because humans are trying to catch and kill them.

T：Now read carefully and find the answers.

T：Who is murdered in the country house?

S23：A wealthy doctor.

T：Wealthy means rich. A doctor who has a lot of money.

T：Why is the tigers' life sad?

S24：They are facing a lot of danger.

Step 7：Further reading

T：Now let's read the guideline again carefully. First, *Sports World*. Is it about football every week?

Ss：No.

T：How do you know?

S25：The programme covers different sports, such as swimming, basketball and football.

T：What is it usually about?

S25：A weekly round-up of what is happening in sport, with up-to-date information.

T：What does "round-up" mean?

A. a short report on the most important information.

B. the act of bringing people together.

S25：A short report on the most important information.

T：In Chinese?

S25：概要,摘要。

T："Up-to date" means "the latest". And if you watch this week's *Sports World*, you can see a number of interviews with famous players and a report on the coming World Cup.

T：People can watch *Beijing Music Awards* to win a prize. What prize is it?

S26：Two free concert tickets.

T：How can we win such a prize?

S26：Write down the answers to the questions and send text messages to 1396.

T：Who is the director of *Murder in a Country House*?

S27：Cindy Clark.

T：Is he a famous director?

S27：No. He is a new director.

T：The director is new. Why does the TV guide recommend his film?

S27：Because the excellent film is full of horror and mysteries.

T：When can you know who the murder is?

S28：You will not know who the murderer until the end of the film.

T：Do you want to watch the film?

S28：No. I get scared easily.

T：Can you give others some advice?

S28：If you enjoy solving mysteries, you might like this film. If you get scared, do not watch it.

T：The tiger in the picture looks so sad. Why?

S29：They are facing a lot of danger.

T：This maybe the purpose of showing the TV programme.

T：How does the TV guide remind people the tigers' situation is serious?

S29：After you watch this programme, you will realize how much danger these tigers face.

T：What should humans do?

S29：Humans should stop hunting them for their fur and bones.

T：If humans stop, the situation will not continue. But if humans don't stop, the situation will continue. Can you find a sentence in the TV guide?

S30：The situation will continue unless humans stop hunting them for their fur and bones.

T：What does "unless" mean?

S30：It means "if not".

Step 8：Complete the passage

T：Now open your books at page 83 and finish B3.

T：Are you ready? Let's check the answers.

Ss：Weekly, interviews, live, Asian, concert, horror, wealthy, mysteries, India, scenes.

Stage Three：Post-reading

Step 9：How does the TV guide encourage people to watch?

T：Which programme do you want to watch?

S31：I want to watch *Murder in a Country House*.

T：Why?

S31：Because I like solving mysteries. I wonder who the murderer is.

T：How does the TV guide encourage people to watch?

S31：The film is full of horror and mystery.

S32：You will not know who the murderer until the end of the film.

T：The TV guide also gives us some advice. What is it?

S33：If you enjoy solving mysteries, you might like this film. If you get scared, do not watch it.

T：What about the other TV guides? How do they encourage people to watch?

S34：If you are an animal lover, you may feel sad about it. You can see scenes in India.

S35：*Tiger Watch* won an award for its amazing photography.

S36：After you watch this programme, you will realize how much danger these tigers face.

S37：If you are a football fan, you will not want to miss this week's programme.

S38：You can win two free concert tickets.

T：OK. The TV guides try to encourage people to watch and offer some advice.

Step 10：Which is the most suitable for Millie? Why?

T：Now let's finish B4. First, what programmes does Millie like to watch?

S39：She loves programmes about animals and films with good stories.

T：So which programmes from the guides does she want to watch?

S39：*Murder in a Country House*.

T: Will she watch *Tiger Watch*?

S39: No. She has to go to bed at 10:30 p. m..

T: What about Simon?

S40: *Sports World*. He will be at home all morning.

T: And Amy?

S41: *Beijing Music Awards*.

T: What about Andy?

S42: *Tiger Watch*.

Step 11: Recommend a programme to your friend or parent

T: Would you like to recommend a programme to your friend or parent? You can choose from the TV Guide or think about one by yourself. Get ready in groups first and recommend one to try out for the voice of Class.

T: Ready. Which group would like to show your recommendation?

Group 3: *Super Vocal* is a weekly singing competition by Hunan TV. Thirty-seven players take turns to sing classical music such as musicals, operas, pop music and also national music in a modern and popular way. Jay Chou will be on of the judges, watching and picking some of the singers to join his team. If you love classical music, don't miss it every Friday on Hunan TV.

T: Wonderful. So the programme is just like *The Voice of China*. Do you like it?

Ss: Yes.

T: Another group?

Group 5: *Running Man*, a South Korean reality show, has turned out to be a great success in China. The show is produced by Zhejiang TV. The members of the Chinese *Running Man* include: Deng Chao, Wang Baoqiang, Wang Cho Lam, Chen He, Li Chen, Zheng Kai, and Angelababy. The interesting shows make people laugh and relax.

T: *Running Man* from South Korean. They really do a good job. How do they encourage people to watch the programmes?

S43：The interesting shows make people laugh and relax.

S44：If you love classical music，don't miss it every Friday on Hunan TV.

S45：Jay Chou will be on of the judges.

S46：*Running Man*，a South Korean reality show，has turned out to be a great success in China.

T：Watching TV is fun. But don't be a couch potato.

Step 12：Homework

Write down your recommendation；Keep a diary about the voice of Class.

第三部分　课例评析

一、学生反响

学生 A：今天这节英语课我们都是在谈论自己喜欢的电视节目，并模仿课本中的电视指南推介自己最喜欢的电视节目。我最喜欢的节目是《一站到底》，我能自己用英语介绍这个节目，感觉很有成就感。

学生 B：冒老师的这节课很特别，在阅读课文时，老师的问题不是很容易能想到答案，而是要去推理、去比较、去概括，感觉很有挑战性。尤其是推介自己最喜欢的电视节目，我们组的四个同学挖空心思，才完成了节目介绍，感觉还不错。

学生 C：在冒老师的引导下，我体会到电视指南语言看起来枯燥，但其实很有意思，也感受到运用英语的快乐。这样的阅读很生动！

二、同行声音

常万里（扬州大学附属教育学院，一级教师）：冒老师的这节应用文阅读课以学生为中心，通过阅读前的对话、竞猜游戏和阅读中的活动，激活学生的认知图式，激发学生参与活动的主动性和积极性；引导学生阅读电视指南，了解这种应用文写作的特点，并小组合作推介一种电视节目，把课堂的时间和空间留给学生，促进学生主动参与课堂活动,促进学生的深度学习。

常松(扬州中学教育集团树人学校,高级教师):我们这套教材改编后,增加了很多不同文体的语篇。冒老师执教的这节阅读课语篇内容是电视指南,他根据语篇特点精心设计教学活动,有利于学生深入理解语篇意义和语篇特点。本节阅读课解决了三个问题:语篇的主题和内容是什么?语篇的写作目的是什么?语篇具有什么样的文体特征和语言特点?实现了学生对语篇意义的理解和有效的表达与交流。

余慧(扬州市邗江区美琪学校,一级教师):冒老师在这节课中侧重于学生思维能力和语言能力的培养。首先,活动设计有梯度。从学习理解到实践运用到迁移创新,冒老师引导学生阅读语篇获取信息、运用所学语篇知识迁移创新,即推荐自己喜欢的电视节目,整节课层层推进,由浅入深,循序渐进;其次,冒老师引导学生分析这篇应用文的文本特点,找出电视指南中那些吸引观众观看的表达,并模仿语篇特点介绍一个电视节目,有助于培养学生的语言能力,学生借助教师搭建的语言支架小组合作,学会表达。

三、自我反思

这节课是译林版教材九上 Unit 6 Reading 教学,是应用文电视指南的阅读课。本节课基于学情和文体做了以下几点思考和探索:

1. 发展学生的高阶思维能力。深度学习的核心特征是发展学生的高阶思维能力。本节课笔者注重引导学生在阅读中分析、比较、评价、创新,发展学生的批判性思维能力和创造性思维能力。笔者引导学生阅读电视指南,分析电视指南作为一种应用文的写作风格和特点;小组合作学写电视指南,培养学生的语言能力和创新思维。

2. 情境中迁移运用。迁移与运用是语言的产出活动。语言学习的关键是学生能够将新学知识迁移运用到新的情境中,实现"举一反三"。理想的阅读教学活动应该将可理解性输入和可理解性输出有机结合,使语言教学形成一个动态的平衡结构。笔者引导学生模仿文本特点,小组合作向朋友或家人推荐一个电视节目,创造性地使用语言。

3. 真实学习的发生。整节课学生思维活跃,阅读与表达相辅相成,教师主导与学生主体相结合,语言输入与语言输出相结合,自主学习与合作学习相结合,学生或两两对话,或小组讨论,在问题解决的过程中,获取新知识和技能,新旧知识获得连接和整合,做中学,学中思,学习在课堂上真正发生。

本节课的不足之处:

1. 因为是借班上课,且阅读开始时的问题设置有一定难度,导致课堂气氛有些沉闷,后经过小组讨论等形式才有所改善。

2. 读后阶段时间偏紧,给学生准备的时间略少,有两个小组未能完成电视节目的介绍。

四、专家点评

点评专家:张利琴

《课标(2017 版)》对不同研读提出了不同层次的要求——从不同角度深入探究语篇的主题意义、内容信息、价值取向等。教师在教学中应首先指导学生对文章进行表层理解,再尝试理解作者的意图和立场,实现对语篇的深层理解。最后根据语篇内容和结构特点,发表自己的见解和观点,进行评价性理解。然而目前初中英语语篇教学大都止于表层理解,对于深层理解和评价性理解指导不足,不利于学生语篇解读能力的发展和提升。

冒晓飞老师的这节课主要有以下几点值得借鉴和学习:

1. 深度解读,提升语篇能力。冒老师的这节课不仅是引导学生对文本进行表层和深层理解,还引导学生根据文本的写作特点和风格模仿写作,向朋友和家人推荐一个电视节目,真正体现了学以致用的教学原则,有利于培养学生的语篇能力和语言能力,促进学生对文本的深度解读。

2. 问题驱动,培养思维能力。语言和思维密不可分。冒老师在本节课中注重培养学生的思维能力,以开放性问题、评判性问题,引导学生对语篇进行理解、分析、比较、概括、整合、评价,培养学生用英语进行多元思维的意识和习惯,培养学生的思维的逻辑性、批判性和创新性。

3. 迁移创新,促进深度学习。崔允漷教授指出:深度学习是指学生基于教师预设的专业方案,经历有指导、有挑战、高投入、高认知的学习过程,并获得有意义的学习结果。或者说深度学习就是学生在教师创设的复杂环境下表现出高度投入、高阶认知参与并获得有意义的学习。本节课中学生小组合作创作电视指南,在具有挑战性的活动中获得对文本的深层解读;学生在活动中高度参与和投入,从理解到应用、从分析到评价,在有意义的学习中获得语言、思维、文化的深度融合。

【点评专家简介】张利琴,教育硕士,正高级教师,江苏省初中英语特级教师,扬州市初中英语教研员。

【名师简介】

冒晓飞:江苏省如皋市外国语学校教科室副主任,教育硕士,正高级教师,江苏省初中英语特级教师;南通市"226"工程第二层次培养对象,南通市初中英语学科基地专家组副组长,南通市英语学科基地专家组成员,江苏省第二届乡村骨干教师培育站导师、第三届乡村初中英语骨干教师培育站主持人,江苏省教科研先进教师,南通师范高等专科学校和江苏第二师范学院兼职教师;曾被评为如皋市德业双馨十佳教师,南通市优秀教育工作者,南通市师德之星,南通市学科带头人,江苏省初中英语教材实验改革先进个人;主张"全·真"英语教学,构建"交往"英语课堂,开设省内外公开课、讲座 60 多场,多项省、市课题研究结题,20 多篇论文发表中文核心期刊,8 篇人大复印全文转载,参与编写教学专著 2 部。

课例 9　整体语篇阅读教学设计与实施的课例研究

第一部分　教学预设

一、教学内容分析

1. 课标要求

《课标(2017 版)》指出英语教学具有工具性和人文性融合统一的特点,强调英语课程对学生语言能力、文化意识、思维品质和学习能力的综合培养，要求教师教学时要注重在主题的引领下，以语篇为载体，将语言知识、语言技能和思维的教学融入到对语篇结构、语言特点和语篇内容的分析中，通过帮助学生从整体上掌握语篇来提升其理解性技能。它对学生理解性技能的要求包括：从语篇中提取主要信息和观点、理解语篇要义；理解语篇中显性或隐性的逻辑关系；梳理语篇中主要信息的脉络；把握语篇中的关键概念和关键细节；根据语篇标题预测语篇的主题和内容；把握语篇的结构以及语言特征。

2. 教材分析

《新概念英语》是一套经典的英语学习教材，问世至今五十多年，其中的文章层次清晰，语言地道，结构完整，适合用作阅读材料。本节课讲授的是《新概念英语 3》的第 26 课 Wanted：a large biscuit tin。文章主要讲述广告商们对人性做了细致的研究并将人性的缺点归类，他们利用人性共同的缺点——我们喜欢不劳而获，作为他们广告营销的重要手段。文章还介绍了一家饼干公司通过广播做广告的事例。这篇文章结构明晰，段落之间衔接连贯做得很好，是一篇十分适合用语篇分析进行教学的范例。笔者想起平日教学中学生对语篇结构的忽视以及学生写作过程中常出现结构混乱、前言不搭后语的现象，决定引导学生从语篇分析的角度来探讨本文结构，理解语篇中显性或隐性的逻辑关系，有意识地关注语篇结构，进而提升英语的理解能力。

3. 重点与难点

教学重点：分析语篇，弄清文章的脉络结构，有意识地关注语篇衔接。

教学难点：深度理解标题，弄清它的意义以及与文章的内在关系。

4. 学情分析

（1）学生心智特征分析。本节课是笔者受邀在扬州大学附属中学"创生教育，启迪智慧"大型公开教学活动中所开设的一节同课异构的公开课。本节课是借班上课，对象是扬州大学附属中学高二学生。笔者与该班英语教师沟通后了解到，该班同学英语基础较好，学习态度认真，考试成绩较好，但性格偏内向，不够自信，上课发言不够活跃。

（2）学生已有知识经验分析。从课前与该班英语教师沟通中获悉，学生获取文本中细节信息的能力较强，但大多数学生对语篇分析的重要性认识不够、语篇结构意识不强，甚至概念模糊。

二、教学目标分析

该课教学目标的定位参照了两个维度,即英语学科核心素养与三维目标。本节课的教学目标设定如下:

在本课学习结束时,学生能够:

1. 清晰认识文章的脉络结构、理解篇章的衔接;

2. 概括文章的主旨大意;

3. 深入理解文章标题的内涵。

三、思路、方法与资源

1. 整体思路

本节课紧扣语篇分析阅读教学的理念与方式,先从宏观层面分析让学生建构语篇结构,再从微观层面探究词、句以及信息之间的衔接与关联,加深学生对文本的理解。从开始的标题预测入手,最后回归标题,让学生进一步体会语篇的连贯与完整。授课过程中,教师通过环环相扣的问题,层层推进,激活学生的思维,最终实现生成。具体思路如下:

(1) 根据标题预测文章内容

邀请学生根据标题本身对文本内容做出预测,教师将学生的回答写在黑板上以备读完后再回到标题。

(2) 从语篇分析的角度阅读文本

① 要求学生快速阅读每一段,归纳段落主旨大意。指导学生归纳的方法:若有主题句则主题句可作为段落大意;若没有合适的主题句,则先找出关键词再连贯成句。

② 从宏观和微观层面分析语篇结构

引导学生关注段落内部句与句之间的衔接,培养学生的篇章意识。衔接是指语篇中句子与句子之间、段落与段落之间存在的某种逻辑联系,它的存在使得篇章内信息逻辑明确、浑然一体,使得文章成为有意义的语篇。

● 分析第一段落中的语言,通过问题链引导学生关注句子之间的逻辑与衔接,最终基于分析,让学生生成第一段的段落结构(见图 4.1);

● 分析第二段落,引导学生关注段落之间的连贯与衔接;

● 分析第三段落,引导学生关注第二、第三段落的衔接;

● 基于上述宏观和微观的分析,引导学生生成本篇章的结构及内在联系(见图 4.2),引导学生概括本文的主旨大意,渗透英文写作的框架意识。

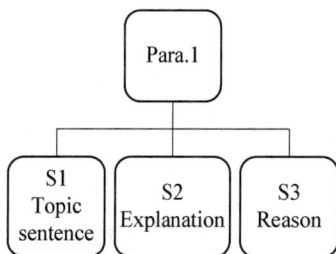

图 4.1

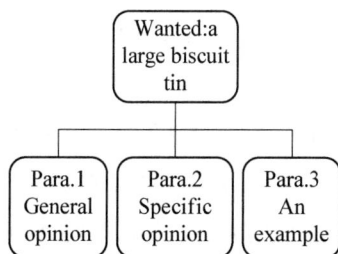

图 4.2

(3) 深入理解标题

① 评价学生课初根据标题做出的预测与文本真实内容之间的相关度;

② 引导学生理解本课标题的深度内涵。

(4) 布置作业

① 根据本节课中使用的语篇分析方法分析一篇新篇章的结构和衔接;

② 思索广告给我们带来的微妙影响是什么,并写下来(通过批判性思维,提升学生思维品质)。

2. 模式方法

(1) 语篇分析理论

系统功能学理论强调:语言事件不是任意的,每一层语言都有自己的系统来表示该层次的意义;它不存在于支离破碎的词语和句子中,而是存在于语篇的链接之中。关于语篇的界定虽然中外学者表述不一,但他们对语篇概念认知的共同点是:语篇是符合语法规则的、具有连贯性和衔接性、能够产生一定语境的、有一连串的语段或句子组合而成的语言单位。因此语篇分析的教育教学研究者提出:英语阅读教学就不应当孤立地以词汇、句子来学习语言，着重讲解语音、词汇、语法和句子，而应该以语篇作为一个整体出发。教学活动要围绕语篇进行教学，语言教学应该从帮助学生理解语篇模式的角度出发，帮助学生认识词汇、语法和句子等是如何联系和构建一个完整语篇的，从而达到理解、学习和使用语言的目的。

语篇知识既是语篇分析教学中的一个重要准则，又是语篇分析教学的主要内容。语篇分析理论指导下的阅读教学对学生和教师提出了更高的要求：要把文章看作一个有机的整体，通过对课文背景知识的了解和篇章结构的把握，明确段落之间所用到的各种衔接手段，领会课文所传递的主要信息及作者的写作意图和观点态度等。

分析语篇时应首先设置相应的问题或任务，引导学生确定语篇的体裁和篇章模式。通过寻找语篇中心段落和段落主题句，准确地分析语篇结构，使学生对语篇有一个宏观层面的把握，理清文章的脉络。其次，教师指导学生寻找段落、句与句之间的逻辑联系语，理解段落之间、句句之间、词汇之间的衔接与连贯，把握作者的写作思路，从而提高语篇理解的能力。最后，通过引导学生在上下文中猜测词义及分析语篇中的长难句，培养学生的语篇分析能力，理解语篇所蕴含的意义。读后重建语篇时，在把握语篇结构的内容的基础上，教师设置相关的巩固性和拓展性练习，检测学生对语篇的框架结构及细节的掌握情况，旨在帮助学生重新构建语篇，培养学生归纳、推理及评价能力。

（2）支架式教学

支架式教学，是建构主义理论中较为成熟的一种教学模式。其基本定义为"支架式教学应当为学习者建构对知识的理解提供一种概念框架。这种框架中的概念是为发展学习者对问题的进一步理解所需要的，为此，事先要把复杂的学习任务加以分解，以便于把学习者的理解逐步引向深入。"很显然，这种教学思想是来源于前苏联著名心理学家维果斯基的"最近发展区"理论。维果斯基认为，在儿童的智力活动中，存在着两个不同的发展水平：第一个水平是学生能够独立解决问题的发展水平，第二个水平是学生在教师的指导下有可能解决问题的潜在发展水平。如果老师的教学处于学生的第一水平甚至第一水平之下，则这样的教学是完全没有意义的，因为学生自己就可以独立完成学习任务；如果老师将教学设定在第二水平之上，则无论教师如何花费心血，学生也很难获得对知识的理解。只有在第一水平和第二水平之间实施教学，才是有意义的教学,才有可能不停顿地把儿童的智力从一个水平引导到另一个新的更高的水平。这两个水平之间的区域就是"最近发展区"。

在"最近发展区"实施教学,必须面临如何使学生从第一水平向第二水平过渡的问题。建构主义者从维果斯基的思想出发,借用建筑行业中使用的"脚手架"(Scaffolding)提出了在"最近发展区"中建立"脚手架"(或者说"支架")的概念,通过这种"脚手架"的支撑作用(或"支架作用")不停顿地把学生的智力从一个水平提升到另一个新的更高水平。笔者在设置教学环节和问题时,环环相扣,层层推进,直至最终顺利生成。教师在此过程中充当了引导者和支架的构建者,避免让学生一头雾水,畏难而退。

3. 推荐资源

(1) 程晓棠. 基于语篇的语言教学途径[J]. 国外外语教,2005(1):24—25.该文章主要将讨论基于语篇的语言教学途径的发展过程和核心思想,并探讨这一教学途径对我国外语教学的启示。

(2) 马志伟. 语篇分析理论在高中英语阅读教学中的应用[J]. 中小学教学与研究,2011(1):24—25.该文章对语篇分析理论在高中英语阅读教学中的应用做了研究,并就研究结果进行了分析,得出结论:语篇分析理论的确能够提高学生的英语阅读能力。

(3) 郭慧. 语篇衔接指导下的英语阅读教学[J]. 前沿,2013(13):123—125.该文章主要利用语篇分析及衔接理论指导英语阅读教学,可以解决英语阅读中常见的问题,有效地使学生熟悉并学会分析常见英语文章的结构模式和提高把握英语语篇整体的能力,从而提高阅读理解水平。

第二部分 精彩实录

授课地点:扬州大学附属中学录播教室。

授课时间:2018 年 12 月 7 日,时长 45 分钟。

听课人员:扬州市教研室、专家及扬州市各校听课代表约 100 人。

授课过程:

Stage One:Greet the students (30 seconds)

T: Good morning! As you can see, there is a beautiful flower on the screen. I know it's cold outside today and I hope I can bring warmth to you, just like the sunflower.

Stage Two: Predict the main idea of the passage according to the title (3 minutes)

T: Today, we are going to learn a passage in *New Concept English*, *Book Three*, Lesson 26. Now read the title of the passage and think about what the passage is about? The first idea is coming into your mind.

S1: It's about a biscuit.

T: Right. But could you be more specific?

S1: A large biscuit.

T: Sure! Sit down, please. Any other volunteers?

S2: Maybe it's about a company wanting to promote its sales and drawing the public attention.

T: Yeah! So it might be about advertising.

S3: It's about comparing different biscuits and choosing the largest one.

(The teacher writes students' predictions down on the blackboard.)

T: Good! We well check your prediction later.

Stage Three: Understand the text

Step 1: Read for the main ideas of each paragraph (5 minutes)

T: Please take out your textbook and turn to page 126. You will have at most three minutes to read the whole passage.

(Three minutes later)

T: What do you think is the main idea of the first paragraph?

S1: The influence of the ads. on people.

T: Yes. Good! Or could you find some original sentence in the text to be the topic sentence?

S1: No one can avoid the influence of advertisements.

T: Exactly! Then what about the second paragraph? If you can find the original sentence, use it; if you can't, then summarize it.

S2: We love to get something for free, and the advertisers devised many different kinds of competitions for people to attend.

T: Try to make it simple!

S2: Advertisers discovered years ago that all of us love to get something for nothing.

T: Do you agree? Do you think the first sentence might be the topic sentence?

S3: The second paragraph is about the discovery and how they made use of it.

T: Which one do you prefer?

Ss: The second one.

T: Me too. Let's move on! What about the third paragraph?

S4: The manufacturers paid more money than they had anticipated.

T: The last sentence? Do you agree?

S5: Not exactly.

T: Then what's your version?

S5: An example.

T: An example of what?

S5: An example of a company's competition.

T: Good! And the main part of this paragraph mentioned different people . . .

T&Ss: baked different kinds of biscuits for the competition.

T: That means people . . .

Ss: responded to the competition.

T: Could you use some adjectives to describe their responses?

Ss: Enthusiastically, actively . . .

T: Good! Could you find the original word?

Ss: Tremendously!

T: Very good! So the last paragraph might be . . . ?

T&Ss: A company offered a competition through the radio, and it received tremendous responses.

Step 2: Read for coherence in Paragraph One (8 minutes)

T: Next, let's dig deep! I'd like to draw your attention to the second sentence of the first paragraph. Could you read it aloud together? (The teacher shows the sentence on the PPT slide.)

T: Good! In this sentence, I have several questions for you? The first one, how to understand "no longer free to choose" here? (The teacher waited for the students to think for a while, and then asked them: "Does it mean we have no right to choose?")

Ss: No.

T: Then what does it mean? Please use your own words to paraphrase it!

S6: It means something influences us.

T: What's the thing?

S6: The advertisements.

T: Good! Then could you express your idea in a complete sentence?

S6: "No longer free to choose" means we are no longer free from influence of advertisements.

T: Great job! Have you noticed the influence?

Ss: No.

T: Why's that? Find the answer in the text.

Ss: Because the influence is subtle.

T: What does "subtle" mean?

S7: It means something is small and not easy to be noticed.

T: Yeah. It means something that is not easy to notice, but not necessarily small. Then how could they influence us without our noticing?

S8: Because we can see advertisements all everywhere in our lives. We are just used to it.

T: Great thinking. Then according to the writer, how could they make it?

S9: The advertisers have studied us closely and they have classified our weaknesses.

T: We have analyzed the sentences in the first paragraph. Then what do you think is the interrelationship of the three sentences. It is easy to know that the first sentence is ...

Ss: The topic sentence.

T: Excellent! What's the relationship between Sentence 2 and Sentence 1?

S10: Sentence 2 is the explanation of Sentence 1.

T: Exactly! Brilliant! What's the relationship between Sentence 3 and Sentence 2?

S11: It's a detailed example of Sentence 2.

T: Do you still remember the last question I asked you concerning paragraph one? How could they influence us without us knowing? Now do you want to change your mind?

S11: Be quiet to follow the teacher.

T: Never mind. Sit down please.

S12: I think Sentence 3 is a reason for Sentence 2.

T: Yeah, exactly! Now we are clear about the structure of paragraph one! You know, the interrelationship between the sentences is called COHERENCE. We need to be conscious of it. And later on, we will try to find out the coherence between paragraphs!

Step 3: Read for coherence between Paragraph Two and Paragraph One (6 minutes)

T: Paragraph two is comparatively easy, right? We have known that this paragraph is mainly about the discovery of advertisers. Then could you tell me together what the discovery is?

Ss: All of us love to get something for nothing.

T: Good! How did they take advantage of the discovery? Don't be nervous! Read the paragraph quickly and find the answer.

S13: The advertisement will begin with the word free.

T: What kind of word "free" is? An adjective?

Ss：A magic word.

T：Great! Then why do the advertisers think the word "free" is magic?

S14：Because they think the ads are attractive to us.

T：Besides using the magic word "free", what else did they do?

Ss：They devise various competitions for us to win money.

T：Yeah! Devise means design. Now look at paragraph one and paragraph two，do you think they are interrelated?

Ss：Yes!

T：Then how are they linked closely?

S15：Paragraph one tells us advertisers have found out some weaknesses of people and paragraph two tells us what the weaknesses are.

T：Great! In the last sentence of paragraph one，the writer mentioned the advertisers have found out our weaknesses but he did tell us what they are. So in paragraph two the writer stated the specific discovery of the study.

Step 4：Read for coherence between Paragraph Three and Paragraph Two（7 minutes）

T：What's the offer of the company?

Ss：They offered to pay 10 dollars per pound for the biggest biscuit ever baked.

T：Why do you think the company made such an offer?

Ss：To get more attention from people.

T：Right! To advertise! And were people attracted?

Ss：Yes!

T：Then why did they respond so actively?

Ss：Because they wanted to win the money.

T：Sure! They wanted to win the competition，win the money，to get something for nothing.

As the writer said，the response was tremendous. Could you find out some evidence to show that the response was really tremendous? You'd better think about the

question from different aspects. For example, in terms of time. From "before long" to
...

S16: to "a little later" and then "just before the competition closed".

T: Any other evidence?

S17: The biggest biscuit is too big, which shows that people want to win the competition so much.

T: What is the weight of the largest one?

S17: 2400 pounds.

T: Yeah! It's too big. Abnormally big.

S17: And also different shapes.

T: Right! Different shapes and sizes of biscuits. And who took part in the competition?

Ss: A lady, a man, a college student.

T: Male, female; young, old. Everyone was involved in the competition. So we can find evidence from at least three aspects: time, participants, shape & size of biscuits. Then look at paragraph two and paragraph three, what do you think the interrelationship between them is?

S18: Paragraph three is an example to prove the points in paragraph two.

T: Well done. Ok. I'd like to ask you an interesting question. Why did the writer mention the radio and TV rather than the Internet?

S18: Because at that time, the Internet hasn't been invented.

T: Very clever! Actually, the article was written decades ago.

Step 5: Conclude the coherence of this passage and summarize the main idea of it (6 minutes)

T: Let's make a summary. The three paragraphs actually have different functions. In the first paragraph, the writer states ...

T&Ss: his general opinion.

T: And in the second paragraph, what did the writer do? Further ...

Ss: Further explain his specific opinion.

T: And what is the third paragraph?

Ss: It's an example to his specific opinion.

T: Brilliant! And I think this is a very useful structure for you to follow when you write your own compositions. Based on what we have talked about, could you summarize the main idea of the article? You can discuss with your classmates if necessary within one minute. Write it down if necessary.

S19: Due to the development of social media, the company wants to win their potential customers and it made their ads with something free.

T: Ok! When you summarize, don't mention to many details. But it's a nice try. Sit down, please. When you summarize, you need to combine paragraph one and paragraph two, and you need to pay attention to the function of the third paragraph. Do we need to mention the specific information of the third paragraph in the summary?

Ss: No!

T: Who'd like to have another try?

S19: Due to the influence of advertisements, the advertisers made a discovery of people's weaknesses, eh ...

T: OK! Due to the influence, the advertisers made a discovery, pay attention to the interrelationship between these two points. Which one do you think might be the reason?

S19: The second.

T: Ok! Then could you revise your version?

S19: The advertisers made a study of the influence of advertisements and found out the weaknesses of people. So the manufactures devised a competition to win people's attention.

T: Better! Well done! Then I'd like to share with you my version.

The teacher's version: Advertisers' discovery of our weaknesses and the use of social media make the advertisement have a subtle influence on every one of us. An example just proved it.

T: Of the three versions, two of your classmates' and one of mine, which one do you prefer?

Ss: Yours!

T: Thank you very much! But I'd like to ask you why? Just because I am the teacher?

Ss: No!

T: Then what might be the reason?

S20: Because your summary mentions all the aspects of the article and the interrelationship of the article.

T: Yeah! A good summary should cover all the key information and has the right logic.

Stage Four: Understand the title (7 minutes)

T: Next. Let's return to the blackboard. Do you still remember your prediction at the very beginning of the class when you looked at the title only? I copied them down just in case you forget it. Then, let's compare your predictions with the real main idea of the passage. Only the second one is close. It seems that the title didn't give you the right guidance. Then do you think it's a good title?

(Students are pretty hesitant.)

T: Don't fall for my trick. Judging from my words, it might not be a good title. But I think it is not that superficial, we need to dig deep. First of all, when you read the title, do you want to find more information?

Ss: Yes!

T: Sure! So the title is attractive. It arouses our curiosity. Well, the second, I'd like to draw your attention to the title itself. "Wanted". What does "wanted" mean? Where is "wanted" frequently used?

(Students seem to have no idea of this word.)

T: Don't worry. I'll show you some pictures.

T：Now could you tell me what "wanted" means in all these pictures?

Ss："Wanted" is usually used to find someone.

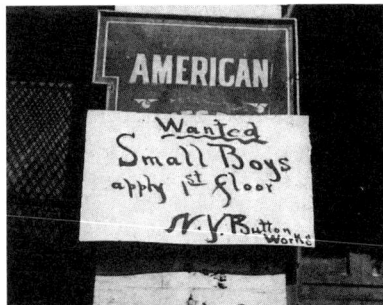

T：Right. In other word，"wanted" is usually used in advertisement. So the second point is that the title itself is an advertisement. It is interrelated to the whole passage. So it's a pretty smart title. Do you think so?

Ss：Yes!

Stage Five：Homework（2 minutes）

First，read another passage handed out and figure out the structure and coherence in it. Second，brainstorm the possible subtle influences of ads on us and write them down.

第三部分　课例评析

一、学生反响

学生 A：这节阅读课下来，我对文章的框架结构有了清晰的理解，能够用自己的语言总结文章大意。这对我来说很新鲜，也很有意义，因为一篇课文对我来说不再是局限于几个单词、词组或几句长难句了。

学生 B：老师整节课思路特别清晰，我特别喜欢老师对标题的处理，她没有简单直白地告诉我们 wanted 的含义，而是带领我们一步步探索，wanted 的含义我一定不会忘了。

二、同行声音

张兆祥(扬州大学附属中学,高级教师):丁老师的这节课让我耳目一新,虽然语篇教学的概念由来已久,但以往很多老师讲语篇时大多停留在把文章划分段落的层面上,比较浅显;但这节课丁老师从宏观和微观层面带领学生分析语篇结构,段落间的衔接,段落内的衔接,层次清晰,层层推进,学生最终能够自然生成,水到渠成。这是一节值得好好研究学习的课。

樊妍(扬州中学,高级教师):丁老师授课时不疾不徐,遵循学生的认知规律,引导学生一步步理解文本,并最终生成。在生成的过程中,她没有将学生的表达限制在预设范围内,而是对学生的自然生成保持开放的态度,并根据学生的即时生成进行评价和改善。

王敏(扬州大学附属中学,一级教师):从这堂课中,我们可以感受到丁老师对学生英语核心能力、核心素养的关注。她对于 coherence 的处理,充分激发了学生的探索精神,兼顾了学生的文本分析能力和逻辑思考能力,通过 paraphrase, questions answering, keyword extraction, analysis of the logic 等形式,对文本内容进行层层处理,探索到文本表层下的 connection 和 coherence。这样的教学形式与教学内容设计是我需要不断学习,不断研究的。

王颖(扬州中学,一级教师):丁老师的教姿教态令人心折,以温暖的向日葵开场,贴近与学生的距离。流利的英语,能轻松 hold 住全场的气势,能缓解学生对上公开课的一点点紧张的微笑,丁老师就是学生英语学习的引导者,引领着他们不断思考,探索与进步。

三、自我反思

课堂教学是一门有缺憾的艺术,唯有不断反思总结才会减少缺憾。

反思本节课,我认为可取之处在于:

1. 教学目标设定合理。《普通高中英语课程标准(2017 版)》对学生的语篇能力提出了较高的要求,这就要求教师在平时教学中要有意识地进行语篇教学,提升学生的语篇分析能力。本节课的教学材料,内容难度适中,但语篇结构清晰,篇章内有显性的衔接,十分适合用作语篇分析教学的材料。从教学结果来看,教学目标顺利达成。

2. 教学设计科学。语篇分析阅读教学相较于常规的阅读教学而言总体难度更高,因为它不是事实性信息的查找,而是根据教师的引导学生要去探索和发现事物之间的或显性或隐性的内在联系,需要他们的深度思考。虽然难度更高,但本节课的教学设计环节依然充分尊重了学生的认知特征,由浅入深,层层推进,环环相扣,没有让学生不知所措的环节和问题。教学结果显示,在层层推进和充分输入的基础上,学生自然会有输出。

3. 教学过程注重互动生成。本节课,教师作为引导者,通过提问、暗示、追问等方式引导学生积极思考,形成自己的观点。在学生表达观点的时候,教师没有将自己的观点强加给学生或者硬生生地将学生的观点往预设的答案上靠,而是基于学生的观点进行互动,很多时候学生在互动后会给出更好的版本,学生的这种生成是令人欣喜的。

本节课亦有诸多不足之处:

1. 因为是借班上课,师生之间的默契度不够高,学生对语篇分析教学方式较为陌生,因此教师在引导和激励上花时间较多,导致某些环节时间控制不够精准。

2. 本节课活动形式偏单一,学生的个人活动多,因此英语理解能力强的学生表现的机会更多更活跃,而基础薄弱的学生参与度有待提高。如何通过活动的创设让不同层次的学生参与进来是需要进一步思考的问题。

3. 授课过程中某些环节可以进一步优化,比如在最后回归标题评价学生的标题预测时,可以请预测精准的那位同学谈谈自己是依据什么做出了这样的预测,通过这样的有声思维可以让其他的同学借鉴方法,以后增强预测的能力。

语篇教学绝不是一节课教学的终点,应当渗透在平时的教学中,这样才能培养和提升学生的语篇意识,进而增强他们的篇章理解能力和谋篇布局的能力。

四、专家点评

点评专家:韩炳华

目前,一线教师对语篇教学的认识和重视程度不一,大部分教师更多的还是利用传统的翻译法进行教学,更多地从词汇、语法等微观层面对文章进行解读,认为阅读文章的主要目的就是学习词汇和语法,较少地让学生从整体上认识和理解一篇文章,忽略了语篇的完整性。而丁薇薇老师的这一课真正做到了从语篇分析角度来进行阅读教学,体现了她较强的语篇教学意识和语篇教学能力。这节课具备几大特点,具体如下:

1. 教学设计完整新颖

本节课的主线条清晰明确,从预测标题进入,而后进行分层阅读,在阅读结束之后,回归标题,用 wanted 点题,前后呼应。以往很多老师在开始阅读之前或者阅读之初都会让学生对标题进行预测,但对预测结果大多不了了之,不做分析评价。丁老师的做法使得标题预测这一任务具有了实际意义,不再是为了预测而预测,值得借鉴。

2. 语篇剖析精准到位

本节课从归纳每段段落大意开始,先进行整体教学,让学生从整体上把握文本,再进行仔细阅读,但这节课的仔细阅读不是专注于词、句的用法意义,而是关注句子之间的逻辑关系,段落之间的逻辑关系。这对于语篇教学极其重要。因为语篇教学的关键词就是衔接与连贯,它指的是信息之间深层的、内在的关系,它是形散而神不散的"神"。语篇教学的意义不仅在于提升学生的理解能力,还能够帮助学生实现更有效的输出,避免写作时出现前言不搭后语,前后句毫无逻辑性的情况。

3. 课堂驾驭游刃有余

相较于常规的阅读课而言,本节课操作难度更大,因为它需要真正激发学生的思维,只有学生真的思考起来,本节课的目标才能实现。丁老师的这节课体现了她对课堂的驾驭能力,一步一步不疾不徐的引导,才使我们听到了学生思维的声音。她流利的口语、抑扬顿挫的语调和具有亲和力的教态也都是这节课能够顺利实现教学目标的不可或缺的因素。

【点评专家简介】韩炳华,扬州邗江中学,英语正高级教师,江苏省中学英语特级教师,江苏省基础教育教学指导委员会中学英语学科专家委员,江苏省人民教育家培养工程培养对象。

【名师简介】

丁薇薇:东南大学硕士研究生,江苏省扬州中学英语教师,扬州市学科带头人。第一届江苏省青年教师基本功大赛一等奖获得者。多次开设国家级、省级、市级公开课,多次受外校邀请参加同课异构教学研讨。在北京、江苏英语同课异构教学评价研讨会活动中,获王蕾教授的高度认可;在省教育厅组织的"名师送培"活动中,赴连云港为高中英语骨干教师开设示范课。曾撰写多篇论文发表至省级刊物。迄今完成三轮高中英语循环教学。

课例 10　基于主题意义探究的英语读后续写教学课例研究

第一部分　教学预设

一、教学内容分析

1. 课标要求

主题为语言学习提供主题范围或主题语境。学生对主题意义的探究应是学生学习语言的最重要内容,直接影响学生语篇理解的程度、思维发展的水平和语言学习的成效。

主题语境不仅规约着语言知识和文化知识的学习范围,还为语言学习提供意义语境,并有机渗透情感、态度和价值观。教师要认识到,学生对主题语境和语篇理解的深度,直接影响学生的思维发展水平和语言学习成效。学生对主题意义的探究是学生学习语言最核心的内容。通过对主题语境的理解和对主题意义的探究,学生把语篇中所呈现的语言知识和文化知识整合起来进行学习,通过语言技能和学习策略等活动的开展,在分析问题和解决问题过程中发展语言能力、文化意识、思维品质和学习能力。

在以主题意义为引领的课堂上,教师要通过创设与主题意义密切相关的语境,充分挖掘特定主题所承载的文化信息和发展学生思维品质的关键点,基于对主题意义的探究,以解决问题为目的,整合语言知识和语言技能的学习与发展,将特定主题与学生的生活建立密切关联,鼓励学生学习和运用语言,开展对语言、意义和文化内涵的探究,特别是通过对不同观点的讨论,提高学生的鉴别和评判能力;同时,通过中外文化比较,培养学生的逻辑思维和批判性思维,引导学生建构多元文化视角。在主题探究活动的设计上,要注意激发学生参与活动的兴趣,调动学生已有的基于该主题的经验,帮助学生建构和完善新的知识结构,深化对该主题的理解和认识。通过一系列具有综合性、关联性特点的语言学习和思维活动,培养学生语言理解和表达的能力,推动学生对主题的深度学习,帮助他们建构新概念,体验不同的生活,丰富人生阅历和思维方式,树立正确的世界观、人生观和价值观,实现知行合一。

2. 教材分析

译林版牛津英语模块六 Unit 4 Reading　UN-bringing everyone closer together 是联合国亲善大使唐宁的一篇演讲,介绍了联合国功能以及她作为亲善大使致力于联合国消除贫穷所做出的自愿无偿的工作,表达了向需要帮助的人伸出援助之手的主题。通过主题意义的探究,教师要着力培养学生作为个体积极参与慈善、公益事业的意识、责任与担当。

3. 重点与难点

教学重点:了解联合国及亲善大使的功能和职责。

教学难点:基于重点主题知识和写作技巧,仿写一篇演讲稿。

4. 学情分析

本课例的授课对象为江苏省大港中学高二年级的学生。他们对联合国这个话题有一定的了解且也很感兴趣。学生的口语表达很好,能够对相关话题提问、讨论甚至对某些观点提出质疑。他们有能力运用略读、细读等阅读策略构建语篇的框架,获取作者对于表示积极态度以及演讲中所表现的热情等信息。但是对于读后体会作者的写作技巧、表达情感等方面略有欠缺,需要在教师的引导下进一步加强。

二、教学目标分析

本课结束时,学生能够:

1. 获取、梳理、描述有关联合国和亲善大使的事实性信息(联合国如何运转、亲善大使如何工作等）；

2. 归纳、总结、报告有关联合国的概况和特点,形成对联合国的结构化知识(联合国应对的问题、联合国的功能以及近期联合国的目标等)；

3. 通过小组合作、同伴讨论、个人思考,分享作者写作的目的和意义,旨在激发学生参加公益事业的热情、责任和担当；

4. 理解作者如何表达表层信息和深层含义,尝试在新的语境中创新迁移主题。

三、思路、方法与资源

1. 整体思路

该课在教学流程上遵循"what — how — why"的顺序对文本解读。第一遍解读,教师引导学生根据关键词联合国和亲善大使来找相关信息,实现主题知识的建构,学生寻找相关知识实现文本结构知识的建构。第二遍解读时,教师可以引导学生思考作者使用了怎样的语言风格和方式来达到目的进行演讲的,同时引导学生与语篇互动,思考作者为什么这样写。第三遍解读时,通过分析演讲写作特色来思考、评价作者写得怎么样;如果你是作者,你又如何来介绍友好大使工作;友好大使工作对人类有何积极的影响;以及你如何看待联合国及友好大使,进而培养学生的批判性思维。

2. 模式方法

本节课采用 KWLA 模式进行教学设计(见表 4.1)。在 K 环节中,教师以标题激活学生相关背景知识,引导学生分享主题相关知识。实施 W 环节时,教师引导学生对

表 4.1　KWLA 教学模式

K: What I have known	Sharing the knowledge of UN
W: What I want to know	Wanting to know the detailed information of UN
L: What I learned	Exploring the information of UN and a strong sense of responsibility to give a hand to those in need
A: Apply what I have learned	Applying what I have explored in the new context

文本细节进行提问,激发学生阅读兴趣。在求知欲驱使下,自然过渡到 L 环节,教师引导学生自主建构主题知识、探究主题意义。完成主题意义探究之后,教师创设真实、全新的情境,引导学生运用所学新知,解决实际问题,帮助学生深入理解主题意义,最终完成 A 环节教学。

3. 推荐资源

(1) 郭颖等. 基于主题意义探究的高中英语阅读教学实践例析[J]. 中小学外语教学,2019(2):1—6. 本文介绍基于主题意义探究的阅读教学的探究维度和设计原则,并结合教学实践案例,分析高中英语阅读教学开展主题意义探究的实施过程。

(2) 李宝荣. 基于主题意义开展阅读教学的思路与策略[J]. 英语学习·教师版,2018(11):5—7. 本文探讨了基于主题意义进行英语阅读教学对学生发展的重要作用,提出了基于主题意义进行阅读教学的整体思路,并从两个方面进行了具体解析。在此基础上,作者结合教学实践案例分析了基于主题意义开展阅读教学的三个实践策略。

(3) 顾雪丹. 初中英语主题阅读时间探究[J]. 中小学外语教学,2019(2):13—18. 本文以 2018 年江苏省初中英语主题阅读研讨会上的课例为例,分析了阅读教学中存在的问题和困境,解读了主题阅读的定义和相关理论依据,并提出了选择恰当的拓展阅读素材、设计综合性阅读活动、实现阅读素养的正向迁移和同步提升、建构课堂内外的交融和互通等实施主题阅读的途径。

第二部分 精彩实录

授课地点:江苏省大港中学高二年级。

授课时间:2018 年 12 月 28 日,时长 40 分钟。

听课人员:夏春来名师工作室、蒯忠山名师工作室以及来自江苏省大港中学友好学校的英语教师。

授课过程:

T:Please guess what organization it is. An organization which was set up by 51 nations in 1945 now has 191 countries as its members. So what's the organization? (If you know the answer, show me your hands.)

Ss: It's the UN — the United Nations.

T: Yeah. It's UN. So what do you know about the UN?

Ss: The UN has a lot of non-profit organizations, such as UNESCO, United Nations Security Council and so on.

T: Good. What does UNESCO stand for?

Ss: UNESCO stands for United Nation Educational Scientific and Cultural Organization.

T: OK. That sounds lovely. Today, we are going to take up a speech "UN — bringing everyone closer together" by a goodwill ambassador. What do you want to know about the UN? You guys can ask questions about the UN with 5 Ws and an H. (面向全班) What are the 5 Ws and an H?

Ss(异口同声): What, who, when, where, why, and how.

T: Now please share with us your questions about the UN.

Ss: Why was the UN set up?

Ss: How does the UN work?

Ss: Who set up the UN?

T: As I mentioned right now, it's a speech by a goodwill ambassador. What do you know about a goodwill ambassador?

Ss: A goodwill ambassador will do his job without getting paid.

T: What else? Then what do you want to know about a goodwill ambassador?

Ss: How does a goodwill ambassador perform his duty?

Ss: What a good-will ambassador do?

T: Would you like to know the answers to these questions? Now it's time for you to read the speech for the answers. (You are not supposed to read the article sentence by sentence, just skim or scan the passage for answers.)

T: Have you guys finished reading, now please answer the questions.

Ss：The UN was set up to promote world peace.

T：What else?

Ss：The UN's four functions are to develop friendly relationships among nations, to work together in solving international political conflicts and promoting respect for human rights, and to be a center for organizing the actions or work of different nations.

T：That sounds so lovely, but what else?

Ss：Apart from the above, the UN also helps to protect human rights and works to improve international laws on child labor and on equal rights for minorities and women.

T：How does the UN work?

Ss：The UN borrows soldiers from different countries and assists the victims of wars and disasters.

T：OK，as a goodwill ambassador, how does Tang Ning perform her duty?

Ss：She visits some countries.

T：Does she visit alone?

Ss：No, she is followed by the press and television.

T：So why?

Ss：To increase people's awareness and encourage people working on the projects and draw people's attention to the situation.

T：Thank you! You did a good job. As is mentioned above, the UN was set up to help to promote peace and solve conflicts. In addition to the wars and conflicts we are faced with, so what kind of problems is the UN going to solve?

Ss：Education（小声）.

T：（走近学生）Loudly, please.（面向全班）OK，guys, do please give your ears to him.

Ss：We are faced with the problems like poverty, starvation, disasters and aids.

T：Um，amazing! I remember that in the speech Tang Ning just included an example in which a program was mentioned. What was that?

Ss：A program in South Africa?

T：What was the program?

Ss：A program about human rights.

T：Was that so? （转向其他同学）Anyone else?

Ss：A program under the umbrella of the government.

T：Exactly，but how did the program work?

Ss：In the program a small amount of money along with funds from local government was collected to help local women to start small business to fight poverty.

T：Good. （面向全班）Now please have a discussion with these three questions：What do you think of the program? Do you think it would work to fight poverty? Why not just give them some money directly?

Ss：The program would have a far-reaching influence，because with the money to start their own business，they would pick up some skills and then therefore be independent some time later.

Ss：As the saying goes，give a man a fish a day，he'll fill his stomach a day；teach a man to fish，you will feed him all his life. With the financial help from the government or the UN，they could build up their own business and finally fight poverty.

Ss：I think compared with the money raised for the project，job-training matters a lot more than money，so some necessary technology together with the money will help them to develop better.

T：So impressive. Go back to the passage and explore how Tang Ning presented the speech?

Ss：Tang Ning included an example in his speech.

T：Why?

Ss：To show us how the UN helps in bringing everyone closer together with the work of a goodwill ambassador.

T：Terrific! OK，please go back to the passage to find the evidence to support the subtitle of the passage —— bringing everyone closer together.

Ss：Help people across the world.

Ss：The UN touches the lives of people everywhere. (Line 16)

Ss：One of the goals is to ensure that clean water is available to everyone. (Line 46)

Ss：Another goal is to ensure all children complete primary education.

T：Wonderful! All the information mentioned above just helps to prove that the UN is doing a good job in bringing everyone closer together.

T：How do you understand the sentences "The organization is helping end some of the world's most horrible conflicts" and "Now let me tell you about the work I have been doing with organization. " As some of you just put it, how did he feel when spoke out these sentences? （微笑）

Ss：（起立，低语）She may feel a bit confident.

T：（微笑）Anything more?

Ss：She must feel so proud and a bit ambitious.

T：So here just pay attention to these two tenses "be doing" and "have been doing". Here two tenses are used to express the strong feelings like being proud and ambitious. And now I'd like to give you another two sentences like "I am pleased …", "I am very happy to …." What did Tang Ning try to convey to the audience?

Ss：He was trying to express his opinion in favor of something in an enthusiastic manner.

T：OK，I want to draw attention to these two to express the positive feeling. What do you think of the speech and what can we learn from Tang Ning as an individual?

Ss：I think the speech helps me get well-informed of the UN and goodwill ambassador. Meanwhile，as a student，we should and must focus on beyond our campus，as an individual we can make a great difference to the world if we like.

T：Very good. Suppose you are a member of a non-profit organization or you are going to start a non-profit club to help those in need. Do please make a speech to introduce your organization or club and your work with it. Now I give you four organizations: UNICEF; OBIS; Project Hope; The Green Great Wall. You can discuss with your group members, choose one and think up a subtitle for your organization.

(Students are discussing while the teacher is going up and down the classroom to see whether any group just need help if necessary.)

T: Any volunteer?

Ss: UNICEF — making everyone child accessible to education.

Ss: OBIS — bringing brightness to the blind.

Ss: Project Hope — not letting any child drop out.

Ss: The Green Great Wall — making the earth look green.

T: Well-done! It's time for you to make a speech for your organization. I'll appreciate it if you can apply to your speech the way that Tang Ning expressed his ideas. What's more, include an example if possible. We'd like to leave it as your homework.

板书设计：

UN -bringing everyone closer together		
UN		**The Goodwill ambassador**
Its four main functions	to keep international- to develop among nations to co-operate -to be a center--	not get paid as a volunteer; visit countries , followed by the television and
Problems it deals with	helps end some of the - assists the victims -- protects human rights;、 improves international laws; helps with other --	increase people's knowledge-- encourage-- draw local people's attention
Goals it ---	to ensure that fresh-----	an example--

第三部分　课例评析

一、学生反响

A同学：整体上我的学习目标达成了这节课老师制定的教学目标，在老师的引导下，我课上全身心投入学习，全然不会走神，因为老师的问题太烧脑了。

B同学：我能积极参与老师给出的小组讨论，能口语表达自己的思想，同时能对同学的观点进行恰当地回应。和其他同学相比我在分析作者写作技巧上略显不自信，在老师微笑鼓励下，我还是大胆回答，尽管答案不够完善，我还是得到老师的肯定和鼓励。

二、同行声音

曾玲玲（大港中学，高级教师）：在主题意义探究的课堂上，教师放手让学生充分自主探究，实现主题意义的自主建构。他采用的 KWLA 教学模式，有效地激活了学生已知，鼓励学生就主题生成一些临时性、探究性的问题，引导学生带着问题深入文本，建构主题知识。当然特别是针对不同观点，教师站在学生的认知视角，引导学生讨论，引发学生讨论、质疑、评判，而不是简单地以自己的解读对学生理解加以评判，避免以自己的解读代替学生的探究。因此，在主题意义探究教学活动中，老师在引导学生主题意义探究以及语篇意义的自我建构的同时，也致力于增强学生探究兴趣、提高鉴别和评判能力。

郭磊（大港中学，一级教师）：我特别关注了上课时教师的形体语言。这一节课教师有很强的亲和力，始终保持微笑，一定程度上缓解了学生学习焦虑，尤其当学生表现出缺乏自信时，教师的鼓励，帮助学生重拾信心，也为学生后续学习扫清心理障碍。

三、自我反思

这一节课通过 KWLA 模式,实践主题意义探究的阅读教学。

1. 注重话题引领,突出交流共享

教师亮出主题,请学生根据已有的知识水平和相关经历、经验去积极思考,努力回忆,用简明单词和词组、句子列出他们已认知的关于联合国的相关主题知识,这样可以激发学生主动学习,同时不同的学生汇报其已认知的东西,汇报的过程实际上是一个信息分享的过程。对于知识丰富的同学,他们体验到了成功的喜悦;对于信息未知的同学,则是一个知识输入的过程。

2. 鼓励自主提问,激发探究兴趣

教师引导学生进入第二个步骤即 W(Wonder),让学生自己思考他们想要了解的信息,感兴趣的有关联合国及亲善大使的信息,充分体现了学生个体的多样性及差异性,可以避免教学一刀切,从而满足不同学生的多样要求,激发了学生探究主题意义的兴趣。

3. 保障持续默读,训练思维品质

在课堂教学活动中,教师应赋予学生自主阅读与思考的时间。本节课虽然只有 40 分钟,教师还是给予学生细读和回读的时间加起来超过 7 分钟时间,学生有足够的时间进行默读、思考,为学生自主探究、合作分享提供了时间保障。同时,教师创设情境,激发学生主动思考,发展学生分析、归纳、推理、创新等高层次思维品质。

4. 需改进之处

本节课虽然注重了学生的主体地位,鼓励学生自主提问和回答,进行主题意义自主建构,但是在学生回答问题之后,只有教师对学生答案进行评价,追问和引导,而没有引导其他同学对回答进行互评,因为这样生生互动更能促进学生的自主探究。

四、专家点评

点评专家：韩炳华

在实施主题意义探究阅读教学中，教师设计一些培养、训练学生高阶思维教学活动，帮助学生深入语篇，对语篇信息进行深加工和处理。训练学生高阶思维的教学活动贯穿于整个教学活动。尤其是在读中环节教师引导学生分析语篇的篇章结构、探究作者写作意图和文化涵义，评价赏析作者的写作风格、语言表达等一系列有助于探究主题意义的评判性思维的活动，同时高阶思维训练也包括读后环节在口头、笔头上的语言输出实现了学生语言知识内化和迁移，释放学生创造力和想象力的活动。特别是在高阶思维训练活动实现读中和读后环节无痕、自然地对接，有助于主题意义的探究。

此外，在实施主题意义探究教学时，教师能联系学生的实际，有效地实现学科育人的目标。设计一系列与学生实际生活关联性强的教学活动，来培养学生语言理解和表达能力，推动学生对主题探究的深度学习，使学生达到学以致用，以激活学生学习英语的内驱力。这一节课很好地践行了《高中英语课程标准（2017 年版）》，在主题意义探究阅读教学活动中，教师能指导学生利用语篇中学得的知识和思想来解决自己现实生活中的问题，实现学科育人的目的。

【名师简介】

董金标：高级教师，现任教于江苏省邗江中学。2016 年 9 月在苏州获得江苏省优质课观摩课评比一等奖，2017 年 11 月在浙江义乌获得全国高中英语教师基本功大赛现场说课比赛一等奖。教学主张：给足时间让学生阅读文本，给每一个学生发声的机会，给足时间让学生完善答案。在《中小学外语教学》《基础外语教育》以及《英语教师》发表教学论文近 10 篇。

课例 11　基于思维品质培养的阅读教学实践

——以 Never Too Late 阅读语篇为例

第一部分　教学预设

一、教学内容分析

1. 课标要求

《普通高中英语课程标准(2017 年版)》(以下简称《课标 2017 年版》)指出思维品质是指思维在逻辑性、批判性、创新性等方面所表现的能力和水平。思维品质体现英语学科核心素养的心智特征。思维品质的发展有助于提升学生分析和解决问题的能力,使他们能够从跨文化视角观察和认识世界,对事物做出正确的价值判断。首先要培养学生的逻辑思维,在此基础上,能够让学生有理有据地进行意义和意图方面的表达。所谓的批判性,强调理性思考,要善于提出疑问,善于通过搜集证据证明自己的观点和判断,或者评价他人的观点是否合理、可信。学生具备了逻辑和批判思维的能力,才能真正在语言运用和解决问题的过程中实现创新。(梅德明,王蔷)

《课标》在思维品质目标方面提出,应培养学生辨析语言和文化中的具体现象,梳理、概括信息,建构新概念,分析、推断信息的逻辑关系,正确评判各种思想观点,创造性地表达自己的观点,具备多元思维的意识和创新思维的能力。在阅读教学实践中,教师应围绕文章主线设计任务,帮助学生理解文本、拓展内涵、发展思维。

2. 教材分析

本节课内容是外语教学与研究出版社出版的《新视野英语教程》第二册 Unit 6 中的一篇阅读文章,原文题目是 Never Too Late to Live Your Dream。本节课是该阅读文章的第一课时,主要内容是作者开学第一天经老师介绍结识了一位新同学——87岁的 Rose,以及通过和 Rose 的相处了解到她的乐观积极向上,从 Rose 的求学经历得到启发：Never too late to be all you can possibly be.

本文结构明了,内容清晰。按照时间发展的顺序可以分为四个部分：

第一部分：开学第一天,认识 Rose。

第二部分：开学后的三个月,与 Rose 相处。

第三部分：Rose 的演讲。

第四部分：学年结束,Rose 带来的启示。

3. 重点与难点

教学重点：如何通过 Rose 的求学经历揭示文章主题：Never Too Late to Live Your Dream。

教学难点：如何理解和提炼 Rose 的演讲,尤其是如何理解和提炼演讲中保持年轻快乐心态、取得成功的四个秘诀。

4. 学情分析

(1) 学生心智特征分析。本课是借班执教的溧阳市级公开课,对象是高一年级学生。据该班任课教师反映该班同学平时上课较为活跃,课堂参与度较好,加上公开课可能带来的刺激和兴奋,预计学生能够较好地参与到课堂学习活动中来。

(2) 学生已有知识经验分析。经过高中近一个学期的学习,学生的语言能力、学习能力、思维品质等有了一定的提升。本文的词汇对于高一学生来说难度不大,虽有少量生词,但学生可以通过联系上下文语境进行猜测和把握。可能对学生构成较大挑战的是：提炼和概括 Rose 演讲中所提到的保持年轻、快乐心态及取得成功的四个秘诀及对 Rose 性格特征的把握和归纳。

二、教学目标分析

根据对教学内容和学生情况的分析,本节课设定了以下教学目标,即经过本节课的学习,学生能够：

1. 分析文本的整体结构以及段落之间的关联,归纳段落大意；

2. 分析和综合文本中 Rose 演讲的关键信息,概括 Rose 的性格特征；

3. 比较和综合语篇信息,正确分析和把握文本逻辑关联,理解文章主旨。

三、思路、方法与资源

1. 整体思路

本节课在整体思路上遵循"把握文本整体结构，分析推断语篇逻辑关系，概括文本主旨"的顺序，注重训练学生思维能力。在具体教学设计上主要有以下环节：文本结构理解、段落主旨归纳、主要人物性格概括、语篇逻辑分析、主题思想拓展。

主要教学环节如下：

Stage One：Pre-reading

Step 1：引入话题

教师提问：When you see the title of the passage，what can you think of?

【设计意图】由于本文标题属于半开放性：Never Too Late，教师在本节课的导入环节充分利用学生的已知知识去联系文本语篇的未知。通过启发学生根据 Never Too Late to . . .思考问题，从而激活学生已有的相关图式，为后续阅读做好语言和内容的铺垫。

Stage Two：While-reading

Step 2：浏览全文，把握文章整体脉络，回答问题：

The passage is mainly organized by _____.

A. providing examples

B. making comparisons

C. following the order of time

D. following the order of importance

【设计意图】此环节旨在通过快速阅读文章考查学生对文章整体结构的理解和把握，尤其是引导学生关注时间状语逻辑关联词，为后续整合细节信息做铺垫。

Step 3：细读全文，划分文章结构，归纳主旨大意

Paragraph	Adverbial of time	Main idea
1—4	the first day of school	

续　表

Paragraph	Adverbial of time	Main idea
5—6		
7—8		
9		

【设计意图】通过对文章结构的理解和划分，归纳段落主旨，有助于帮助学生更好地理解行文逻辑和脉络发展，也为后文深层阅读、分析主人翁性格特征作好铺垫。

Step 4：细节深层阅读，分析人物性格

教师要求学生根据 Rose 演讲中的 four secrets 分析 Rose 的性格特征。

	laugh and find humor every day	humorous, positive
four secrets	have a dream	
	grow up by always finding the opportunity in change	
	have no regrets	

【设计意图】为让学生读懂、读深、读透文本，挖掘文本字里行间所蕴含的信息，教师设计该任务帮助学生透过文本表层信息挖掘文本所折射的情感态度。通过对人物性格特征的分析和提炼，有助于加深对人物精神的理解，更有助于学生准确深刻地理解文章主旨。

Step 5：分析把握文本逻辑关联，填补信息空缺

Where should the sentence "There is a huge difference between growing older and growing up." be put in paragraph 8?

A. ①　　　　B. ②　　　　C. ③　　　　D. ④

【设计意图】根据段落语篇的逻辑关联，通过对文本信息的重新加工，旨在帮助学生从深层次上厘清文本逻辑，从而培养学生语篇分析和推断的思维品质。

Step 6：细节信息深层理解和推断，升华主旨

教师设问：By mentioning "One week after graduation Rose died peacefully in her sleep. " in the last paragraph，which of the four secrets the writer wants to emphasize?

【设计意图】在理解文本的表层信息之后，读者也要理解"散落在文本各处"的信息点之间的相互关联。(葛炳芳，2013)教师在解读文本和设计问题是应凸显文本的核心主线，寻找各信息点之间的相互关系。(刘阳，南美善，2019)此问题的设计旨在帮助学生进一步理解 have no regrets 在 Rose 身上的体现。同时，也为后面回归标题埋下伏笔。

Stage Three：Post-reading

Step 7：回归标题

教师通过引领学生关注全文最后一句话：It's never too late to be all you can possibly be. ，并再次关注和拓展文章标题。

【设计意图】此环节的设计在于引导学生回归标题，加深对标题的理解，从而启发学生对本文所要表达的主旨进行深层理解，进而提升学生的深度思维能力。

2. 模式方法

本节课主要采用 PWP 教学模式，将阅读教学分为 pre-reading，while-reading 和 post-reading 三段教学模式，其教学目标与教学活动在三个阶段有着各自特点。

读前教学(pre-reading)的核心任务就是为阅读做前期认知和心理准备。主要包括背景图式的激活、话题的切入、兴趣的激发和语言、策略准备等。本节课的读前环节非常直接明了，以标题快速切入，教师通过设问：When seeing such a title, what can you think of? Or usually, we say, it's never too late to . . .？激起学生背景知识储备，直接切入本文表达的主旨，在引起学生表达欲望的同时，也激起学生阅读探索的渴望。

读中教学(while-reading)是阅读教学的核心，各种阅读能力的培养都是通过这一段教学完成的。从具体信息的识别，到推理判断能力的培养，再到各种逻辑关系和篇章结构的分析，阅读能力中的知识层面、理解层面、分析层面一般都是在这一段完成的。(王笃勤，2012)因此，教学活动的设计必须具有层次性。本节课围绕学生思维品质的培养这一目标主线，结合文本逻辑的立体多层分析，在读中教学中展开了丰富多样的教学活动，由浅入深，循序渐进：文章框架结构的整体把握、段落划分和主旨的归纳、人物性格的分析和提炼、语境逻辑的分析和推断都离不开文本逻辑的多层分析和理解，离不开分析、综合、归纳、判断、评价等各种思维活动的参与。

读后教学（post-reading）一般侧重知识的运用和综合，一般教材中普遍运用的 reading and writing 中的 writing 就属于读后活动的范畴。如果把阅读分为 read the lines，read between the lines 和 read beyond the lines 三个层次的话，读后阶段完成的就是第三层次。学生在联系实际的基础上，对阅读中所获取的信息、感知的词汇和句法、认知的策略或理解的文化等方面的运用。（王笃勤，2012）而本节课在读后环节的处理上将语言运用实践主要放到了 assignment 部分。

3. 推荐资源

（1）葛炳芳. 英语阅读教学的综合视野：内容、思维和语言［M］. 杭州：浙江大学出版社，2013. 本书主要探讨英语阅读教学的综合视野，强调在英语阅读教学过程中，阅读教学绝不是信息解读、思维培养、目标语言点学习、阅读策略体验等的简单相加，必须将内容、思维和语言有机整合起来，帮助英语教师形成整体阅读教学的意识。

（2）梅德明，王蔷. 改什么？如何教？怎样考？高中英语新课标解析［M］. 北京：外语教学与研究出版社，2018. 本书以问题为导向，用案例进行阐释，对学生核心素养的培养做实践性的指导。这些问题大多与教学实践紧密相关，比如：如何能够在原来综合语言运用能力的基础之上，进行整合和提升，构建好英语学科的核心素养？基于活动观的教学设计有什么样的特点？等等。

（3）王笃勤. 英语阅读教学［M］. 北京：外语教学与研究出版社，2012. 本书的每个章节均以案例入手，引出阅读教学中的各个相关主题，并围绕主题介绍相关的理论知识。每个章节都设置了实践反思环节，教师们可以通过具体案例的分析内化相关的理论知识，通过实践提高相关的技能。

（4）刘阳，南美善. 基于思维品质培养的阅读教学实践——以 Life in a Violin Case 阅读语篇为例［J］. 中小学外语教学（中学篇），2019(2). 本文以"培养核心素养，关注学生发展"为主题的一节公开课教学实践为例，着重从教学主线设计、教学活动设计层次、阅读策略的指导几个方面阐述了如何在阅读教学中培养学生思维品质。

第二部分　精彩实录

授课地点：江苏省溧阳市光华高级中学高一（6）班教室。

授课时间：2018 年 11 月 30 日。

听课人员：溧阳市教研室专家代表、常州市各高中英语教师代表共 60 人左右。

授课过程：

Stage One：Pre-reading

Step 1：Warming-up and lead-in

（教师呈现 Never Too Late to . . .。）

T：When seeing such a title，what can you think of? Or usually，we say，it's never too late to . . . ?

S1：to begin.

S2：to start.

S3：to learn.

S4：to enjoy life.

S5：to love.

. . .

T：Now，let's read a story to see what the writer intends to tell us it's never too late to do.

Stage Two：While-reading

Step2：Fast reading for the first time

T：First of all，please go through the passage quickly and find the answer to the question：

The passage is mainly organized by _____.

A. providing examples   B. making comparisons

C. following the order of time   D. following the order of importance

（大约 1 分钟后。）

T：Which one to choose?

S1：C.

T：Why?

S1：Because we can find some adverbials of time.

T：Where are they?

S1：In the first paragraph, the first day of school; in paragraph 4, every day for the next three months; ...

T：Good job.

Step 3：Fast reading for the second time for the structure and main ideas of the passage

T：Based on your analysis, we can divide the 9 paragraphs in the passage into 4 parts in this table. Please read each part again and try to get the main idea for each part.

（大约 3 分钟后。）

T：Are you ready?

（部分学生回答 Yes,教师随机点了一名学生。）

T：What's the main idea of Part one?

S1：It's about what happened on the first day of school.

T：What happened?

S1：We saw an old classmate.

T：Just saw? What did you know about her?

S1：Her name, her age and her dream.

T：Very good. So can we say the first part is mainly about how we got to know Rose?

Ss：Yes.

...

Step 4：Detailed reading

T：Please read the first part again in details and answer the question：what made Rose in college at her age?

（大约 1 分钟后,教师点了一名学生。）

S1：To meet a rich husband, get married, have a couple of children, and then retire and travel.

T：Why did she jokingly reply to me?

S1：Because she is humorous.

T：Since she is humorous. What do you think is the real reason for her to be in college?

（该生又浏览了一下文章。）

S1：Oh, she dreamed of having a college education.

T：Yes, her dream of having a college education made her in college at her age. Well, when it comes to her age, how old was she?

S1：Eighty-seven years old.

T：Since she was so old, why did I ask her "Why are you in college at such a young age?"

（该生似乎没有听懂这个问题,教师又重复了一遍,该生还是笑而不答。）

T：Do you think I had a sense of humor?

S1：Yes.

T：Why do you think so?

S1：Because you are always smiling.

（很多学生哈哈大笑,该生显得有点尴尬,似乎意识到自己犯了什么错误。教师赶快介入。）

T：Oh, I am sorry. I didn't put it clearly. I mean do you think the author also had a sense of humor like Rose?

S1：Yes.

T：Why?

S1：Because the author asked an old lady "Why are you in college at such a young age?".

T：Quite good. You've got it.

Step 5：Further reading for discussion (pair work)

According to paragraphs 5 and 6, what can we learn about Rose's characteristics?

（学生在阅读过程中,进行同伴合作讨论,气氛较好。约2分钟后,教师提出以下要求。)

T：You are supposed to find some details in the text to support your opinion. OK?

Ss：OK.

(之后，教师连续点了好几名学生回答问题。)

S1：Easy going, because "We became instant friends' in paragraph 5. "

T：Well done.

S2：Friendly and outgoing.

T：Why?

S2：Because she shared her wisdom and experience with me and easily made friends wherever she went.

T：Oh, very good.

S3：Positive and energetic, because she tended to be highly motivated, responsible, and deeply involved in class participation. In spare time she had someone hang out or go to bars with. She even participated in some form of athletic activity.

S4：Enthusiastic.

T：From the sentence in paragraph 5 "Every day for the next three months we would leave class together and talk nonstop. " What can we learn about Rose's characteristics?

S5：Talkative.

T：Wonderful.

Step 6：Detailed reading for further understanding

T：What are the four secrets in Rose's speech?

(大约 2 分钟后，教师点学生找出四个秘密。)

S1：Staying young, being happy, and achieving success.

(部分学生一阵骚动，窃窃私语。该生似乎很快意识到大概答错了，露出想要纠正的神态。)

T：Is this one of the four secrets?

S1：No. The first secret is to laugh and find humor every day.

T：Yes，quite good. Thank you.

S2：Have a dream. Have no regrets.

T：Good job，you find two more secrets. What about the forth one?

S3：Have many people walking around.

T：Any other opinion?

S4：Grow up by always finding the opportunity in change.

T：Why don't you agree with him?

S4：What he found belongs to the secret — have a dream.

T：Well done.

（老师转向之前的那个学生。）

T：Do you agree with her?

S3：Yes.

T：Now we've found the four secrets. But based on each secret, what can be inferred about Rose's characteristics? For example，according to the first secret — laugh and find humor every day，we can say Rose is humorous and positive. What about the other three secrets? Rose said we should always have a dream and so we can say she is ...

S1：Hopeful.

T：Good. Any other different opinion?

S2：Ambitious.

T：Wonderful. What about secret 3?

S3：Positive.

S4：Active.

T：If someone grows up by always finding opportunity in change，we can say he or she is ... and do you think such a person takes responsibility for himself or herself?

S5：Responsible.

T：I like your answer. Thank you. What about secret 4?

S6：Brave.

S7：Determined.

T：Perfect. You did a wonderful job.

Step 7：Further reading more

T：Where should the sentence "There is a huge difference between growing older and growing up. " be put in paragraph 8?

A. ①　　　　B. ②　　　　C. ③　　　　D. ④

T：If you come across difficulties, you can discuss with your partners.

（大约 1 分钟后。）

S1：I think the sentence should be put in place 2.

T：Why?

S1：Because it mainly talks about the difference between growing old and growing up from place 2. So the sentence should be put here to introduce the following text.

T：Oh，excellent explanation. You analyzed the discourse well. But，boys and girls, how do you understand the underlined part "lived them out" in paragraph 8?

S2：According to the context "She challenged us to study the words of the song and lived them out in daily lives"，we can see them here refers to the words，so live them out should mean turn the words of the song into reality.

T：Excellent. Thank you very much. Would you like to enjoy the song?

Ss：Yes.

（教师播放歌曲 *The Rose*，并呈现歌词。）

T：From the song we can see "Just remember in the winter far beneath the bitter snows lies the seed that with the sun's love, in the spring becomes the rose". Do you think the old lady, Rose, also became a rose finally?

Ss：Yes.

T：Why?

Ss：At the year's end Rose finished the college degree.

T：Yes. I agree with you. In the last paragraph, which one of the four secrets does the author intend to emphasize by mentioning "One week after graduation Rose died peacefully in her sleep"?

Ss：Have no regrets.

Stage Three：Post-reading

Step 8：Appreciating a poem

T：According to the last sentence of the passage — It's never too late to be all you can possibly be，we can complete the title again-never too late to be all you can possibly be.

Actually，in our daily life，we will often find it never too late to do many different things．Let's read all the sentences here altogether．

（呈现以下句子,让学生齐声朗读。）

It's never too late to change．

It's never too late to clear up the past．

It's never too late to right your wrongs．

It's never too late to try something different．

It's never too late to go after your dreams．

It's never too late to be what you can be．

You're never too old，never too bad，never too late and never too sick to start once again．

Step 9：Assignment

Make a speech with the title：Never Too Late to ...

Tips：1. Complete the title；

2. Make your speech based on your own experiences；

3. Focus your speech on why and how；

4. Try to use the words learned if necessary.

第三部分　课例评析

一、学生反响

学生 A：这篇文章我们老师以前讲过,但没想到,可以像今天这样讲。老师把课文挖得很深,有点费脑子。

学生 B:有点紧张,活动很多,而且要动脑筋。很喜欢课上播放的歌曲。

二、同行声音

狄建忠(溧阳市教师发展中心英语教研员):蒯老师的课让我们看到了全国一等奖的水平。特别是对文本逻辑的深度分析,有助于培养学生的思维品质。其中对文本的分析、概括、提炼、推断,尤其是对文本的重组,对学生阅读能力的提升大有帮助。

姚超英(江苏省溧阳中学):蒯老师的教学设计环环相扣,特别注重学生对文本逻辑的分析和把握,对学生思维能力挑战较大。学生要能够分析文本,还要运用语言,辨析语言现象,还要分类概括,进行自己的语言表达。

沈亚君(溧阳市光华高级中学):作为和蒯老师进行同课异构的老师,我感到差距非常大。蒯老师的教学设计和课堂教学很有深度。当然,这需要教师具有扎实的基本功。

郭皓(溧阳市南渡高级中学):蒯老师这节课注重对学生的逐步引导,引导学生的思维由浅入深,对文本的加工逐步深入。有概括,有归纳,有推断,其实对于学生来说,难度不小,但蒯老师很巧妙地引导学生逐步解决问题,效果很好。当然,估计上完这节课,学生会有点累。

三、自我反思

本节阅读课采用 PWP 三段教学模式,注重在文本逻辑分析的基础上训练学生思维能力,培养学生思维品质。

1. 本节课的成功之处

(1)教学活动的设计层次分明,由浅入深

从整体快速阅读活动开始,到归纳每一部分的主旨大意,再到文本的深度分析和理解的活动中,无论是语言理解难度还是思维挑战的强度,都循序渐进、由浅入深有序地开展。每一个活动的设计和完成都为后面的活动做好认知的铺垫和思维的准备。从教学效果来看,整节课,学生的课堂专注度和参与度都很高,较好地达成了预设的教学目标。

（2）注重文本逻辑分析,培养学生思维品质

本节课每一个教学环节的设计和课堂学习任务的完成几乎都离不开文本逻辑的分析,和在此基础上不同程度的思维参与来解决阅读理解过程中的实际问题。尤其是在读中阶段,通过层层任务设计,帮助学生分析和理解文本、整理和加工信息,引导学生进行比较、分析、判断和归纳等思维活动,促进理解,训练思维,使学生一直处于积极、主动的阅读探索体验之中。

（3）注重阅读策略的指导,帮助学生获得成功阅读理解和解决问题的成就感

本节课中,学生对文本的整体阅读、细节阅读、深度阅读都有教师给予的阅读策略的指导。在整体快速阅读时,教师提醒学生在阅读过程中定位关键信息、关注时间状语线索。在细节阅读时,教师要求和指导学生关注上下文语境中的支撑信息。在深度阅读时,教师指导学生关注逻辑层次,并分解问题,帮助学生搭建"脚手架",降低任务难度的同时,让学生逐步体验成功解决问题的喜悦和信心。

2. 本节课需要改进之处

读后活动一般应该侧重语言知识、文化知识和语言综合技能的运用,而本节课在读后环节的处理上缺乏一定的语言运用实践。由于考虑到时间紧和追求公开课形式上的完整和流畅,忽视了学生在联系实际的基础上,对阅读中所获取的信息、感知的词汇和句法、认知的策略等方面的运用。

四、专家点评

点评专家：夏春来

英语学科核心素养是可以通过课堂教学来培养的,就思维品质看,要注重学生从认知角度对文本进行分类、概括和归纳,进而形成或建构新的认知。同时,教师还要注重引导学生对语篇知识进行分析、推断、评价和创造性地表达,学会独立思考,进行个性化、创造性的表达,进而培养学生深度思维品质。

教师在这节课中,对文本价值深度挖掘,同时选取恰当的点来设计由浅入深的学习活动。教师在课堂上,借助有效、合理的教学设计,帮助学生对文本进行逐层解读,多元理解,多层次加工,随着阅读进程的逐步深入,学生不断进行思考,完成与文本人物、文本作者深度对话。

同时,教师通过有效的提问促进学生思维能力的训练和思维品质的培养。从事实信息类问题到理解应用性问题,再到分析综合类问题及评价性问题,在增强学生对文本内容、思想、情感、主旨深入理解的同时,也使得学生思维逐步走向深入。

另外,在以学生为中心的课堂上,教师积极引导学生自主合作学习,主动思考和解决问题,通过层层递进的问题设计为学生提供了阅读、合作、质疑、讨论、思考和表达的空间,在师生互动、生生互动中,优化学生思维习惯,提升学生思维品质。

【点评专家简介】夏春来,江苏省句容高级中学,正高级教师,江苏省教学名师,江苏省"333"工程高层次人才,镇江市夏春来名教师工作室领衔人。长期致力于信息技术与英语学科融合教学,在《中小学外语教学》《中小学英语教学与研究》等中文核心期刊发表文章 13 篇,人大复印报刊资料全文转载 4 篇,1 篇文章被人大复印资料中心评为"十二五"期间基础教育英语学科最具影响力论文。先后应北京师范大学、江苏大学、江苏省师培中心等邀请做专题讲座多次。获省优质课一等奖,省杏坛杯青年教师教学展评特等奖,一师一优课部优、省优。主持省市级课题 8 项。曾获镇江市十佳教师、镇江市优秀教育工作者、镇江市教育领军人物培养对象、句容市劳动模范等荣誉称号。

【名师简介】

蒯忠山:江苏省大港中学英语教师,镇江市英语学科带头人,镇江市丹徒区英语名师工作室领衔人。获得 2011 年江苏省高中英语优质课评比一等奖,2012年全国高中英语教师教学基本功大赛一等奖。被授予江苏省五一劳动奖章,获第二届全国中小学英语教师名师、镇江市优秀教育工作者、镇江市十佳教师等荣誉称号。长期致力于高中英语阅读教学研究,注重学生阅读思维的培养。

课例 12　基于英语学习活动观的高中英语阅读课例

第一部分　教学预设

一、教学内容分析

1. 课标要求

根据《普通高中英语课程标准(2017 年版)》,英语学习活动观是指学生在主题意义引领下,通过学习理解活动、应用实践活动、迁移创新活动等一系列体现综合性、关联性和实践性等特点的英语学习活动,基于已有的知识和认知水平,依托不同类型的语篇,在分析问题和解决问题的过程中,促进自身语言知识学习、语言技能发展、文化内涵理解、多元思维发展、价值取向判断和学习策略运用。

2. 教材分析

教学文本是美国奥斯卡获奖影片《阿甘正传》的剧本(节选)。该影片讲述了一位智商低于正常人的美国青年阿甘(Forrest Gump)从一个受人歧视的小男孩逐步成长为国民偶像的励志故事。文本选取了阿甘成年后回忆自己第一天离开母亲独自上学时,在校车上受到冷遇,却结识了一位名叫 Jenny 的善良女孩的场景。文本前配有导读文字,简要介绍了阿甘的性格特点和整部电影的背景信息,旨在启发读者思考文本主题与电影主题的内在联系。文本作为电影剧本的语篇特征十分鲜明,由台词、舞台指令和画外音组成,语言通俗易懂、内容真实具体、文化内涵丰富。具体来说,作者通过阿甘与母亲、司机、冷漠少年、Jenny 之间的言行交流以及成年阿甘的自述,表现出阿甘单纯善良的性格力量,由此引发读者对"单纯是一种生活智慧"这一人生哲理的思考。

3. 重点与难点

教学重点：依托剧本语篇特征,理解文本背后隐含的人物性格特点。

教学难点：通过理解文中细节,感受人物的性格力量,从而超越文本升华主题。

4. 学情分析

学生心智特征分析。本课是借班执教的江苏省阅读优质课评比活动中的一节课,对象是高一学生。据该班的英语教师反映该班同学英语基础较好,学习态度较认真,考试成绩较好,但多数学生性格偏内向,上课发言不够活跃。

学生已有知识经验分析。从课前调查中获知,学生已基本具备在阅读中获取细节信息的能力,但多数学生在理解和整合知识、逻辑推理和分析论证观点方面能力比较欠缺。从与该班学生交流中发现,该班只有少数学生经常看英文原版电影,对电影剧本的体裁特征不甚了解。

二、教学目标分析

教学目标的制定要遵循活动观的三个层次,即学习理解类活动、应用实践类活动和迁移创新类活动,要能够反映出学生对文本主题意义探究的过程,要体现核心素养四要素的相互渗透、关联融合和协调发展。基于文本解读和学情分析,教师确定了如下教学目标:

学生学完本课后,应该能够:

1. 通过阅读,获取剧本的基本信息,如主要人物、场景设置、主要情节等。

2. 分析文中人物的台词、动作和画外音等信息,分析和概括阿甘性格单纯的具体内涵,并形成结构化信息。

3. 结合文中细节信息,分析和阐释阿甘单纯友善的性格力量。

4. 对阿甘的性格特点做出自己的评价,并联系个人生活,谈论自己对"单纯是一种生活智慧"的看法。

三、思路、方法与资源

1. 整体思路

该课基于英语学习活动观的教学理念,立足分析问题和解决问题,以主题意义探究为教学主线,依托文本的语篇特征,遵循活动观的三个层次设计教学活动,并在活动中设计指向学生思维品质的问题,通过环环相扣的问题链,使主题意义探究层层推进,最终达到学科育人的教学目标。具体思路如下:

活动层次	解决问题	活动内容
学习理解类活动	What is simpleness?	① 感知与注意:学生通过浏览文本前的导读文字,初步了解阿甘的性格特点,并预测文本的大致内容。 ② 获取与梳理:学生通过浏览文本的主要内容,获取核心信息,梳理剧本的语篇特征,并验证先前的预测。 ③ 概括与整合:学生通过细读文本细节,概括并整合阿甘单纯性格的具体内涵。
应用实践类活动	How powerful is simpleness?	① 推理与阐释:学生运用文本的语言特征,推断和创作阿甘的台词,并阐释创作的理由。 ② 分析与判断:学生分析阿甘的单纯带来周围人态度的变化,由此认识到阿甘的性格力量。
迁移创新类活动	Why is simpleness a kind of wisdom?	① 批判与评价:学生联系自身实际,讨论单纯友善的性格与成功的关系,并在全班交流想法、内化语言。 ② 想象与创造:学生完成课后作业,用自己生活中的经历,论证自己对"单纯是一种智慧"的理解。

2. 理念方法

本课的教学设计遵循新课标提出的英语学习活动观的教学理念。英语学习活动观指向学科核心素养的发展,强调主题意义的引领和课程内容的整合性学习,体现学习的认知层次和活动的本质特征。英语学习活动观的实施路径是从学习理解到应用实践再到迁移创新。这三个层次的活动从基于文本的信息输入,到深入文本的初阶输出,最后到超越文本的高阶输出,这种逻辑的进阶、发展、提升能够实现基于内容、聚焦文化、学习语言、发展思维的深度学习的目的,从而落实英语学科核心素养。英语学习活动观尽管并非某种固定的教学模式,但它明确了课程实施的宏观路径。具体来说,教师在基于英语学习活动观设计教学时应关注以下几个方面:

（1）深入研读文本，把握核心内容

教师可以从文本的主题、内容、文体结构、语言特点和作者观点五个角度深入理解和把握文本的主题意义，梳理出结构化知识并解读出各个环节是如何为主题意义服务的，以形成深入而独特的见解；然后，运用解读的内容尝试回答 what（主题和内容）、why（主题和作者）、how（文体和语言）引出的三个问题，确定文本的主题和内容是什么，它的深层含义是什么，承载的价值取向是什么，作者为了有效而恰当地表达这样一个主题意义，选择了什么样的文体形式、语篇结构和修辞手段。以本课的教学文本为例，教师应在研读文本的基础上解读出以下信息：

［What］（主题和内容）本课文本是一部电影的剧本（节选），描述了智商低于常人的青年阿甘回忆自己第一天离开母亲，独自在校车上受到冷落时，一位善良女孩 Jenny 向他伸出援手的场景。作者通过阿甘与不同人物的对话过程和动作描写，表现了阿甘单纯友善的性格特点以及不同人物对待阿甘的态度。作者还通过成年阿甘的画外音，表达了阿甘对 Jenny 的终生感激。

［Why］（主题和作者）教材编者在文本前的导读部分简单介绍了阿甘的性格特点和他后来具有传奇色彩的人生经历，是希望本课的学习能让学生懂得：单纯是一种人生智慧，这是本课文本的中心思想。教师在引领学生探究主题意义时，不能仅停留在阿甘单纯的行为表现上，更要分析阿甘的单纯引起周围环境怎样的变化。

［How］（文体和语言）本课文本是典型的电影剧本，由角色台词（line）、舞台指令（stage direction）和画外音（voice-over）组成。台词和舞台指令生动形象且通俗易懂，让读者充分感到人物鲜明的个性和态度，如阿甘的口头禅"Momma said"体现出他的单纯可爱，阿甘台词中的语病也体现出他的智商较低，校车司机的微笑和 Jenny 的主动握手体现出他们对阿甘友善的态度，等等。成年阿甘画外音的出现，表现出他对初见 Jenny 的场景记忆犹新，画外音运用了排比、反衬、比喻等修辞手法，使阿甘对 Jenny 的感激之情溢于言表。以上表达方式和表现手法，都凸显了文本的主题意义，为学生探究主题提供依据。

（2）树立问题意识，创设合理情境

英语学习活动观强调培养学生在情境中利用形成和内化了的结构性知识去分析问题和解决问题的能力。为了达到这一目的，教师要在设计教学时树立问题意识，力求使解决问题成为学生学习的出发点和落脚点。每节课的教学设计,教师都应设法思考基于本课主题内容学生需要解决什么问题,并设法结合学习内容,将要解决的主要问题转化为几个具体的问题,并基于这些具体问题设计和组织教学,引导学生通过学习、思考、合作、探究等,找到解决问题的答案。围绕要解决的问题,教师还需要创设合理的情境,通过让学生运用预测和验证等阅读技能,激活学生的已知经验,激发他们的探究热情。创设的情境一要真实,以增强学生的融入动机;二要简洁,以节省足够时间开展探究活动;三要开放,以激活学生的思维和表达欲望。以本课的教学为例,教师应确立要解决的中心问题:阿甘的单纯是否是一种生活智慧?为此,教师将这一问题转化为三个具体问题:阿甘的单纯具体有哪些体现?阿甘的单纯引起了怎样的积极变化?阿甘的单纯和他后来的成功有何关联?在探究以上问题前,教师先让学生预测:单纯的阿甘第一天上学可能会遇到什么问题?他最需要的是什么?这一情境的创设简洁有效,悬念感强,有利于激发学生阅读文本的兴趣,并启发学生思考阿甘的单纯是否有助于解决他人生经历中遭受冷遇的问题。

(3)设计教学主线,追求意义探究

英语学习活动观强调对意义的探究,教师要改变脱离语境的知识学习和碎片化的教学方式,把主题意义探究作为教学活动的主线。在教学设计时,教师应树立主线意识,在深入研读语篇、把握核心内容的基础上,依托语篇类型,梳理文本的意义主线,形成结构性和可内化的知识,使三个层次的教学活动逻辑关联、层层递进、环环相扣,成为融合课程六要素的有机整体,自然而然地达成指向学科核心素养的课程目标。就本节课而言,教师围绕阿甘的单纯个性,设计了"单纯的内涵—单纯的性格力量—单纯是一种智慧"的教学主线,通过三个层次的活动设计,形成一个围绕主题意义探究的、逻辑递进、循环上升的活动链。

(4)依托语篇内容,关注活动层次

英语学习活动的设计应以促进学生英语学科核心素养的发展为目的,围绕主题语境,基于口头和书面等多模态形式的语篇,通过学习理解、应用实践、迁移创新等层层递进的语言、思维、文化相融合的活动,引导学生加深对主题意义的理解;帮助学生在活动中习得语言知识,运用语言技能,阐释文化内涵,比较文化异同,评析语篇意义,形成正确的价值观念和积极的情感态度,进而尝试在新的语境中运用所学语言和文化知识,分析问题、解决问题,创造性地表达个人观点、情感和态度。以本课为例,教师以主题意义探究为教学主线,设计了三个层次的学生活动(详见"整体思路"的表格部分)。

(5) 优化问题设计,指向思维品质

思维品质是英语学科四大核心素养之一,是思维在逻辑性、批判性、创新性等方面所表现的能力和水平。思维品质的发展有助于提升学生分析和解决问题的能力,使他们能够从跨文化视角观察和认识世界,对事物做出正确的价值判断。提问是教师在阅读课堂上组织英语学习活动最重要的手段。阅读教学中设计的问题包括展示型、参阅型和评估型问题。教师应注意将三种类型的问题设计与三个层次的英语学习活动结合起来,在主题意义的引领下,逐步提高问题的思维层级,形成环环相扣、层层递进的问题链,最终达成基于内容深度学习、发展思维品质的目标。以本课为例,教师首先通过展示型问题让学生在导读部分直接获取阿甘的性格特点,再借助参阅型问题让学生结合文本细节分析阿甘单纯性格的具体内涵,最后设计评估型问题让学生联系自身实际探讨阿甘的单纯带来的启示。整节课以文本的主题意义为活动主线,实现了从逻辑性到评判性再到创新性的思维品质的培养目标。

(6) 合理开展评价,确保教学效果

完整的教学活动包括教、学、评三个方面。课堂评价活动应贯穿教学的全过程,为检测教学目标服务,以发现学生学习中的问题,并提供及时的帮助和反馈,促进学生更有效地开展学习。为此,教师应处理好评价与教和学之间的关系,实现以评促学、以评促教。具体而言,教师可以通过提问和追问,评价和促进学生对语篇的深层次理解;也可以鼓励学生相互评价,通过学生观点的相互碰撞,促进学生的课堂生成。学生思维的活跃程度是一节课教学效果的重要指标,教师应通过合理的评价活动使学生的思维始终处于应激状态。为此,教师应尽量减少预设,放手让学生探究文本主题;只要学生言之有理、论据详实,教师应平等看待学生的思维成果,尊重学生的个性化表达;同时,教师还应注意避免将自己的观点和想法提前透露或强加给学生,以限制学生的思考空间。当然,教师在尊重学生主体地位的同时,也要适时发挥自身的主导作用,在学生无法回答或回答不完善时,应通过等待、追问、暗示等方式帮助学生自我纠正或补充答案;在得到学生的精彩回答后,应给予他们个性化的积极反馈。本节课评价环节的师生对话详见第二部分"精彩实录"。

3. 推荐资源

(1) 张凌敏. 基于英语学习活动观的初中英语阅读课教学活动设计[J]. 中学外语教与学,2019(2):19—22. 该文概述英语学习活动观的内涵,并结合教学实例,指出教师应从基于语篇的学习理解类活动、深入语篇的应用实践类活动、超越语篇的迁移创新类活动等三个维度进行教学设计,并在每类活动中有机融入语言知识学习、语言技能运用、学习策略应用、思维品质发展和文化意识培养,从而达到培养学生英语学科核心素养的课程目标。

(2) 王兰英. 对六要素整合的高中英语学习活动观的认识与实践[J]. 中小学外语教学,2018(12):7—12. 该文对六要素整合的英语学习活动观进行了深入剖析,进一步阐明了活动观的内涵和要素,提出了符合学习活动观的设计策略,并结合具体案例阐释了关联、整合、发展的教学活动设计理念。

(3) 张秋会. 在初中英语阅读教学中落实英语学习活动观的实践[J]. 中小学外语教学,2019(1):1—7. 该文介绍了英语学习活动观的内涵与意义,提出了实施英语学习活动观的教学设计应遵循的基本理念,并结合实例阐释了如何基于文本解读,遵循英语学习活动观设计和实施阅读教学,实现培养学生英语学科核心素养的目的。

(4) 高洪德. 英语学习活动观的理念与实践探讨[J]. 中小学外语教,2018(4):1—6. 该文分析了课标提出的英语学习活动观的内涵及其对英语教育的意义,讨论了如何正确对待现实英语教学中各种学习活动的价值,并通过案例介绍了学习活动观的实践方式。

第二部分　精彩实录

授课地点:江苏省靖江高级中学。

授课时间:2018 年 9 月 27 日,时长 45 分钟。

听课人员:江苏省教研室专家、各大市教研员及各地听课代表约 400 人。

授课过程:

Step 1:Leading-in (5 minutes)

(The teacher writes the title "Forrest Gump" on the blackboard.)

T：Guys，today we will enjoy a touching story of a little boy named "Forrest Gump". Do you want to know about him?

S：Yes.

T：Now，please go through the introduction of the story and find out some information about him.

S：He is a simple boy with a warm personality，but his IQ is only 75.

T：So，he is a simple，kind but unintelligent boy. In your opinion，for such a boy，what will he probably meet on his first school day?

S1：Maybe some people who will laugh at him.

S2：Maybe some people who refuse to make friends with him.

T：Right，that is to say，he will meet some cold strangers. So，what does he really need?

S3：He needs love and care.

S4：He needs some help.

T：Good job! He really needs kind helpers. So，please go through the story right now and find out who cold strangers are and who kind helpers are (Q1). Meanwhile，you need to answer another two questions：where is the story set? (Q2) And what happens to Forrest Gump? (Q3)

Step 2：Exploring the script (7 minutes)

(The students skim the script and give their answers to Q1，Q2 and Q3.)

T：Based on the three questions，what do you think we should pay attention to when reading a story?

Ss：Characters，setting and the plot.

T：Excellent! But do you think it's just a story?

Ss：No，it's also a script.

T：What do you think makes it a script?

(Showing the students part of the script on the screen)

Ss：The lines，the stage directions and voice-overs.

T：Can you give more details about them?

S1：The lines show what the characters say.

S2：The stage directions show how the characters behave.

S3：The voice-overs show the voice beyond the screen，but we can't see the speaker.

T：You are very smart! All these pieces of information will help us to dig out the theme of the script，right? That's what we're going to do next!

Step 3：Exploring the meaning of simpleness（18 minutes）

[**Activity 1**] The teacher shows Slide 1 on the screen and has the students discuss：What's the attitude of Forrest Gump towards his mother?

S1：I think he is respectful to his mother because he likes saying "Momma said".

S2：He always obeys his mother's words，so I think he is obedient to his mother.

S3：He loves his mother so much that he bears everything she said in mind.

（The teacher writes the words "respect/obedience/love" on the blackboard.）

T：You're so clever! But I wonder how you understand the words "I sure will，Momma."

S4：He is making a promise to his mum.

T：Good. So when the driver asks him if he gets on the bus，he hesitates. Why?

S5：He doesn't want to break his promise to his mum.

T：So what kind of boy is Forrest Gump?

S6：He is an honest boy.

S7：He is a faithful boy.

S8：He is a loyal boy.

（The teacher writes the words "honesty/faithfulness/loyalty" on the blackboard.）

[**Activity 2**] The teacher shows Slide 2 on the screen and has the students discuss：Why does the bus driver smile at last?

S1：I think she is laughing at the boy.

T：Sounds an interesting idea. What about the others? Do you agree?

S2：I disagree. I think the boy is innocent, not foolish. The driver maybe feels he is lovely.

S3：I disagree. I think the boy wants to make friends with her. She should give a kind smile.

S4：I agree. The boy seems to be too naive.

T：All of your ideas sound reasonable. Now let's go back to the beginning of the dialogue. What do you think of the bus driver's mood with "Are you coming along?"

S5：She is kind of impatient.

T：So after talking with the boy, she smiles. Do you think she gives a positive or negative smile?

S6：I think she begins to love this boy for his innocence.

S7：I guess she smiles because she likes his friendliness.

S8：I think she is touched by his kindness.

（The teacher writes the words "innocence/friendliness/kindness" on the blackboard. ）

[**Activity 3**] The teacher shows Slide 3 on the screen and has the students discuss：What's the attitude of Forrest Gump towards the cold guys?

S1：The boy ignores their coldness.

S2：The boy is very confident.

T：Confident? How do you know that?

S2：Because he doesn't respond to the guys and looks around.

T：What does he look around for?

S2：He looks around for kind guys who would give him a seat.

T：So does it mean he is confident or ... something else?

S2：I think he is positive about life.

T：Good point！In your opinion, the boy is very optimistic.

（The teacher writes the word "optimism" on the blackboard. ）

[**Activity 4**] The teacher shows Slide 4 on the screen and has the students discuss：

How does the boy feel about Jenny's kindness?

S1: The boy feels grateful for Jenny's kindness.

(The teacher writes the word "gratefulness" on the blackboard.)

T: Why do you think so?

S1: Because his voice-over says "Next to Momma, no one ever talked to me ..."

T: Good job! But can you find other evidence in voice-over to show his thankfulness to Jenny?

S2: In Line 27, "I don't remember being born. I don't recall what I got for my first Christmas and I don't know when I went on my first picnic. But, I do remember the first time I heard the sweetest voice in the wide world."

S3: In Line 33, "I had never seen anything so beautiful in my life. She was like an angel."

T: Wonderful! But can you tell me in what ways Forrest Gump conveys his feelings to the fullest?

S4: He uses a comparison when he says "she was like an angel".

S5: He uses emphasis when he says "the sweetest voice in the world".

S6: He uses contrast when he says "I don't remember ... I don't recall ... I don't know ... But I do remember ..."

T: Excellent job! But strangely, there no Voice-over about the bus driver and the cold guys. How do you understand?

S7: Because Forrest Gump is a simple man. He ignores the cold people.

T: I can't agree more with you! By now, we have found out the different meanings of Forrest Gump's simpleness. Let's take a look at the blackboard and review what we've got.

Step 4: Exploring the power of simpleness (8 minutes)

(The teacher shows the following content on the screen and asks the students to create a line for Forrest Gump.)

> JENNY: Are you stupid or something?
>
> FORREST: ▲
>
> *Jenny puts her hand out toward Forrest. Forrest reaches over and shakes her hand.*

S1: I think he probably says "Yes, I'm a little different from others."

T: Do you mean that Forrest has to admit he is a little stupid.

S1: Yes, I think so.

T: But have you noticed that afterwards Jenny puts her hand out toward Forrest. Can you explain why?

S1: Oh, I'm sorry. He probably says "I'm not stupid."

T: Something like that. But please pay much attention to his simpleness. Do you have a different idea?

S1: I think he says "Momma says I'm not stupid."

T: Very close to the original answer. Do you want to know it?

(The teacher shows the original answer "Mommy says stupid is as stupid does.")

T: How do you understand this answer? Do you like it?

S2: It means that stupid people do stupid things.

S3: It shows Forrest doesn't think he is stupid because he never does stupid things.

S4: It shows Forrest doesn't care about being called stupid. He has a firm belief that he isn't stupid.

S4: I like it. It shows that he is an innocent but confident boy.

S5: I also like it. In his opinion, those cold people are stupid people.

T: You are all great thinkers. I appreciate your ideas very much. Next, let's discuss what makes Jenny put her hand out toward Forrest?

S6: Maybe she is pleased with his simpleness and wants to make friends with him.

T: Great! It's the power of simpleness that has made a difference to others, right? Can you find out some other evidence to show the power of simpleness?

S7：It makes the bus driver smile.

S8：It can make Jenny invite Forrest to sit down.

S9：It can make Jenny and Forrest "like peas and carrots from that day on".

T：Brilliant ideas! However, it can even make Forrest live a truly amazing and successful life.

Step 5：Exploring the wisdom of simpleness（7 minutes）

（The teacher puts some pictures on the screen to show Forrest Gump's amazing and successful life later on.）

T：Do you think Forrest Gump's success has anything to do with his simpleness? If yes, what can we learn from his simpleness? Let's have a discussion.

S1：I think yes because he is honest and loyal, which brings him some true friends.

S2：I think yes because he stays positive in face of trouble. He always keeps a good state of mind.

S3：I think no because if a person is too simple, he will be easily cheated by bad people.

T：It's an interesting point. The others, do you all agree with her? Show your opinions!

S4：I disagree with her. Being simple is not being stupid. We should learn from simple people to be honest and sincere with others.

S5：I disagree. Even if a simple man comes across bad people, they can be protected with their true friends.

S6：Every coin has two sides. A simple man is faithful to his friends, but he should still learn to protect himself from bad people.

S7：I disagree because simple people are not stupid. They usually stick to their life values and keep moving forward to their goal. They may suffer some losses for the moment, but they can achieve success in the long term.

T：I appreciate all your ideas. I'd like to join you by sharing my own idea. Do you want to know it?

Ss：（in chorus）Yes!

（The teacher puts a little poem line by line on the screen with the movie background played. The teacher takes the lead in reading aloud and more and more students join in. ）

A simple man

A simple man is an honest man;

he keeps his word to his friend.

A simple man is a sincere man;

he treats friends with full trust.

A simple man is a merciful man;

he forgives and never goes mad.

A simple man is a positive man;

he can fail but never lose heart.

A simple man is a loving man;

he is so kind as to give his hand.

A simple man is a grateful man;

he extends thanks to the world.

Stupid is as stupid does.

Being simple is not being stupid.

Being simple is another kind of.

（At the end of the poem, the teacher pauses and waits for students to speak out the last word. ）

T：Being simple is another kind of ...

Ss：(in chorus) Wisdom!

Step 6：Assignment

Please write a short essay in response to this script. The following information should be included：

☻ A summary of the plot in the script.

☻ Your own understanding of simpleness.

☻ A specific experience to support your own idea.

板书设计

Forrest Gump

To his mum：honesty/faithfulness/loyalty

To the driver：innocence/friendliness/kindness

To cold guys：optimism

To Jenny：gratefulness

PPT（部分课件）如下：

Slide 1

Slide 2

Slide 3

Slide 4

第三部分　课例评析

一、学生反响

学生 A：本来觉得课文内容太简单了，上课时没想到老师的问题都那么烧脑，不过这样的课让我觉得特别有收获，比一味地讲解词汇和语法有趣多了。

学生 B：这节课让我真正懂得了什么叫"大智若愚""大道至简"。上完课以后，我一定要去看一下这部奥斯卡电影。

二、同行声音

张小红（吴江区英语教研员，高级教师）：本节课的最大特色是运用追问策略由浅入深地探究文本的主题意义，在此过程中实现了学生思维品质和情感、态度、价值观的培养。本节课构思精巧，环环相扣，最后的主题升华，给人一种水到渠成的感觉。

王明霞（镇江市英语教研员，高级教师）：这节课中，教师充分尊重了学生的主体地位，师生互动过程是平等融洽的。教师没有将自己的想法强加给学生，也没有打断学生的发言，而是放手让学生说出自己的想法。如果学生们的意见相左，教师自己也没有评判，而是鼓励学生之间互评，形成观点碰撞，充分激发学生的思维。

余文元（邗江中学教研组长，高级教师）：这节课的教学设计遵循 2017 版新课标提出的英语学习活动观理念，合理安排了三个层次的教学活动，从学习理解类活动探究单纯的内涵，到应用实践类活动探究单纯的性格力量，再到迁移创新类活动探究单纯与成功的关系，最后得出结论"单纯是一种智慧"，整个教学活动设计前后递进、思维进阶、浑然一体，体现出教师对英语学习活动观理念的精准理解。

丁宏强（邗江中学，高级教师）：这节课的主题是"大道至简"，其实本身的设计也体现出"大道至简"的智慧。首先，导入部分非常简洁明了，不兜圈子，为后续的探究活动留足时间；其次，教师通过简化课件内容，减少预设，为学生的探究生成留足空间；再次,教学活动不花哨,整节课看似不够热闹,但并不缺少学生思维碰撞的火花。

三、自我反思

本节阅读课基于英语学习活动观的理念,其优点主要体现在以下四个方面:

1. 教学目标指向核心素养

本节课的教学目标体现了英语教学的人文性和工具性的统一,学生在探究主题意义的过程中习得文本语言,并使用习得的文本语言进行思考、表达和交流,提升思维能力,并树立正确的人生观和价值观。

2. 教学内容依托语篇情境

本节课的教学设计没有割裂语篇,而是在主题意义的引领下,围绕情节内容,探究语篇的各个部分和语篇主题的关系,教学活动层层递进,思维进阶,过渡自然。

3. 教学设计聚焦主题意义

本节课的教学设计没有停留在聚焦语言知识的表层学习上,而是遵循意义优先的原则,优化教学活动,梳理主线,逐级递进,在关联学生已知的情境中不断推进意义探究,并有效地呈现意义探究的结果。

4. 教学过程注重互动生成

本节课中,教师通过提问、暗示、追问等方式,使学生始终处于思维的应激状态;在互动过程中,教师未将自己对主题的理解强加给学生,而是引导学生从不同的角度思考主题,鼓励学生发表自己的看法,尊重学生的个性化表达,最终使课堂上出现了许多精彩的生成。

本节阅读课仍存在以下不足:

本节课的互动方式以师生问答为主,虽然有学生主动举手回答,也有学生之间不同观点的碰撞,但学生组内分享交流的时间不足,致使本节课成为了少数优秀学生的展示舞台,而大多数中等生由于反应慢或自信心不足,作壁上观,错过了许多表达的机会。

四、专家点评

点评专家：韩炳华

本节课很好地落实了课程标准所提倡的指向学科核心素养的英语学习活动观。通过一系列相互关联的语言、思维、文化、策略有机融合的活动,李凯老师引导学生基于书面语篇所提供的主题情境,通过获取与梳理、概括与整合、实践与内化、分析与评价、迁移与创新等一系列相互关联的学习活动和多种互动交流方式,梳理、整合、阐释和评判语篇所传递的意义,让学生感知文学作品的魅力,获得积极的人生观。活动中学生积极地表达个人观点、抒发情感和自己的态度,在参与学习活动中学会运用学习策略与方法,提升学英语和用英语的能力。

本课设计的学习活动是在主题意义引领下的学习,是一个意义探究的过程。教师带领学生多层次、多角度地研读语篇,以语篇为载体,以意义为中心,以师生或生生有意义的互动为手段,以问题设计为核心,依据语篇的基本意义、价值取向、文体风格及语言特点等,将语篇分析问题化,问题兼顾"理解、应用、分析、评价和创造"不同思维层次,以由具体到抽象的、渐进性和累积性的思维活动,帮助学生深刻理解语篇,把语言学习与意义探究融为一体,充分有效地实现深度学习。

【名师简介】

李恺,扬州大学附属中学英语教师,扬州市中青年骨干,扬州市韩炳华名师工作室工作教师。曾多次在扬州市教研活动中进行公开课展示,并在 2016 年扬州市高中阅读优质课评比活动中荣获一等奖,在 2018 年江苏省高中英语阅读课评比活动中荣获一等奖。长期致力于高中英语阅读教学研究,在省级及以上期刊发表论文十余篇,其中有六篇论文发表于国家级核心期刊《中小学外语教学》和《中小学英语教学与研究》。目前参与省级课题一项,主持市课题一项。